C000274514

BLISSTEARS

Bliss, the root of all suffering

∾

KARL RENZ

BLISSTEARS

Bliss, the root of all suffering

∾

KARL RENZ

Edited By
Manjit Achhra

A DIVISION OF MAOLI MEDIA PRIVATE LIMITED

Happiness is just overrated bullshit.

– KARL RENZ

Blisstears: Bliss, the root of all suffering

Copyright © 2019 Karl Renz

First Edition: February 2019

PUBLISHED BY

ZEN PUBLICATIONS
A Division of Maoli Media Private Limited

60, Juhu Supreme Shopping Centre,
Gulmohar Cross Road No. 9, JVPD Scheme,
Juhu, Mumbai 400 049. India.
Tel: +91 9022208074

eMail: info@zenpublications.com
Website: www.zenpublications.com

Book Design: Red Sky Designs, Mumbai
Cover Image: © Karl Renz

ISBN   978-93-87242-32-6

Printed By
Repro India Limited

All rights reserved. No part of this book may be reproduced or transmitted in any form or by any means, electronic or mechanical, including photocopying, recording, or by any information storage and retrieval system without written permission from the author or his agents, except for the inclusion of brief quotations in a review.

Contents

Other Books by Karl Renz

- Undecided: *Neti-Neti*
- Commentaries On The Gospel Of Thomas
  Excerpts from the Marsanne talks
- A Little Bit Of Nothingness
  81 Observations On The Unnamable
- The Song of Irrelevance
  Meditation of what you are
- Heaven and Hell
- Am I - I Am
- May It Be As It Is
  The Embrace of Helplessness
- Worry and be Happy
  The Audacity of Hopelessness
- Echoes of Slience
  Avadhut Gita Revisited
- The Lies About Truth
- Peace Off
  And Be What You Are
- Soy Yo - Yo Soy (Spanish)
- Mythen in Tüten (German)
  ES macht nix

ACKNOWLEDGEMENT

The Publishers wish to thank Anjali Walsh,
for her invaluable help in making this book possible.

~

Self-love is the root of all suffering

∾

Q: Is there something called as a pre-sense?

K: Yes. That what is the pre-sense. That what can never be sensed is the pre-sense.

Q: It sounds like a contradiction...

K: No. It's not a contradiction. That what can never be sensed is what-you-are because you can never sense what-you-are, whatever you can sense is not what-you-are... it's just a sensation. Pre-sense means prior to the presence. The presence you can sense, the absence you can sense. Absence is the sensation of absence of sensation, so even absence is not it. So pre-sense is neither the absence nor the presence because both can be sensed. But that what is sensing the pre-sense can never be sensed. Clear?

Q: So far...

K: I try to make it very easy and not so complicated that at first there is Awareness, then consciousness and then there are all these steps. No. It's very simple. The 'I' cannot see the 'I', the knife cannot cut the knife. The nature cannot know the nature and the nature you can know is not the nature of the nature. The nature doesn't know any nature and that what knows nature is mind. So, never mind.

In deep-deep sleep there's no sensation and still you exist. That is called pre-sense. Without any sensation or no-sensation you exist. Your Absolute being never needs any sensational experience of being or no being to be what it is, that's all. And just to know yourself as That what doesn't need to know itself to be what it is, is Knowledge. The rest is ignorance. And you cannot get closer to it. There's no bridge to That. There's nothing to cross. You can never be aware enough to be That. You never left it, so you cannot go home. No way – that's Buddha – no way home.

That's the very problem. You never left what-you-are but by trying to get back you live an imaginary life... an imaginary idea that by various steps you become that what-you-are. By that, you become an object of time because only in time there's closer and further away. So, what to do?

Q: There's no notion of getting closer or getting there?

K: It's a phantom notion. The lover who's in love with itself, it's the mind minding itself. The caretaker taking care about the caretaker, consciousness taking care about consciousness. Consciousness is a phantom which takes care about itself permanently, minding itself. But what you are is in spite of consciousness. Being conscious or not conscious, being aware or not aware, you *are*; never *because*.

That you cannot reach by anything. And there's no need to reach it because you are That. And whatever you do is futile. Be happy that everything is failing, failing, failing. All attempts are futile. Resistance is futile because you cannot resist yourself. To resist it needs two and there are no two. How can you resist yourself?

Q [Another visitor]: The Absolute is present everywhere...

K: No. The Absolute is never present. There is no presence of the Absolute. There is no presence and no absence of the Absolute. The Absolute is neither present nor absent. The Absolute is just the Absolute – neither present nor absent. Whatever you call it, it's not.

Q: But...

K: There's no 'but' in it. The Absolute is! Finished.

Q: If you are That...

K: There's no 'you' in it, there's no 'me' in it. The Absolute is what-you-are but you are not the Absolute. That's the switch. The Heart is what-you-are but you are not the Heart. There is no ownership in it, you can never own it. It can never be yours, not by understanding, not by any realization. There is no ownership in it. Whatever can be owned is shit. Whatever you understand and call it, is shit. The Tao that you can name is not the Tao. Whatever you give it as a name or frame you make it opposite to something else. Then you're in the fucking mind again. The mind always fucks around, always tries to define it. Then you want to control it by seeing that everywhere it is present. You think that if you see that that Absolute is present everywhere, then maybe you're fine. You want to define it, 'I see everything myself, I made it!'

Q: That was not the question... [Laughter]

K: [Laughing] But I see what is behind the question.

Q: There must be...

K: There is no 'must be'. I understand that out of tendency of love you want to know yourself but by that you suffer, you know that. I can only tell you that you will never know yourself by any means. There is no way of knowing yourself, no way of defining yourself. But you may try and it hurts because by that you miss yourself, all the time.

Q: You said that even Consciousness is a concept...

K: Consciousness is an experience but that what is experiencing the consciousness is not consciousness. Who is the owner of consciousness?

Q: That's the question...

K: That is the question. Who owns fucking consciousness? Who owns Life? It's all about ownership. This little 'my' life, 'my' understanding, my, my, my... And the 'me' is misery, you know that. Mine is 'me' and there is *my*sery and *me*sery. But how to get rid of it?

That's why I sit here and say that you cannot get rid of what does not exist. That's the whole problem. You cannot get rid of something what doesn't even exist. There is no mind in Reality, never was there. How can you get rid of the mind? How can you kill the mind which is not even alive? There's no such thing as mind, come on!

Q: How much is belief involved in all this?

K: Ten thousand Euros. The price is high. [Laughter]

It's all believing. Because you believe in yourself, you left yourself. You believed in the tree of life and now you're the leaf and the leaf wants to become the tree. It's a be*leaf* system. You will never become the tree, you are the tree. But now you believe to be a leaf and because of that you left yourself and now you try to go home. But as much as you go closer to home, you go further away. When you think you're closer, you are furthest away. Everyone thinks that now he's closer but he's as furthest away as he can be. Always confirming that there is two. Because the phantom can only exist in separation, in twoness. It cannot survive in that what is. So, it needs to make it something, like an object. Without making it an object, it cannot remain as an object. It fights for its life, all the time... Mein Kampf.

The inner Hitler always tries to hit himself. Hit me, beat me up, because when you beat me up, I exist. It's a permanent S-M connection. You are the sadist and the masochist in the same moment. Because you suffer, you exist, that's your confirmation and the phantom always needs a confirmation that it exists and suffering is the cheapest one and always available. [Whining] I don't know, I'm suffering, but for that I am. I suffer, for that I am. The French say, I think therefore I am, that's the same.

What would you do without suffering? Could you exist without suffering? Or missing something? Is the phantom able to exist without a little discomfort? It needs discomfort. So let it have its discomfort, who minds it? You cannot end it, that's the story of consciousness, always hunting itself; inquiring permanently what it is. It is a love story of consciousness – the lover, the loving and the beloved. The highest success is knowing the beloved. But consciousness will never know consciousness. How can it know that? Then there would be two Consciousnesses, one consciousness knowing another consciousness. How could that be?

Q: Self Awareness?

K: Whose self-awareness would it be?

Q: Consciousness being aware of itself...

K: Consciousness is already lower than Awareness, come on! Then does the lower know the higher? Like Auro-bingo, the superior consciousness?

Q: It's a problem of different terminology...

K: No. It's not a problem of different terminology.

Q: There can be awareness together with consciousness...

K: But it's all a phantom. It's all part of the realization but not the Reality. It's the highest consciousness you can say but the highest is not high enough. You can use it as a terminology, but for what advantage?

Q: But who is then aware?

K: Who is aware? Is there any 'who' in it? Doctor Who and the cannibal.

Q [Another visitor]: Is awareness aware if I'm aware or not?

K: No. Who would confirm that it is? When you are in deep-deep sleep who cares about awareness? Only when you wake up, you ask someone, 'Was I aware? Did you see my body when I was asleep?' And then he confirms you, 'Yes there was someone. Your eyes were moving and you were dreaming.' But you don't know. You don't even know if the world exists or the universe exists during the deep-deep sleep, during the absence of any sensation. Even the absence of presence of awareness is not there. What is there?

But still you exist, as that what you are. So, your nature doesn't need any awareness to be what-it-is. But it starts with Awareness. The beginning and the end. But in the beginning you don't begin and in the end, you don't end, that's the main thing. You don't start with awareness and you don't end with awareness. You are in spite of it – you were, you are and you will be, in spite of presence or absence of any Awareness. All this terminology is part of the dream. So even awareness is the beginning of the dream and the end of the dream. But you are in spite of the beginning and the end, that's all. In the beginning you don't begin and in the end you don't end. What else do you want? How can you be more Absolute than That?

But the question always is, what do I get out of it? Does it make me happier in anyway? Isn't that the question? What do I get out of it? What kind of advantage would it be if there would be the Absolute? Is there an advantage in it? That's always the question of the mind – What do I get out of it? This businessman always trying to get something out of it. It's like if I'm a bit more aware then maybe I'm a bit calmer. Then 'I' have more silence, 'I' have more peace. Crazy!

And I'm talking about the absolute advantage – being what you are – that doesn't need any advantage. It doesn't even know any advantage or disadvantage. And that what needs an advantage or knows any advantage, is by nature a permanent disadvantage. Even if you become permanently aware, it is a disadvantage because there's still something that needs to be aware, to be. So even the highest advantage is a disadvantage. That's why when I say fuck it all, I mean it. Fuck it totally! Fuck it all and be what you are. Because you cannot not be, that's what I'm pointing at. You cannot escape, there's no way out, you are That what is the Absolute and this is your fucking realization. You cannot leave it because you are not in it. You will never be aware enough to leave it. You think Awareness is the way out of it. You will be fucked forever I tell you – the eternal fuck! [Laughing]

Who can take that? No one! If you try to take it as a phantom, it's impossible. You will resist it because it will kill you. You will never allow that as your truth. There'll always be some 'may be' or 'if' or 'when'. For what-you-are, there's no problem, you are That anyway. There's nothing to take for what-you-are. You are That. But for the phantom it's difficult to realize that because in that realization it would kill itself and it will never allow that. There's always a survival system running. 'If', 'When' and 'Then'...if I just have more peace, more awareness, more of this, more of that. Help me God!

All the teachers tell you that – I did it my way and maybe you can follow my way and then you will be where I am because you want to sit where I am sitting now. Then some have already bought their dresses in case they may sit there sometime. [Laughter] I know some people like that.

Q [Another visitor]: So, preparation...

K: Preparation is only for the animals that need to be stuffed, flesh out and foam inside so that you prepare it for later, like mummification. You want to have your mummy forever. The Buddhist tradition was like that. They prepared themselves for twenty years to mummify themselves in meditation, eating little, drying out. Then by dying they don't die because the mummy is still there. [Laughing]

Q: Is this true?

K: There are books about it that you can read, especially in Thailand.

Q: So we are sitting here waiting to be struck by the random lucky stick?

K: No. You are sitting here because resistance is futile... Puff... Puff... Puff...

Q: Deflating...

K: You may realize that you cannot realize. You may understand that you cannot understand. You may realize that resistance is futile and you cannot not be. Then the movie continues but for no one. There was no director, no actor, no whatever. Nothing ever happened by anything that happened. Silence is not that something does not move. Silence means that in moving nothing moves; in coming nothing comes and in going nothing, nothing goes. That is silence. But it is not silence that is different from movement. You always make something up because you think that stillness is something where there's no movement.

Q: I have my silencing headphones now...

K: You are phony anyway, a phony head having headphones.

Q: I'm trying to use technology to have some silence...

K: Then they go to Himalayas and try various technologies to have silence. That's all fake silence. Silence is your nature. In nature nothing comes and nothing goes, life is never coming and never going. That's silence but it's not something that's not moving. You always think that not moving means silence.

Q: Sometimes there's an experience of that...

K: Of what?

Q: Of silence...

K: You cannot experience silence.

Q: Stillness?

K: There is no experience of stillness. For experience it needs movement.

Q: So, stillness happens...

K: It never happens. It's always there, it's permanent. Silence never comes never goes.

Q: Maybe something drops?

K: There's nothing to drop. Now she thinks she's a cloud and someday she'll drop as rain, that's draining.

Q: But...

K: You see? The fighting of the phantom continues. Whatever has a butt needs a but.

Q: In life living life...

K: Nothing comes, nothing goes, that is life.

Q: What is core splitting honesty? Is grace...

K: Another fucking idea. If you want to bless yourself, put your hand on your head. [Laughter] You don't need anyone else to bless yourself. Just bless yourself. Don't look for any fucking guru for any blissful bullshit.

Q: What is this idea of grace then?

K: Grace Kelly.

Q: She was pretty...

K: She was just a greedy business lady. What kind of role do you play today? Any role you play is a stupid one. Everyone wants to have a different role because no one is satisfied with his role; 'There must be a better role, I want to play the main character and not this supporting act'. [Laughter]

Q: Someone has to be a supporting act...

K: The best you can get is a supporting-ex... Ex-boyfriend, ex-husband. Ramesh Balsekar in Bombay would say you play all the roles. So you don't have to be jealous of the other roles because you play them all. Whatever is, is consciousness and you play all the roles. If you understand that then maybe you have peace of mind. Or maybe you don't have a thinking mind anymore and have just the working mind. [Laughter] Then you become a banker because then you have an interest. It's fun... so many goals and no one wants to be the keeper.

Q [Another visitor]: What is right listening?

K: When there's no listener. Right listening is listening without a listener, hearing without one who hears, ears without a head. [Laughing] How do you listen? I have ears without a head. Thinking without a thinker, living without one who is alive... sounds all good. Can that be the goal? Can you decide? Can you choose? Does life needs to choose what's better, the personal or the impersonal? The impersonal would be listening without a listener and the personal would be listening with a listener, trying to get something out of it. But does life care if it's personal or impersonal? Does life get more if it's impersonal and less when it's personal experience? Is personal life less than an impersonal life? Innocent questions. Would life mind if the mind is thinking or working? What would you say? I always have to answer and now I ask something and no one answers me. [Laughter] But I'm self-guilty. After a while no one has any question anymore.

[Pointing to a visitor] Yes, Hamburg? Would a person from Hamburg call himself a Hamburger? A person from Berlin would never call himself a Berliner because that's another name for a donut. It's like someone says, I'm the Self, it's already too much. You may say you are That what never says anything, never defines itself as what-it-is. It defines itself in everything but never defines that what is defining everything. But now you try to define that what defines everything.

The definer is already the defined but the definer that's part of this definition is not that what is defining the definer. So even the definer is not fine enough.

Q [Another visitor]: Trouble comes when...

K: Trouble doesn't come, it's always there. The moment you wake up... trouble. The trouble-maker wakes up. When this shit factory wakes up, it makes trouble. It always wants something. A needy bastard wakes up, always needy, always more, never satisfied. There's no satisfaction in this body, always wants something. This body, this brain, everything is a shit factory, a needy bastard, never satisfied. There is no satisfaction in anything.

And I sit here and tell you, there's no satisfaction for you and the beauty is, what-you-are never needs to be satisfied by anything. That what tries to get satisfied is Mick Jagger but it will never be satisfied. Consciousness will never be satisfied but you believe that consciousness will satisfy you. Then you become a slave of a fake master. It's fantastic! You give all your freedom to a fake asshole called consciousness. You enslave yourself. And now you have a tendency that you want to break free out of that slavery but the more you want to get free from that slavery, you give importance to that slavery. Then you become more enslaved by that. The more you want to be free, you are imprisoned. Then even freedom becomes like a prison. So, what to do?

Q [Another visitor]: Every intention from the person confirms...

K: The worst intention is trying to have no intention – you know that. The wish of having no wish is the biggest bullshit wish. It's such a wishy-washy. The wishlessness of your nature can never be reached by any wish or no wish.

Q: But if you feel that no wish will do something to you then you compare...

K: But who cares about the one who's wishing or not wishing? Do you think I care that you wish or don't wish? Or if you're a dar*wish*? It's never clean enough. It's like you clean something in front of you and when you look back you find all the dirt behind you. I think all the housewives should be realized. [Laughter]

Q: Not knowing what is clean or not clean...

K: But not knowing is still too much. No way out. Now you step into the same 'next' trap. Knowing doesn't work and not knowing doesn't work either.

Q: Maybe you can say by knowing and by not knowing...

K: You are! You are in knowing and in not knowing, in wishing and not wishing. Does wishing make you less and not wishing make you more? What you are never gains or loses by anything. There's no gaining in gaining and no losing in losing, no birth in birth and no death in death. Nothing ever happened by anything, nothing ever comes, nothing ever goes. What to do? You don't become cleaner when you're more purified by awareness. All the ideas of purification are the dirtiest ideas that you produce.

Q: This survival system always wants to puts something...

K: Of course! It lives by dirty ideas. It's a dirty bastard. So, when I say, when it wakes up, a dirty bastard wakes up, I mean it. Out of dirt comes dirt.

Q: By not standing in the way...

K: Who wants to control existence by not standing in the way? [Laughing] You are fucking in love with yourself. You think if I go on the side, if I devote myself, if I'm not in the way anymore... 'Life, I allow you to live now. You can now do whatever you like'. [Laughter] 'I was blocking you before but now I'm unblocking you'. And you think life feels very grateful and gives you peace and you get what you want. [Laughter] Someone finally worked it out. Life is like a bull and I'm like a Torero, I just have to step aside and let it go through. I'm so aware of what's coming. With all the Vipasanna, I already know what's coming next. [Laughter]

Q: Some say I'm just a hollow bamboo flute of the existence... [Laughter]

K: In short, I'm just a Pfeiffer (German for whistler or Piper), I don't know who's blowing me. It's amazing, everyone wants to control himself. There's a permanent self-control... out of love. You cannot even blame yourself. You're so fucking in love with yourself that you want the best for you. The best would be, 'I give myself freedom'. 'I' give myself freedom, 'me' the glorious. I'm so generous, generosity is my nature, I allow everything to be as it is... whoa! Wonderful! Half of Tiruvannamalai talks like that. I allow existence to exist. I don't mind anymore.

Q [Another visitor]: Sometimes it feels so hard and stressful. It feels like you have been defeated by life...

K: You are always defeated by life. Life always wins, I tell you. But sometimes you realize that and you feel bad.

Q: Sometimes lots of bad things happen...

K: Whatever happens is bad. You don't have to wait when they happen, they happen all the time.

Q: Sometimes...

K: There's no sometimes, it's all the time.

Q: Sometimes it's more concentrated...

K: Sometimes it's just that your energy is not strong enough to take it and then you break down and start crying... poor me.

Q: It's a common experience...

K: Why is that a common experience? [Pointing to another visitor] He never complains.

Q [Another visitor]: Me? [Laughter]

K: It's always interesting how people excuse themselves and blaming the circumstances and then having self-pity... poor me.

Q [Another visitor]: But sometimes there's not even time to complain...

K: Then there's no time. How can there be a stressful situation without time? What are you talking about?

Q: I'm talking about events when you have to work in the world and face practical situations...

K: [Pointing to another visitor] I think you both should work together. He gives the pills and you talk about it.

Q: Sometimes there's a bad situation and you have to face it...

K: Should I allow her to continue? [Laughter] Shall we vote? Some Marijuana maybe. Doctors are always good for that. Whenever their job gets too much, they take a pill. Doctors are the biggest junkies on earth. What's your question?

Q: When...

K: Not 'when', just have a question. You're just telling a story, just have a question.

Q: Are the difficult situations moments that train you to go deeper?

Q [Another visitor]: I really want to know her question... [Laughter]

K: One can imagine. If one feels really helpless and the situation is so overwhelming that you cannot know what to do anymore, then what to do?

Q: Yes, that is indeed the question...

K: Now I have to be intuitive. [Laughter] I say that's the case all the time. The circumstance always dictates everything and you're just a witness. That's the highest you can gain – being the witness of the circumstance that dictates everything. You were never in control in anyway.

Q: Sometimes it feels like there are easy moments...

K: There is no 'sometimes'. There are no easy moments. Look I cannot even control what your questions are. What am I here? [Laughter] If someone would say that he had choice to say what he wants to say and wants what he wants, I would kill him right away. In that way I see myself in this helplessness and controlessness in trying to pronounce what does not come. Otherwise I could never do this job, if I really think that I was somebody who could control himself and what kind of questions come. If there would really be someone sitting here who could control himself in any way, I would just shoot him with a machine gun. [Laughing] It hurts, but if there really would be someone who's the doer, the torturer then I would be in a torture chamber.

In that way it's fun, there is no control. Life cannot control life. Life cannot decide in what way it lives itself. There's absolutely no control in anything. This almighty, this all absolute life cannot control the way it lives itself: if it's personal, impersonal, aware, witness or anything, there's absolutely fucking no control in anything as there are no two lives. Life cannot control life because there is no second life. So, what's there to do? It's stupid to sit here, but it's as stupid not to sit here. It's always stupid.

There's a place in Germany called Böhme and it's unbearable to live there, it's the most boring city. Then there's a saying that everywhere else is as shitty as Böhme anyway, so I'd rather live in Böhme. Shit is everywhere, so I'd rather be in Böhme. Or sitting here and listening and echo reflecting the questions. It's all an Echo of Silence, that's why there's a book with this title. It's an echo and the echo cannot decide what it echoes. Everything is echoing, there's no ego in it. It's like there's a drop dropping in water and then there are ripples. Can the ripple decide where the ripples are and how big are they?

Where did this start? Everyone wants to find the beginning of something, like who is guilty or something. Maybe there was never any beginning, just ripples. Sometimes they call it a tsunami and after a tsunami, the 'me' is gone.

Q [Another visitor]: I was reading a book from Siddharameshwar Maharaj and he says generally the masters prefer having fewer disciples because every action of the disciple is a burden...

K: Even one is too many. So if even one is too many, then there could be millions, who cares? It's like Ramana never took any disciples. But now how many disciples are running around in Tiruvannamalai? How many people sitting there, claiming to be from the lineage of Ramana? For the guy who said there's no fucking lineage and that what has a lineage is a fake one. Now how many people sit there now? Happy Nappy, how are you today? In Tiruvannamalai I call him happy-nappy. In the Self you become like a child and he was presenting that. [Laughter]

Nisargadatta or Ranjit never took any disciples. There's 'I' to 'I', no master no disciple, there's just Self talk – life living. There's no one talking from a higher position and no one talking from the witness position like I am the witness and you are still fucking ignorant personal consciousness. Poor you, I'm already better off.

Q: Osho took many disciples...

K: Yes and then he took Valium and laughing gas. [Laughter] Otherwise he could not bear it. It's unbearable, even one is unbearable... imagine two million!

Q [Another visitor]: So, what are we to you?

K: A piece of meat, pleased to meet you. What are we to you? [Laughing]

Q: So, are we friends? [Laughter] Friends of Karl Renz...

K: I'm always happy not to have friends. No friends, no enemies. It's like being in a military, one against another and then you make friends so that at least one doesn't shoot at me. Then the friends especially shoot at you by asking 'How are you today?' Family, relatives! Imagine you have relatives, that instantly makes you relative. Fuck! I have relatives and my relatives like me. Do I like my relatives? Or do I want to kill them all? Maybe I want to kill them all because that makes me relative. It's a nice word... my relatives. My family... because then I'm famous, everyone knows me, everyone knows me and gives me attention... Good morning!

Q [Another visitor]: If there are teachers that talk about it is all God's will and you don't have any will...

K: That's Ramesh Balsekar from Bombay.

Q: This is all empty anyway...

K: It's just to make your life a little bit easier. It's on the level of a personal life because if you see everything is God's will, you don't blame you or someone else. Then life becomes more peaceful. So, there's an advantage in it. It's all about making life a little bit easier. But it's not to realize yourself. These are two different teachings. There are teachings for the relative life, that you may have a better life, a more comfortable life, that you don't mind so much anymore and there's advantage in it. And it's okay for me. It's like psychotherapy, there are psychotherapist gurus. Whenever there's a guru, there's a psychotherapist. That's the nature of a guru. Out of compassion of sitting there, trying to make life better.

Q: Then there's one teacher who said once to me that you can step into your soul...

K: That really hurts, I tell you. If you step in your soul... whoa! First you have a soul, then you have to step into it. You enter the spirit... whoa! You enter the void. Imagine there could be one who could enter the void. It's a very famous thing, you enter into the void. But then there would be no void anymore because that would be one too many. You really have to avoid that. [Laughter] That's amazing... entering the void. I'm Johnny Depth. Entering the void. [Laughing] Maybe the void enters you, then you are in trouble. Can you avoid the void? Or is it that you are fighting for survival, always avoiding the void? Then even by entering the void, you try to avoid the void. I wish you all the best of English luck. I asked every Englishman, what is this fucking English luck? Everyone uses it but no one knows why?

Q: What about the concept that life is endlessly repeating itself and you can try to get out of it...

K: By trying to go out, you are in it, that's the problem. You can try forever, you cannot get out of something you are not even in. But the moment you get out of it, you're in it by imagination. Your belief system puts you into that trouble. Sounds good. Some even claim that they went out of it by some technique. Mr. Ken Wilber says he has reached to the twenty eighth level. There are many who create this Jacob's ladder. When you climb up the ladder, you get to closer to... whatever.

Q: There was a teacher...

K: Who? I want the names.

Q: You don't know him...

K: That doesn't matter.

Q: His name is Peter...

K: Peter the liar? When someone asked him about his master, he lied three times. Only Judas – he told them where he was. That is core splitting honesty and not this bloody Peter. Then all these Churches are built on this bloody Peter. It's a re*peter* – the repeating of Peter. So, what does Peter say?

Q: He says that there is an energy that goes across various lifetimes and he goes to the source of the energy and releases them...

K: Unknotting the knots. Just say it like that, don't make it a complicated thing. Like Mother Meera, the karmic knots get unknotted by her rearranging your energetic body. That's called unknotting the knots.

Q: As you say, it leads to an advantage position...

K: You may succeed and end up with more knots. You start to believe that you can do something, that something needs to be done and if you succeed in it, that's even worse. It makes you a *suck*sessor... succeeding in bullshit. This ownership of having knots, that's the main thing. That there's someone who has knots. Then there's another teacher who confirms that there's one who has knots and that he can help him. Fuck this bloody Peter! [Laughter] They read some books and repeat it, that's Peter. They always tell you there's something wrong with you and that makes them relevant.

Q: Also that then there's someone to forgive...

K: This bloody forgiveness. That's the biggest bullshit. Who are you to forgive anyone? Not even yourself. Who do you think you are that you can forgive something? That makes you something that you could've done or not done. How arrogant can you get that you can forgive something? To who? You forgive that what you have not done. What arrogance! Forgiveness is pure arrogance. Devotion, the biggest arrogance! As if you have something to devote to anything. What is yours anyway? Fuck! Devotion! I'm a devotee! Like a king devoting himself to a guru or an idea. I'm a devotee of Ramana... whoa! And I only choose the best ones. Ramana in my eyes is the best and I devote myself to Ramana. 'I' do something, 'I' devote myself, 'I' am full of devotion. Did you hear me? I would never devote anything to you... whatever you are. [Laughing]

All these concepts have ownership in it.

Q: It's a hundred percent ownership...

K: Absolutely! Absolute arrogance of one who believes that there's something that does not belong to life. That there's a doer; that there's an owner and for that he needs to be punished by all the Upanishads. [Laughter]

Any moment you believe that you have a life, you are punished and you suffer by that ownership. And it's absolutely right that you get punished by that arrogance, that you own something that does not belong to that what is existence. Come on! As if you have ever had anything what was yours. And for that you get punished and that's absolutely right. And this punishment is not severe enough; if I could, I would make it more severe but I cannot. If I would be existence, I tell you... [Laughing]

It's fantastic! Then you want to control suffering, you want to control the misery that comes back... my life, my, my, my. No way out!

Q [Another visitor]: But isn't this desire...

K: Then comes the psychotherapy. [Laughter]

Q: Isn't this part of life itself?

K: You see? That was like an 'Excuse me... can I help it?' Yes of course! You can be what you are and fuck yourself!

Q: No...

K: Not no. Yeah! [Laughter] 'Excuse me I cannot help myself, isn't it part of life?'

Q: It is life itself, there's no need of judging anything...

K: Of course, I like to judge. It's fun. And life doesn't mind. Who says judging is wrong?

Q: No...

K: Thank you very much!

Q: But controlling is part of life and if that wants to control, let him do it...

K: For that he should be punished, I just said it. Judgement is a permanent day, it's only a judgement day.

Q: There's nothing to exclude...

K: It's all inclusive. [Laughter] You can eat and drink as much as you like. Especially when there's a fixed price, you eat and eat because you don't have to pay more. Then you come home and you're fed like hell. These all-inclusive holidays are so fucked. Then they make a big buffet and it always has to be full even if the last one comes. Then what doesn't get eaten gets thrown. For that humanity should be punished. There should be a tsunami all over the world. [Laughter] I think the moon should hit the earth. There will be trouble for few minutes and then everyone's gone. Maybe it would happen anyway.

Q [Another visitor]: It's very devastating...

K: No one can control that one day it will be gone. That whatever is will be gone. That even humanity is just a disease, it came and it will be gone. All the gurus and all the Upanishads and all the Vedas... already gone.

Q: It's devastating...

K: It's not devastating, it's fun. That's joy that nothing is permanent. Even the most precious and the highest and the lowest and truth and all those ideas... are gone. They didn't even exist in the first place. The Bible, the Vedas, the Upanishads and Yoga-Fascista. Imagine! Puff... A little blow job of existence and it's gone. All these little problems come and go and you think my little problem is the worst ever. Be happy that it's all a fleeting bullshit, that it's all a shadow.

Q: I haven't hit that happiness yet...

K: It's the happiness that doesn't need to be happy, that's the nature of happiness. But you want to own happiness. You want to make it 'your' happiness and by that you suffer and you should suffer more severely, you know that... by trying to own bloody happiness. [Laughter]

I just say it as it is, the more you want happiness, happiness runs away from you, thank God! Because happiness could never be owned by anyone. 'My' reality! Come on! 'My' joy. Watch out if there's joy; you will not be there.

Q: And how's that?

K: It's quite joyful. It's full of joy when there's no one who's enjoying it. That's called the joy of silence. There's no ownership in it, there's no my joy, no higher joy, no lower joy, no bliss or anything. If you want bliss you get blisters in your brain, you know that.

Then they all say, how can you talk like that? What can I do? [Laughing] Then they ask, don't you like humans? If there would be a human, I'd kill him. Empathy, oh my goodness. When there's compassion, there's no one having compassion. Then you are that what is That... that's compassion and not one who has compassion. That's just pity... self-pity. Thank God no one could ever reach compassion. That's why the Buddhists try and fail and in failing to have compassion maybe the owner disappears. All the intellectual debates that they have in Buddhism is only so that you can fail. No one can ever have compassion for anyone. In compassion, there are no others. There's no two. How can there be one who has compassion with someone else? How can there be someone who has empathy? What you can feel is pity... poor you. And then you already feel higher by putting someone else down.

Q: I just feel about not being hurtful...

K: I hurt everyone... I heard.

Q: Are you hurting now?

K: I hurt everyone. Everyone believes that he owns something and I'm hurting that one. That what I am is hurting because he thinks that he is apart from what he is. By being apart from what it is, it hurts. In that way I hurt him.

Q: And there's a carelessness in it...

K: Why should I care about it? If I would care then I would be in the same boat as the other one and then I would be paddling for life. Whoever comes here, comes for carelessness and not for someone who cares about your little trouble. Or someone who gives them an answer to make them feel better today; no, you should feel worse... if I could help it. But even I have no power.

That's the main thing, when you are power you have no power. You cannot control anything. But by that you control everything, just by being what you are. There's not even a need of trying to control it. Just by being what you are, you control everything. You are That, more is not possible. But when you are not That, there is... puff... puff... puff... [Laughing] Little hamster in a wheel who thinks he's going somewhere. That's the symbol, a hamster running continuously in a wheel, thinking one day he'll reach his goal. That's a seeker. A seeker seeking and thinking by seeking, he can find that what the seeker is. No one is sicker than a seeker. Show me a seeker and you show me a patient.

Q [Another visitor]: In the play of darkness and light...

K: There is no play of darkness and light. Darkness in its nature is light because darkness is just the non-movement of light. The non-movement of light, you cannot experience, you experience it as darkness. But it is the same light as the light in motion. The light in motion you experience as light, but the light in no motion is darkness. But both are light. There is no 'between' because in nature there's no difference.

Q: So, there is no bad or evil?

K: There is bad or evil... I'm very bad. But evil? I still have to work on that one. [Laughter]

Q: But they have no real power?

K: Why should it have any power? The question always is who calls something bad or evil? It needs a reference point and if you are a person, you already have a reference point.

Q: And there are good and bad things but if there's no reference point...

K: Even that's a reference point. Then you have a hope that if you would not have a reference point, then you would be fine. Ha, ha, ha! Another way of controlling it.

Q: So, it's neti-neti…

K: Neti-neti is just a pointer that it's not that or that. It's neither control nor no control. It's neither having a reference nor no-reference point. It's neither. No reference point is the reference point you cannot lose anymore, so it's the worst one.

Q: So, there's no way out?

K: That I repeat all the time… no way out! But you wanted to be quiet. So be quiet that there's no need for a way out. And the one who needs a way out… [Laughing] Even people who claim they found a way out, where are they? Are they still talking to people who are not there? I'm out, I don't bother anymore, not me, I gave up. Then they even say that because of grace I'm very special because grace chose me and if you follow me it will come to you as well.

How can you leave what you are? Come on! That's the main thing. And who needs to leave what he is? An idea. I will be better off when I'm out of it. Who is better off by what? The only answer is 'me'. And what is a 'me'? It's sometimes there, sometimes not. If you look for it, it's gone and then the moment you think you lost it, it comes back… Hello! Did you miss me?

No. You cannot get rid of your shadow. The 'me' is just a shadow of that what you are. And trying to bring light to the shadow is the worst. Then the light is in the shadow. You think I have to bring light into the shadow, especially 'me'. I am the king of existence. You must be jo-king!

That's why I say the darkness is as much light as the light. It's just a different way of experiencing the light. It's the light of Shiva in two different directions, in darkness or absence and in presence. The presence is the light in motion and the absence is the light in no motion… as experience. But both is light. And silence is if Absolute starts to wake up, there's no waking up in it. If the God particle starts to move, it moves in Absolute speed. Absolute speed means in whichever direction it goes, it already instantly ends up where it started. So, nothing happened. That's Absolute speed. There's not even any motion in it. That's 'nothing ever happens'. That's silence. And no one ever suffered enough to reach that. That's just another hope. No heart will break because there was never anyone who owned any heart that could break. That is heart breaking. The idea that you have a heart that needs to be broken, that keeps you alive.

Q: Is there no some 'one' in an avatar?

K: There's as much someone in an avatar as you. Avatar's are born enlightened, isn't that fantastic? Ammachi, the hugging Kali, Sai Baba. They're all part of the show, come on! And they never helped anyone.

Q: It's so easy to see that they're standing outside...

K: Yes. They're standing outside but even to stand outside, there has to be an inside, it is part of the game. There has to be an exception to the game but even an exception is not exceptional.

Q: It seems they have so much knowledge and control to go into the things and change it...

K: Yeah, wonderful! Sai Baba for a while manifested Swiss watches. Then suddenly there was a ban of Swiss watches so automatically the watches from Hong Kong started getting manifested.

Q: You sometimes say that everything that is inside has no power and the one that's outside doesn't need it...

K: Outside? What are you talking about? What drug did you take this morning? The most famous drug is the 'one' who woke up. Then you're drugged into life.

Q: But you have no power because...

K: There's no one who owns power anyway. There's no ownership in anything. No doership, no ownership. It's all imaginary.

Q: It is power but not power over something else...

K: Even that there's power is an idea. Ask power, 'Do you know power?' Ask Reality, 'Do you know Reality?' Ask Life, 'Do you know life?' Silence. No answer.

Q: Everything disappears when there's no reference...

K: For that there has to be something in the first place so that it could disappear. For who did it appear and for who does it disappear? 'Me'. And you think that the answer disappears everything and suddenly there will be silence and it was such an immensely deep silence… because my understanding went so deep into the nature of Reality and I realized my true nature and then there was silence. Then now I tell everyone… there's only silence. Come to me and I'll show you silence.

Many years ago I was in Holland in the Science and Non Duality gathering. There I met Unmani and she said she came to Tiruvannamalai and didn't feel anything and said if you realize your true nature before you arrive there, then you don't feel it anymore. [Yawns] [Laughter] That left me speechless. I was like, okay, bye-bye. Be happy with your true nature.

Who makes this difference between the true nature and the false nature? Who was false before and suddenly he becomes true? Who thinks it was wrong earlier and now it's right? It's very nice to see the videos of awakening of the five so-called masters. There was Mooji, Adyashanti, Tolle… All of them had a before and after story, like a beauty salon. Before it was all despair and everyone was down and didn't feel good. Then suddenly after this event, everything was fine. It was like, I was plugged into the knowledge of existence and it came loading in my system. There was a download in my little system from cosmic consciousness. Woah! [Laughter] I'm not joking, it sounds good. And everyone wants the same, that's why they have many followers because for them there was a before and after. And you're also looking for that, now it's a before and after that everything would be fine. You promise yourself that you go somewhere now and you work for it because without a promise of later, without a prize, without a gain, you would not go for it. It's a trap of existence. But even the masters step into it. It's fantastic! The so-called masters of self-realization… as if the self needs to realize itself, to be the Self. What kind of Self would that be which needs a self-realization? Another false one. But it always sounds good and it sells good.

So, if I would like to have a thousand or two thousand people, I should use beautiful words. And I have to tell my story of how it was before and after and you can have it too if you listen long enough to me. But when you are what you are, would you really cheat yourself like that? Tell me. Should I promise you something? Would you like that? Tell me. Do you want to be cheated? Yes, you want to be cheated because you want to believe. Of course, you want to be cheated. Something knows it is shit. But you want to be cheated because you want to believe that there's something after suffering, where there's no suffering anymore. You want to believe. That's why you look for it, you listen to it and your hope is running wild. If there's one who gives you hope, you go… 'Yes I want to believe'. Of course you want to believe, what else can you do? I cannot even blame you.

Q: May be it's about disbelieving what you believed before …

K: Then you believe that disbelieving is a way out of believing. Then you believe in disbelieving, that's another belief, believe me. [Laughing] And whatever starts with a 'may be' is like, I may be or may not be. May be in May I am and in June I am not but never in July.

But that you can even doubt that you are, you have to be. That you can even doubt, you have to be doubtlessness. So be what you are because doubtlessness is what you are. That you can even imagine that you are not That, you have to be That. It's crazy! To claim that you are not, you have to be. That's Ramakrishna's famous single sentence. That you believe not to be, you have to be. That you doubt yourself, you have to be That what is doubtlessness in nature. Without being the Absolute being, there cannot be doubtlessness of existence. But you want to have more, you imagine it cannot be so easy. But what do Zen Buddhists say? Easy is right and right is easy. But you want to have it complicated. Why not? Does it make you less if it's complicated? I like complications too, doesn't make me more or less, so what? Let it be complicated, let it be easy. If it can be complicated, it's very easy because it's complicated anyway. Did anyone follow? [Laughter] Follow me if you can.

Q [Another visitor]: What about memories in the human mind?

K: Never mind. Your personality is based on memories. So why not? Let it be based on memory or no memory. If there's a little thing in your brain called dementia, then all the personality is gone, isn't it fantastic!

All your personal memory is gone in one second. Who are you? All your precious insights, all your precious realizations. Imagine Mooji gets a dementia or Eckhart Tolle forgets about the 'now'. And everyone around is yelling at him, Eckhart 'now' and he asks, what 'now'? What do you want from me? [Laughter]

Dementia is like you die before you die. The person disappears and the body just decomposes. Where is your memory? In your left ear or the right ear? My left ear always hears something different than my right ear. Just in one instant, you're gone. As every night when you fall asleep, you're gone but still you are. So know yourself as that who doesn't need any presence of anyone or absence of anyone. What else do I talk about? I talk about that what you are, what doesn't need anything, never had any necessity of anything. That is satisfaction. That's why it's called joy, the joy of not needing joy. The peace that doesn't need peace. So peace-off!

The rest is fiction. The fiction wakes up in the morning. It's all science fiction. All the realization of so-called realized or non-realized, is fiction. The fictive realized, the fictive unrealized and a fictive enlightened... the before and after. Who wants to live forever?

Q [Another visitor]: They are trying to invent a pill that helps you forget...

K: They have already done it in Switzerland. They drop it into the water in the Rhine and then the Germans drink all that water and have dementia. Then all these old people who have the number accounts in Switzerland, they forget the number. Switzerland is living only due to dementia. All these banks are living by the fact that no one comes and claims. That's why they invented dementia and they put it in the water everywhere. The Germans always thought of Swiss as the milkmen who milked our cows but now they're milking us. [Laughter]

All your precious understanding, all your realization, all your gurus, will disappear like.... Ping... Where was I? Where was I not? Who am I? Who am I not? So, what are you after? What's in your bucket list for this life that you're still planning to do? Enlightenment? Meditation?

Buying house? Whatever you accumulated in this life, reading all the books, all things will blow away in the wind... *c'est la vie*. All your meetings with Shakti masters, shanti masters, puff... puff... Was there really something? I need to look into my calendar on that day. Where was Papaji? What did I read? But it was good energy. Did it trigger something? No. Was it real? And all the orgasms that you've had... puff... puff...

Q [Another visitor]: Even the so-called love between two people...

K: The only thing that remains is laughing. That's why in Buddhism they have the laughing Buddha. He doesn't know anymore what to laugh about, he's just laughing. That's the joy that you don't need to know why you're laughing. You don't have to understand the joke to be the joke. When you're the joke, you laugh. What else can you do?

Q: Laugh and love...

K: Love is too much. [Laughter] That's effort again.

Q: Some people say love, love, love...

K: [Singing] Love is in the air. Do you remember when we met first? Oh, I love you so much.

Q: They say all what remains is love...

K: That's why I say, all what remains is laughing. Laugh about yourself, about how stupid you are because you cannot escape your own stupidity. How can you? It's stupid to wake up in the morning, but try not to wake up. Try. What would you say? Can you succeed? That's called *vipasanna*, they always try to be awake for waking up, not to wake up. Because in waking up no one wakes up. That's *vipasanna*. But they fail in that because for maybe five days it works and then on the sixth day, they forget. Suddenly they're not there when they wake up and then they think, oh shit, I have to sit a bit longer. Every satori comes and goes. It doesn't bring anything, it doesn't take anything away. Just sitting down and looking at the wall because the body is so uncomfortable, so painful that the perception just disconnects from the body. Then they call it satori and then you're one with the spirit. Then for few months it holds because the perception is still disconnected but then by whatever event, it connects again. You get glued again to that. Then shit happens and you have to sit again. So, you fail again and again.

Q: What about this sacred feeling that we get?

K: Sacred is the most un-sacred idea you can have. What a fuck! Holy shit, I tell you. Something what's pure, is the dirtiest.

Q: All these people and all this respect...

K: You ask me something not because you want me to respect you. I don't anyway. There's no respect. Why should I respect for myself? Respect yourself, love yourself, all these impossible things you try, you suffer by that. The moment you try to love yourself, you suffer, you create an object of love. Then you're relative. What to do with this love? If you cannot escape it, you enjoy it. It doesn't bring what you want but...

Whatever is, is bad and for me that's good enough. If there's one thing that's good, that would be the worst. If everything is bad, it's fine... bad, bad, bad. That comes natural. If something is good, then you're in trouble.

Q [Another visitor]: What about this landscape?

K: Do you want to escape into this landscape? I disappeared into the sunset. And then in the morning, there's sunrise again. I disappeared into the beauty. There was a peace of art, I disappeared into it. The perceiver and that which was perceived was one. I disappeared and then I was in this oneness of pure bliss... whoa! Always sounds promising.

Q: But maybe it helps?

K: Yes, it helps to sell the paintings.

Q [Another visitor]: Sometimes there are saint's talk about the past lives...

K: That's totally insane. If there's a saint, there's in-sanity.

Q: You say all lineages are lineages of shit. When people say, Ramana is here, they don't refer to Ramana, they just refer to its essence...

K: Why then do they call it Ramana? Why not call it shit? Because even the essence of shit is knowledge. For me chit and shit is no different. When everything is shit, it's all chit because shit doesn't know shit and that's knowledge. If everything is shit, then it's chit because that what is shit doesn't know shit. You only know shit when there's something what is not shit. That's the mind... when there's something that's shit and something that's not shit. If everything is shit, that becomes chit, its knowledge. But if something is real and something is not real, then it's unreal. Reality doesn't know any real or unreal. It doesn't even know Reality. But the moment you know Reality, there's something what is not reality.

Q: If Ramana says that there are a lot of holy beings here, then someone thinks that they are somewhere in the corner where I cannot see them. There may be holy beings here since you are here...

K: They come for me? What to do with them? Have a party maybe, candlelight dinner with all the saints. [Laughter] They cannot even help themselves, these bloody saints. And they, for sure, cannot help you.

Q: Papaji sat under a tree and all the holy beings start to come...

K: Yeah. Krishna came there and then Rama came and Papaji realized they are not real. [Singing] Da, da, da... [Laughter] Then Mooji repeating these things that Papaji realized that even Krishna is not real. It's all fairy tale, but it's fair enough. Guruji, Papaji. Four years ago in Rishikesh, there was an advertisement of Mooji saying, Shri Shri Moojiji. Oh God! Meet the Shri Shri. If I hear the word tradition, I could just kick their ass! As if Ramana had a tradition, as if there's a tradition of the Self.

Q [Another visitor]: So, where did this need of rituals come from?

K: From you! You're guilty. It's a romance of the Self, they all come from the aroma. It's the essence of the Self. And you're the origin of all that shit, especially you, only you. Then she's like standing in a court case, 'It was not me'. [Laughter] 'I'm not guilty.'

Q: When I was a little girl...

K: [Singing] Kay sera sera... whatever will be will be, when I was a little girl I asked will I be rich... *kay sera sera*, the future is not ours to see, *kay sera sera*. That's a Ramana song. That's Ramana gita. [Laughter] The grace of Ramana was Grace Kelly... *Kay sera sera*. It was not me, I was not guilty...

No! You're fucking guilty, I tell you. You're the only one. The one and only who's guilty. It's all the story of the Self. You cannot take one bullshit out of it. It's the romance of self with itself. It's like an imaginary romance. You cannot take one imaginary aspect out of it. All of that is what you are in romance with yourself, but an imaginary one. You cannot take any event, not any experience out of the totality of life living itself. Impossible! Otherwise the Absolute would not be Absolute. No way! And you're Absolute stupid. When you're stupid, you're Absolute stupid. But the most stupid is that now you want to be the Absolute Self. But you're anyway Absolute. You cannot be more or less Absolute. That's the point. Then you make it dimensions of Absolute. Absolute dimensions, not to mention.

You cannot be less stupid. You're especially stupid when you don't want to be stupid. But what to do? Stupidity hurts, but what to do? Then you try to know yourself, you want to get out of stupidity and that's really stupid. That really puts you into ignorance. If you don't want to be ignorant, than you're really ignorant. You are ignorance and the nature of ignorance is knowledge. What's the problem with ignorance? And who owns ignorance? That's the main question. It's never your ignorance. Ignorance owns you, if at all.

Q [Another visitor]: People say...

K: Don't start like that.

Q: How should I start?

K: Just say 'I say' and not people say. When you say people say, you already call them stupid. Then you're saying people say and not me, I would never say that. I'm much more clever but people say that. So, what do people say?

Q: I often heard that...

K: That's even worse. Now you even repeat it. Earlier I recorded something and now I'm stupid enough to play the same record. So, what's your recording?

Q: Spiritual beings are working with us. What does that mean? What are they working upon?

[Laughter]

K: That's very deep. But people say that, you don't say that. You already know that there are no beings, I know. But you want to know why people say that. But you want to know if there's something right or wrong with it. Just be honest, don't hide behind people.

Q: I find these ideas attractive because it seems there are beings in other dimensions...

K: Yeah. They die there – *die*mension. Whatever has a dimension is dead. That's why it's called *die*mension. And by believing in that, you die in it. That's the only suicide you can commit. You murder yourself by being in a dimension. It's a murder and you will be punished for that. You murder yourself, any moment you believe that you're born or you're in any dimension. It's a murder, you're a criminal and for that you need to be imprisoned in that bloody body. That's the worst imprisonment you can have, being in the bloody body, being born a piece of shit.

Q: Even in the light body?

K: That's the biggest shit, the light body. That's lighter shit and this is heavier shit. [Laughter] You're right, even that's an idea, a concept of shit. As if the matter here, this gross body is lower than the higher light. Who makes that higher and this one lower? Do enlightenment ones fart light? And don't they stink anymore because it's a light fart? Do enlightened ones shit? And what comes out? Enlightened shit? That's why in India they collect the urine, the shit, they wash the feet of the guru but if it comes out from normal people, it's all dirty. For the enlightened one they collect the hair, the finger nail, everything gets collected somewhere. Fantastic! Then you build *samadhi's* everywhere like Ramana being mummified and then everyone comes to suck some light from his light body.

What to do? Everyone is suffering and everyone wants to get out of it. So, whatever gives them hope... and there is some energy in different level and resonance field. Everything is there. So, there's some different resonance. Then there are *poojas* and the body becomes a lingam later. But all of that is the story of the Self in different levels but the levels are not real. It's like seven different ways of realizing yourself or experiencing yourself. But the only Reality is the Absolute experiencer you are but not the way you realize yourself and there's nothing higher or lower in anything. Nothing is more pure or impure or anything. There's only purity because there's no second to anything. But even to call it purity is impure. You better don't call it anything.

Q: No higher beings?

K: Only you. You hire beings that help you. [Laughter] Sounds good, who did you hire today? I have this higher being, that higher being, my cleaning lady that comes later is my higher being. She was very expensive so I took another higher being. My washing machine is my higher being.

Q: The spiritual healers they claim that they work with entities...

K: Everything can happen. It may work. Everything is possible, even lower beings.

Q: But even that's based on beliefs?

K: No. It's just the way life lives itself; it's just fine. But there's no one who has an advantage or disadvantage with it. It's like a theatre or a play where no one goes home after the play because there was no one playing. In this Absolute dream of Parabrahman, everything is possible, everything is there. Whatever you can imagine, is there. Everything! Whatever you can imagine, is the Absolute imagining whatever has to be, has to be. You cannot take one thing out of it. If you could take one moment of suffering out of this life living itself, you could destroy life. But you cannot. All has to be there. All little whining and crying. That I'm supposed to sit has to happen. Imagine if I could avoid it! Fuck it all!

The moment you try to avoid suffering, you become the sufferer. What can you do? How can you not try to avoid it? And love makes you try to avoid it because in love for yourself, you want comfort and comfort would be the absence of suffering or misery. The Self-love is the root of all suffering. You cannot imagine that the love for yourself is the root of all misery because there's a 'me' involved, a lover and a beloved, the subject and an object. Instant misery. And now it's too late. You have to be in spite of it because it will never stop. It never started and it will never stop, this passion... Passion for yourself. Enough hopelessness?

That Shiva note had to be mentioned. It's like orchestral manoeuvres in the dark. That what's playing doesn't know what to play, it's just Orchestral Manoeuvres in the Dark.

20th July 2018 Talk 1
Ladakh

It's not about awakening,
it's about falling asleep again

∾

Q: The idea of not having any continuity is a bit scary...

K: He's still afraid and wants to know what comes next. No way out. There's always this curiosity and then you look towards the light. People have not killed themselves because they're just afraid that they miss something. They want to know what comes later. You don't want to miss the party, maybe there is something and I don't want to miss it otherwise you'd kill yourself already. What next? What shall I do next? What comes next? Maybe I miss something. Then I come and ask is there someone who's concerned in deep-deep sleep later? Now when you have a body, you think you're incarnated, then you're concerned about your *carne* (the Spanish word for 'flesh'). Then you have a carnival... the dance of the flesh. Then you say, no rock is not good for me, I want to have another body.

Q: Do you believe that reincarnation exists?

K: Of course! Look, consciousness reincarnates every moment, everywhere. This next moment is a reincarnation of consciousness from the moment before. But there's no personal reincarnation. It's not 'you' reincarnating. It's consciousness reincarnating moment by moment, again and again, infinite incarnation of consciousness... re-born again and again. This moment dies and the next moment gets born again... always rebirth, rebirth, rebirth. We need some birth control, an anti-baby pills for consciousness.

The seeker is seeking an anti-baby pill for consciousness because he wants to stop time. He wants to stop consciousness, stillness, silence. 'I want to stop it. I'm fed up with this moment and this rebirth and the next moment and the boring moment, never-ending moments.' Try harder. You will not succeed. This potential moment creates the next moment and the next moment. Never ending story. So, there's reincarnation but no one gets reincarnated because there's no one incarnated here now. How can someone who's not incarnated here get reincarnated? All what you can experience, is consciousness incarnating again and again. But never gets tired. So, there's no retirement for you. [Pointing to a visitor]

Q: But you told him he has to retire…

K: You will be retired.

Q: Once you spoke about the string of reincarnations…

K: He's so concerned about his genetic design. He knows exactly how much percentage he's Italian, German and the rest, he knows all the numbers. My finger is Italian, my thumb is maybe German. He's so concerned about the lineage he comes from. His back is Russian. [Laughing]

Q: I just cannot accept that there's no sense in this whole thing…

K: That makes sense. [Laughter] You cannot accept that nothing makes sense, there has to be some sense. No one can accept that it's all for nothing here. It's all for fun. No one can accept that, everyone thinks there must be some reason; there must be some sense. I have not suffered for nothing. All the while I was seeking and suffering and I went so deep in myself and penetrated myself from left to right and all for nothing? I went so deep into the void and then came out of it, and all for nothing? That's too much. I have kids… that must make sense!'

Q [Another visitor]: I'm missing something here, I don't seem to get the joke…

K: Right now you are the joke and for the joke it's not necessary to understand the joke. Just be the joke.

Q: Be the eye that cannot see the eye…

K: Like Ramana said be the 'I' of the 'I'.

Q: What cannot go through the eye of the needle?

K: The owner. There's a story in Israel that a camel goes through the eye of the needle but not its owner. The owner cannot enter the kingdom of heart because heart cannot be owned. No one comes to me with anything; you have to be the naked existence not knowing what you are and what you are not. With that nakedness you enter the kingdom of heart. But he still wants to know what clothes he wears next time. The translation is not correct when they say you have to be naked in front of the existence, everyone thinks he has to be naked in paradise. Nakedness means the absence of presence of any idea of what you are and what you are not. Naked existence that doesn't even know existence.

Q [Another visitor]: The way things happen, it seems like there's a plan...

K: When you look back you see there was a plan but if you look into the future, you want to know what the plan is. Then you go to a fortuneteller who is maybe already in the future and tells you what the plan is.

Q: Order seems to be the law of nature...

K: No. These are scientific problems. It's all science fiction. The quantum physics now says they don't know anything. All they can say is maybe there's a cat or maybe not. There's no proof of anything. They cannot find energy, they cannot find matter. They cannot find anything.

Q: In nature you find seasons, biology...

K: You don't find it. Didn't you listen right now? Now the climate changes and the seasons are gone. So, where's the order of nature?

Q: What about DNA?

K: [Pointing to a visitor] Look at him! Does he seem to be in order? Coca-Cola is in his blood. He had Coca-Cola transfusion. [Laughter] He proves that there's no rule, no order in nature because he can live by Coca-Cola. So what about the order of nature? You are an Italian you cannot even think like an Italian. It's amazing to think that even

Italians can think. If there would be an order in nature, they'd only drink espresso and not think. [Laughing] When one is afraid, he needs order. The Germans are very famous for that. We need order otherwise everyone does what he wants. That's not possible, we need order. Then there are mutations out of nature.

It's so simple that it doesn't need anything. Who sees the seer? Who sees the seeing and who sees what is seen? Who experiences the whole scenery but is never part of the scenery? Is there any 'who' in it? That you can say, is the Absolute Self experiencing itself in all possible ways? It seems to be that there's an order in it. There's a seer, seeing what can be seen. It's like a scenery, the presence of the scenery and the absence of scenery. The Absolute seer is in the presence of the scenery and in the absence of scenery what it is. So what is there to know?

That's the only thing to know – to be That what is in spite of presence and absence of any scenery, any sensational… whatever! Because the Absolute seer doesn't need to see anything to exist but the relative seer you believe to be always needs to see something.

Q: Does the relative seer disappear?

K: It cannot disappear because it never appeared. You cannot kill him because he doesn't have his own existence. It's never alive; it's just a phenomenal experience. But the noumenon experience never depended on the way this phenomenal experiencer experiences itself.

Q: This intellect seems such a…

K: Whenever there is an inter-lect there must be an outer-lect. [Laughter] Someone leaks inside and the other one leaks outside. You're inter leaking and outer leaking. It's like a baby coming to earth leaking. Then you need a pamperer. Then when the baby gets old, it goes to a guru – to another pamperer. Existence should take care, pamper me, pamper me, give me what I need. Everyone wants to be pampered. The baby never stops. Is there an order in it? The sucking baby trying to suck the universal tits of existence – 'Satisfy me please!' The never satisfied baby. The tit is never big enough, the milk is never good enough. Maybe for a moment by understanding there's stillness and then it starts again. The sucker never stops.

The phantom 'I', the so-called sucker 'I' can never get satisfied by what he's sucking. That's the way it is. Consciousness can never get satisfied by anything. Whatever happens, there's no satisfaction in anything. And that's the best for me. I cannot get satisfied by anything. Let's try... why not? But if you expect to get satisfied then you suffer and then you complain. You become a complainer, 'Why me? Why not him?'

Q: I like what you say that you can never get satisfied by anything...

K: And then you remain as That what never needs any satisfaction. If you just see this, it's just a never-ending story of non-satisfaction. You experience yourself in non-satisfaction because satisfaction cannot be experienced, cannot be owned. You cannot get satisfaction. It's like Mick Jagger, 'I can't get no, but I try'.

Q: That's the whole thing to keep trying to get satisfaction but you never get satisfaction...

K: So, there will never be any end because satisfaction cannot be reached. What you are is satisfaction in nature because it never needs anything. There's no need for anything. There's no hunger in what you are. But you experience yourself as permanently hungry. There's no end of being hungry for yourself.

Q: Sometimes there are just some breaks...

K: Yes, like falling asleep or occasionally there's a five minute understanding and then you want to go deeper. You want to find the end of the light of Shiva because you think then you would be satisfied. If I really find the end or the beginning. You want to find the beginning and then you say Awareness is the beginning. If you reach awareness, then you make it. Then you reach awareness and still you are not satisfied. Or maybe it takes a bit longer to be unsatisfied because there is no time in that. In no-time there's a phenomenal satisfaction because you think it's so peaceful here but even that is still different from something that's not peaceful. Sometimes you land somewhere where it's more comfortable. Then for sure you go back to that what's not so comfortable. In Tao they say that you can stay there for thousands of lifetimes but out of the blue there comes an intention. Then you're back in the market place and you're thirsty as before. The glass is still there because there was no time in between. In no-time thousands of lifetimes is nothing. Then the next moment is already there and you're as thirsty as before.

No escape! And I sit here and show you that you cannot escape what you are. And you have to experience yourself in satisfaction and in dissatisfaction, both come together. Both are ideas. There's comfort and discomfort. Absence is comfort and presence is discomfort. Heaven and hell permanently. But who is in heaven and who is in hell? It's just two ways of realizing yourself. Two faces of your nature. The two faces of Shiva. So, what to do? You cannot rip off your faces. But you only want to experience one face and that's called suffering. Having a preference of comfort.

Q: I experienced that yesterday, once I woke up from sleeping that I was trying to create a preference for the absence...

K: Everyone here has a preference of sleep because everyone here would rather be asleep than awake. Absence is better than presence. If you could sleep forever you would never wake up again. But you wake up again and again. You want to avoid discomfort and that creates the 'me'. That's the misery, the avoidance of yourself because this is what you are, not more not less. You are as Absolute you are in Absolute presence as in Absolute absence. Absolute hell and Absolute heaven.

Q: So why would Ramana Maharshi ask for abiding in Self for longer periods of time. He said at first it would be intermittent...

K: No. He talked about getting initiated into that. You get initiated, the light gets lit. It's just like you have an 'Aha, there's no way out'. That's the 'a-ha' of no way out. You cannot leave what you are. In that you abide in that what you are because it has no problems with it. What you are has no problems with presence or absence. But if you are in presence as one who is in the presence then you have a problem.

Be as you are, be Absolute. That what he's pointing at, 'Abide as that what you are' means be Absolute and the Absolute can never get more or less by anything. So you don't get more by presence or less by absence, that's what he's pointing at. Establish yourself in that what never needs to be established in anything because nothing is more natural than being what you are which never needs any establishing in anything. Abide in that what never needs to abide in anything. That's always a paradox. It's always like a *koan* that you cannot break. Be that what you cannot not be. But it's not something what you can do.

Q: That's the issue…

K: That's what I say – the highest is silence, being quiet. Just be quiet and by nature just abide in that what is quiet, what never moves. You don't get established in that, that's just a pointer. You just abide as that what never needs to abide in anything, where there's no necessity of anything and this pre-taste of that is lighting the fire of the Self. This lights the fire for loving that what is the Self and breaks the love for the imaginary self because it shows you that the imaginary Self can never be satisfied. The only satisfaction is being what you are. And it's always available, it's always present. You cannot not be That. It's more than natural, it doesn't need any effort. It is laziness itself. Nothing has to go, nothing has to come for you to be what you are. So, abiding in that is impossible but you have to try and you will fail. And maybe in that failing you are That what will always fail… failing not to be what you are. You fail not to be.

That's why it is meditation. Meditation is *neti-neti*, you stay in the middle. You are neither present nor absent – that's meditation. But there's no meditator possible. You just be what you are and that's meditation. There's no expectation in it. There's no one who meditates and wants to have more peace, 'Oh I became so peaceful, I became more aware.' Ha, ha, ha. That's fucking work but not meditation. That kind of meditation is expectation. It's for sure not meditation. Meditation is being that what is in the centre of existence. Then there are two faces and you are neither that nor That, you just stay as you are. Neither time nor no time. But it's impossible to do. People come to me and say that today I meditated for five hours. Wonderful! Sounds very nice.

In Ramana ashram they come to the meditation hall sitting

somewhere and looking around if anyone is looking at them. [Laughter] They want people to see them meditating and looking at their nice and relaxed face. I'm working so hard for my peace of mind and don't you dare disturb me otherwise I'll kill you. Go to Tiruvannamalai and look at them after meditation, everything disturbs them. Everything! They're the most easily disturbed people ever. They are so touchy – 'Leave me alone, I just meditated.' [Laughter] That's the meditator!

No. It has to be twenty-four seven, and three hundred and sixty five. If you meditate just for two hours for world peace – peace off! What is twenty-four seven, and three hundred and sixty five? You are! Just that what is uninterrupted, in presence and absence of... whatever. So, meditation is your nature. You meditate in presence and you meditate in absence. There's nothing but meditation. Meditation is the way you realize yourself. What else can you do? But you want to make it right. You want to bring order into it, then you're fucked. You want to control it. Then you have a preference. I have a preference to be Renz. I'd rather be Renz than anyone else. That's quite a prefer*enz*.

Q: As you say, you cannot do it. It can't be done because that's just the mind...

K: But you cannot not look for it because the misery is so intense and you want to get out of the discomfort. What can you do? That's why I see that you cannot help it. You have to look for so-called enlightenment or awakening because this is unbearable. Any moment not being what you are is misery... just by nature. That's the order. Any moment you're not the Absolute nature, you miss it and missing is misery. What can you do? The only way of ending this misery is being what you are but not by you trying to find it. It's not something you can find or you can achieve.

Only by failing you are. Failing is wonderful, it's joy – 'I failed again!' How many times have I failed again? Infinite times. A student asks a master, 'What's the difference between you and me?' The master says, 'You fail sometime, I fail all the time.' If there's really any difference between a master and a disciple, it is that a master fails permanently and the student fails sometimes. And then he fails more and more times until there's no time anymore between the failings because there's faaaailing. [Laughter] Uninterrupted faaaaaiiiiiiling. Presence failing and absence failing. I can only repeat it... there's an uninterrupted joy in failing and there's a misery in finding yourself. Right now you found yourself as a body, as a person. Finding is a problem. Succeeding to know yourself and you know yourself that you're in a misery. You fucking know yourself that you're in suffering. So, my dear knowers.

Then they say be as a baby because the baby doesn't know any baby. Ask the baby, are you a baby? And it just looks up blankly. Brmmm... brmmm... brmmm... Then when it is three years old mother succeeded. Mothers are always guilty for all the misery of the world. The hand on the cradle creates a war in the battlefield. But still I love my mama because she had a mama too. So whose mama is guilty? The mama of the mama, mama, mama... That's why he [Pointing to a visitor] wants to have a genetic lineage. Where was the first mama who did this for the first time? Was it Eve?

If you don't even know if you are or if you are not, who can suffer? This not knowing what you are and what you are not. Where is the suffering in it? You only suffer because you know who you are and what you suffer about. There has to be knowledge about something, some concept about your existence. You fall in love with an image of yourself and now you want to break that love but as much as you want to get rid of that image... out of love again. So love is the mother of invention, inventing everything. Actually I show you what you cannot do.

Q [Another visitor]: Did you say that there's no relative seer?

K: There's no Reality in the relative seer. It does not have its own existence. So it cannot be real. But you are in love with a phenomenal, sensational, non-existing existence. Then you want to make that real. You have an existential crisis right now because you feel intuitively that there's something that's fleeting, fragile. You want to make it stable. You want to become real. The unreal now tries to become real but the unreal cannot become real. It's impossible, you will fail. The real doesn't need to become real because the real doesn't even know what is real and what is not real. And that what now knows what's real or unreal, who wants to become real, will never become real. The real and unreal can only exist in non-reality. It's fantastic! And there's no bridge between that because there're no two.

It's a joke! You want to confirm that what permanently needs confirmation. You got baptized by the bloody church. You need all the strings attached, the family, relatives just that your fleeting existence can survive. You need all these bank accounts and your numbers and all your memory effects and all your order... The last year it was like this and it should be like this. My last lover did it like this so it has to be like this otherwise maybe I'm not so stable. Then you touch and say there must be some reality in what I can touch. It's proven that it hurts. Who needs to prove himself? Only a phantom needs proof. And it permanently needs proof, I think therefore I Am... like the French. For Italians it is, maybe I fuck therefore I am. [Laughter] The actor always needs to be active to prove that there's an actor. That's consciousness – always needs action. Action please!

How to kill that actor? And who needs to kill that actor? That's the main question. Who has the necessity that something has to stop? Me! If I could control actions then I am in control. Then I'm the king. But there's no king in the kingdom of heart. The king cannot be there. When you're king, you're king doomed because you believe you're the king and no one does what you want. Then you always complain. My kingdom, my body, my thoughts. Then you try all the techniques to control your thinking. Actually all the exercises are for the reason that you don't want to feel the body because you want to have comfort. Comfort means healthy. I'm healthy means I don't feel my body and I want to continue doing that. Then you have doctors who cannot even help themselves.

Q [Another visitor]: I'm trying to replace my Italian blood with Coca-Cola...

K: That you already did. [Laughter] *Morfine*, Heroin... all the drugs are made for that. That's called the bar meditation. Go to a bar and drink as much as it's needed to drink yourself away. Then you feel that there's a joy of absence of 'me'. Then the 'me' comes back with double strength in the next morning. It's like five times 'me'. They hangover everywhere. [Laughter] Then you have to drink again.

The people who meditate do the same. If they do not meditate for one day then they are really angry... 'I did not meditate today, I have to sit down.' All junkies. You experience that in the morning. The moment you wake up, what wakes up is a junkie. You're always looking for some drug. Even enlightenment is a drug, the blissful drug. Whatever happens then is a drug. You're drugged by drugs, by hope. Hope is a drug, grace is a drug, bliss is a drug. All drugs, drugs, drugs. Then you have an idea, you go to AA (Alcoholics Anonymous) or SA... Seekers Anonymous group. Then you're very proud... My name is Hans and I haven't been seeking for thirty days. [Laughter] Then the next one comes, my name is Fredrick and I've not been seeking for a hundred and twenty days and if you need some help, I can help you.

Why do I have to make fun about everything? I cannot help making fun about myself, always talking to what I am. For me that's absolutely amazing that there's myself believing that he exists in this relative way. It's unbelievable. I'm still amazed by how it functions that you fall in that trap. But I see you cannot avoid the trap because the trap is made by yourself. And the one and only biggest trap is love because only love can make you so stupid to believe in yourself... only love. There's no other power that can be so stupid that you believe that you have a body. Fantastic! And you cannot kill that bastard... love. It's so famous and everyone writes about it and everyone wants it. Love is the biggest drug. Trying to get attention and that someone loves me because when someone loves me, it confirms my existence since I don't love myself. There's no one here who loves himself otherwise you would not sit here.

Q [Another visitor]: It's like being your own Facebook wall...

K: [Laughter] Likes, likes, likes... Even you don't love yourself but then there should be others who are stupid enough to love you. Then you wear make-up just to be loveable. Men make money to be loveable. Then they make babies because it's all a make-up of existence otherwise no one would have babies anymore.

Q [Another visitor]: The worst-case scenario is when no one agrees with you...

K: This problem I have all the time. They are all quiet because maybe they're afraid what I answer. No one ever agreed with me. When they're clever, they are quiet and they say, let him talk. [Laughter] Everyone inside thinks, no this cannot be, it's bullshit.

Q: If this person disagrees with you, is that the worst-case scenario?

K: No. I wouldn't mind.

Q: Okay, I agree eighty percent...

K: We can work on the last twenty. It could be twenty years, twenty life times, twenty centuries, let's see how long it takes. I have time, infinite time. The last time I told you the same.

Q: Disagreeing is not good...

K: Why not? I have no idea of good or bad so I agree with you... maybe. I can always say I don't know how it is to be what I am. I don't need anything. This blah, blah, blah just comes out of... whatever. It's not because I know something. There's no need for knowledge. I am with and without... whatever. And for me whatever comes out is as good or bad as anything. It doesn't need to be proven. I don't have to be right to be right. I'm right anyway. I'm always right, that's my problem. What can I do? I'm especially right when I'm wrong because it's more fun.

If existence doesn't need to be proven anymore, there's nothing to gain or to lose in anything, what's the problem? Who needs to agree with me? Everyone can just go away and think this is all bullshit and I would be fine. I don't have to convince anyone of whatever.

Q: But the problem is for me...

K: But that's not my problem.

Q: I know...

K: I thought you wanted to make it my problem. I have many who wanted to make it my problem. And sometimes they even succeed, then we have a problem but not for so long. It comes and goes. So I'm not even afraid of a problem, that's quite a problem. Having a problem doesn't make me less and having no problem doesn't make me more. Problem, no problem, who fucking cares? And who counts the percentages? Eighty percent, ninety percent or anything? Agreeing or not agreeing. You are in agreeing what you are and you are in not agreeing what you are. I don't need your agreement.

Q: I agree but I don't know why...

K: You don't know what is agreeing, that's the best. I need some people who don't agree with me; that's more fun.

Q [Another visitor]: Is it possible to have any problem when there are no expectations?

K: Yes.

Q: I disagree...

K: Why?

Q: From my understanding a problem is caused by expectations of what it should be and what it is at the moment.

K: But the problem with that is you think you know what it is.

Q: If I had no expectation...

K: There would still be one too many who has no expectation and that one has a preference of no expectation. Then he's very proud that there's no expectation and I have no problem with that, that's actually everyone. There's a joke, how to know if someone is Vegan? Just wait for five minutes he tells it by himself. [Laughter] That's like the same with one who has no expectation. Go to Byron Bay, there are Papaji left overs saying, I called off the church (search). [Laughter] They tell you immediately. They are very proud inside. I understand that I don't expect anything anymore, not me. Then they make a church out of it, like a religion, a non-expecting church. All the other religions believe that God should satisfy them but I don't expect anything so I don't need any God. God is only for people who expect something but since I don't expect, I don't need anyone.

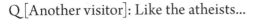

Q [Another visitor]: Like the atheists...

K: In Texas now the atheists have a special group that kills believers. They say that believers create all the wars and all the bad things on earth. Everyone has a different God. I don't believe in any God so I shoot the believers as they are the problem. I could never imagine that an atheist could become a terrorist, fighting for their non-existing God. [Laughter] They really believe in God because they believe there is no God. And to believe that there is no God, there has to be God who cannot be.

I agree that it would be a personal advantage not expecting anything. But there's a disadvantage that there's one who needs not expecting something to be content. There's a need in it, there's a condition in it. Even if someone says I love you unconditionally, if you don't do what I want, I'll kill you... Ha, ha, ha. [Laughter] I take you in my heart but now you have to behave because whatever is in my heart has to behave. I own you now in my heart so do what I want. I don't let anyone else in my heart, you are the only one. What a prison!

Why not expect everything? I expect everything from everyone, always the worst. I expect the worst. I'm always positively surprised that it's not so bad. Nothing helps. Even this sounds like a hope again that when I don't expect something then I'm closer to that what is my nature. That's the next trap, the non-expectation trap.

Q: It's not about getting closer...

K: But you want to have peace.

Q: It's just surrendering to life...

K: Who surrenders what? Who the fuck are you who can surrender something? 'Look at me, I surrendered. I surrendered everything to life. Life owned me anyway before, but still I surrendered.'

Q: But the previous ideas make up all a lot of suffering...

K: The non-sufferer is still a sufferer, I tell you. The non-seeker is still a seeker. There's no way out. The no 'me' is still a 'me'. It always sounds promising but it's an empty promise. It's all empty. Whatever is different is empty. If accepting life would be better than non-accepting life, what would that be? Would life be more natural in accepting or non-accepting? What kind of life is that? A relative needy life. Is that worth being? Depending on that you have a little pleasure or less suffering because now you don't expect anything anymore? For the person, I agree maybe he has a better life. But in that what I talk about, I have no interest. If you are happy with it, I don't mind. I don't want to change you. If you're fine with non-expecting and life becomes a bit more easy, that's fine for me but don't ask me any further. If that's your goal, go for it... having an easy life. Ramesh Balsekar was a very good psychotherapist in this area, one of the best. If you really follow him step by step, you would have an easier life. No complications anymore because you don't expect, it's all God's will. If you really follow that, there would be a so-called *better* life. If that's your goal.

Q: But if you struggle all the time...

K: That's what I said. If you want to have a better life because you think this is not so good and something else is better. Not expecting is better than expecting.

Q: Having peace inside...

K: But what kind of peace is that? It's a peace of shit. [Laughter] It's a peace of shit, depending peace depending on a special circumstance. What kind of peace of shit is that? A shitty peace because you're fragile that it could be destroyed any moment. God will cut you down, I tell you... by your so-called achievements. There's no chief in life but everyone wants to be the chief, chief of police, chief of a tribe with feathers all over... Chief Broken Knee. [Laughter]

You can achieve whatever you want to achieve in this life. You can become like a chief, an avatar, the chief of the universe, you can control all the energetic movements just by intention. You can control the entire universe but you'll only control shit because you cannot control yourself. It's the same as using acceptance as a tool for achieving something. You'll always fail because that what you achieve will be taken away because it's already given by life and it will be taken away by life. It's not your achievement if you like it or not. It's never your doing, never your achievement, never your effort who did that. It's given by life, it will be taken away by life, your so-called little pleasure. It's very fragile, very depending. So what to do with it? Enjoy it as long as it lasts. But see that it will end and you still will be what you are. It'll be different again and again. And you'll always step in the same trap again. The trap is perfect. What to do?

Q: Why would it be step in the same trap?

K: Love. What did I say before? A memory. Last time it was so nice, let me try again and again. Hate it. Hate is so natural. Hate comes by nature, love by effort. Love is work, I hate you anyway is easy. Unconditional hate. It's just the opposite, unconditional love and unconditional hate. Both are bullshit. But just to make it in harmony I say it's so nice to be in unconditional hate. You don't have to fight for that. No one wants it from you. You can keep your unconditional hate. You don't have to prove it.

But if you tell someone that I'm in unconditional love, you have to prove it all the time. Then you're fucked, permanently. When you say I don't expect anything anymore then everyone comes and tests you. You don't expect anything? Let's see. There will be a challenge. But if I hate you anyway, everyone is fine. They don't fight against you. But if you say that I love you anyway, ha, ha, let's see what I can do against that. I will behave in a way that maybe you stop loving me. That's called marriage. [Laughter] Because no one allows anyone to control him by anything. You will make sure he hates you because that proves that he cannot control you.

So far so bad!

Q [Another visitor]: Isn't there anything spiritual about silence?

K: Who can be in silence? What can be in silence? What does silence mean? Is there any existence in silence?

Q: No...

K: So, what are you talking about? What a joke if someone says I was in silence. Who can define silence? Who can experience silence? If you're not there, who experiences silence? You can maybe experience the absence of 'me' and you call it silence but that's not silence. Silence is not the absence of a 'me'. Silence is in presence and in absence of whatever you can imagine, that's silence and that's your nature. But no one can *be* in silence. Giving it a name 'silence' is already a mistake. Silence would never call itself silence. That what you call silence is just an absence of disturbance. So, its bullshit.

Q [Another visitor]: How to see it as bullshit when it feels so nice?

K: It's like an orgasm and you want to have it again and again. Then you suffer when you don't have it. This little happiness experiences make you suffer. You want to have it permanently again and again. You suffer any moment that you don't have it. Happiness makes you suffer. Comfort makes you suffer because you want to have it permanently so comfort makes you suffer. So, experiencing comfort is discomfort. Experiencing happiness is unhappiness. The experience of happiness is experience of unhappiness.

Q: It's like someone gives you a lot of money...

K: Then depend on him. Then you have to be fucking grateful.

Q: You can lose that anyway...

K: Money never makes anyone happy anyway. That was not a good example. Maybe it makes you happy if your girlfriend does not complain one day but then you're afraid that the next day it comes for sure. So, it's better that she complains all the time because then you don't expect anything anymore.

You have to see that when there's happiness, there's also the opposite of happiness. They come together. Comfort comes with discomfort. Light comes with darkness. All comes together. If you have a preference of light than darkness is bad.

Q: Is it that absence is the silence you're searching for?

K: It's not the silence you're searching for. Every night there's absence. You're an expert of absence. More than ninety five percent of the day there's absence... there's no one there. There's only five percent a day of disturbance where you exist as a 'me'. Only in disturbance there's a 'me'. During ninety five percent of the day you don't exist. Everything happens automatically. Only when someone steps over your feet, then you exist as a 'me' as the one who's disturbed. If it's more than ten percent, then you're already in the mad house because your nervous system cannot take it. You get crazy. If it's eight percent you already take drugs. If it's five percent you can just balance. Then the enlightened one is maybe one percent. Then already he's a saint. Woah, he's only one percent disturbed today like Dalai Lama. I like him because they always complain that he's still angry and shouting against his assistants. He has some real temper. Then they ask him, 'You are Dalai Lama, you must be enlightened. Why do you get angry if something is not right'? He simply says, 'Why should I care about the genes of my father?' In Moscow this joke was translated as Dalai Lama is angry because of the blue jeans of his father. [Laughter]

In that sense when you drive in the car now and you get angry or mad, it's not you. It's just your ancestors running through you. Sometimes you hate someone and you don't know why. Maybe your ancestor had an issue with someone with a similar face and now you wonder why do you hate this guy? Or why do I like her? Maybe one of your ancestors had a good sex with that person. Then you expect it again. You never know why you have affection towards someone or hatred. Sometimes you can't stand the smell of the kitchen. Maybe one of the ancestors was burnt in the kitchen by the same smell. All of this runs in you. All the bloody past and the future. And it's not yours, it's just ripples. Ripples, ripples, ripples... Sometimes you feel like a cow and you don't know why.

To care or not to care, is that the question? This trinity of mind, no-mind, never-mind. It's like caring, not caring, who cares? Who cares if there's caring or no caring? Or acceptance or non-acceptance? Who cares? The question always is who has the advantage in anything? Who needs that advantage? And the answer is always 'me'. What is this 'me'? A fleeting shadow of sensational cluster of memory effects of genetic design of whatever. It's not stable, it's totally fleeting. Every morning you wake up as someone different. You never wake up as the same person; always slightly different. You have to recollect yourself. Recollect yourself to know how you are and you need all the family and friends and partner to tell them how you are – I'm never like that, I'm always like that. And you have to all the time talk about how you are because you're so afraid that you'll forget who you are and how you are. What a fear! You cannot imagine that you are even without knowing how you are. Fuck it!

That's why you have friends to talk. You call them in the morning and ask, how are you today? Yesterday was like this and blah, blah, blah... like sewing machines making your clothes stitch by stitch. So much existential fear that it always tries to remember how it was yesterday and how you are. Otherwise you would not even know how you are or how you react to anything. So I ask you, surprise yourself. You don't have to fear to be whatever. What's the problem to be different? You're different anyway. No moment is the same. It's maybe similar but not exact, it's always unique. Every moment, every sensation is totally unique. But you still believe that this body behaves like this and if I don't behave like this then I don't know myself anymore. Then I'm afraid that I don't know myself anymore. Then I don't know how I'd react. Then what if something happens and I cannot control.

Q [Another visitor]: Is it just like a survival mechanism?

K: No. It's just trying to keep friends. Surprise your friends. If your friends are still your friends if you behave as you are, we can talk about it.

Q [Another visitor]: What are friends?

K: One confirmer confirms another confirmer who needs a confirmation. It's like an agreement of phantoms – friends. The friends confirm that you exist and you confirm that they exist. And you know how they are and they know how you are, that you behave as a friend, as long as it's in a frame of acceptance. If they step over the limit, over the border, then suddenly the friend becomes an enemy. The same person, the same friend – instantly you'd like to kill him. The love affair turns into a hate affair and you don't even know why, just by some little behaviour. Some little event suddenly turns everything into opposite. Someone notices a phone number of a friend and you become suspicious and then there's a seed of doubt. Then suddenly you start hating the friend, then you don't trust him anymore. All of that collapses very easily. It's a very fragile thing – friendship. Love affair is even more fragile.

Q: If you don't feed these relationships, then they are over. You have to be connected...

K: This year I have received a golden confirmation. But who wants to meet them again? Friends!

Q: You said before that we carry all the things from our ancestors...

K: Yes. All the genes and behaviour comes as a mixture from your past ancestors. It's not yours; it's just a cocktail of tendencies, cocktail of behaviours of whatever. It's not yours. If I look at my father I know exactly where something comes from. It's not your fault, you cannot help it. Trying not to be like that is the worst because then you're permanently trying not to be your father or mother. But you are your father and mother. You are your grand, grandfather and mother. This moment is a result of all the moments before. Or maybe what comes... maybe the future decides what comes now so that the future can be as it already is. Imagine! The future demands what you do now so that the future can be as it is. You've never done anything. It's a demand of... whatever. It's a product of the past and the demand of the future and in between you are sandwiched. Then you try to become a witch to control it. You even want to change your past because you always lie about your past you know that. Everyone lies about their past. You think no one would like you if you told the truth. Everyone is bad – criminals. Whoever you meet is a criminal. Thieves! All thieves! They are stealing your attention. They are all attention thieves.

Q [Another visitor]: There's a certain effort to stay here...

K: That's why I talk you to death. Then it becomes more and more like an effort to be present. Then by nature you are suddenly that what is the pre-sense. Then there's something unbelievable, indescribable, something that you don't know. Nothing is more pleasant as being that. It's pleasure itself. Then you come back but you have to make effort to stay here. Then I talk you again to death then you are pre-sent where you are not even absent, there's just pre-sense. Every effort is too much because laziness takes over. Laziness is so attractive; nothing is more attractive than laziness. If you taste that laziness everything else becomes empty. It's all pale and empty. This is the Absolute intention of what I'm talking, what I'm doing that I talk you to death because this is the initiation of laziness.

Q: That's very attractive...

K: I just tell you all the secrets, all the magic. [Laughter] For a while you fight to be present but you get exhausted because that what is the self is so attracted by that what is the Self. In that, effort cannot remain. That's why after a while many people just fall asleep, they cannot be present anymore.

That's why I say it's never about awakening. It's more about falling asleep in that what you are by being present. It's never about waking up from something. It's not about an awakening; it's more like falling asleep again. Just being – not even knowing what is. It's not waking up to your true fucking nature. There's no waking up to anything. That you woke up from something, that's the problem. The waking up is the problem and not the falling asleep. Being asleep while awake. I know what they mean by awakening, but...

Q: And what do they mean by it?

K: They think you're in the false identification and you should go to the right identification. You identify yourself into something what is false. The false nature and the true nature. So you wake up from your false nature to your true nature but there's still one too many who woke up to his true fucking nature. Who defines true and false? So you better fall asleep to that what has no bloody idea about true or right. There's no fucking concept about right or wrong or anything. That's the pleasure of your being, the joy of what you are and not now waking up to your true fucking nature. Then telling others, you should wake up too. I woke up, so you should wake up too. I'd shoot them right away and then maybe there's more peace. They all want something from you as if something is wrong with you. I'd say everything is wrong with them, these awakened ones.

Andrew Cohen talks about evolution of consciousness. What fucking consciousness needs an evolution? No he's back and has mastered his ego. There's now a master-bation again. I should talk with him one day.

Q [Another visitor]: Is it like dementia?

K: It's self-forgetfulness but how can you forget yourself? You never need to remember you don't have to forget. Self-forgetfulness is again a personal advantage.

Q [Another visitor]: It takes some effort to be alert and relaxed at the same time...

K: But that everyone tries... being alert and relaxed at the same time. [Laughter]

Q: So, why do we fall asleep? I just fell asleep and I was not even tired...

K: The interest just disappears. The perception has no interest and then it goes to the absence, that's all. That what is sensing everything senses himself as the presence or the absence and sleep is just an absence. That what is the absolute sensor, what is not a sensation, you cannot have any attribute on it. The Absolute experiencer cannot even be called as an experiencer. You don't have to know what it is. Sleep is just opposite to waking state. Presence is waking state and in absence there's nothing. Nothing and everything. So, you don't fall asleep it's just that your perception goes to the other side where there's no perceiver. There's no story, no memory. Then you call it sleep as there's no one there who makes a story out of it. Then when the sensor senses again, it makes a story out of its perception. I perceived and my reference point and all of that. There's an absence of all of that. But you're never not what you are.

You are the Absolute experiencer and you permanently realize yourself and you realize yourself as the presence or the absence. It doesn't make any difference for what you are if you're present or absent. It's totally indifferent. You're Reality realizing yourself in the so-called presence of being awake and that what you call the absence of the presence. What to do with it? When you don't expect anything more in the presence, you go to the absence. Then by nature you go back to the presence. When you have an exhausted self and the body is exhausted, then you go to the absence because the tool is burnt out for the moment and then you fall asleep. It's like a camera without energy. Then you go to the other... You don't even go there, there's one face and then there's another face. Actually right now here and now there's presence and absence. There's no presence without absence and there's no absence without presence. It's not as if you shift anything. It's just that your attention goes to the absence, which is already here. It's not something that changes.

The form and the formless are permanently there. The form is the presence and the formless is the absence. That what is the formlessness is here now. You don't have to wait for it. Without the absence there could not be any presence. How can there be any presence? In what? The presence can only be in the absence and the absence can only be in the presence and both are in nature not different. So, what to do with it? And no way out! Your body is resting but you never rest, you don't need to rest. You're the restlessness and the rest and the no-rest are just two faces of what you are... death and life.

Q [Another visitor]: This is a new concept for me, putting you to sleep rather than awakening...

K: Sounds good, just invented it. I have to remember that. [Laughing]

Q: Everybody talks about awakening...

K: I know! And they claim that they're awakened otherwise they would not tell you that awakening is better than what's happening now. And awakening always happens in the future. Eckhart Tolle would say, 'Now? Where's the awakening? Is there anyone who's asleep now? Think about it... but now!'

What would you say? Is the now already too late? Or is the now too early? What do you think? They put something in time what's never part of time. It's amazing! Awakened ones and non-awakened ones. Where do they exist? Only in a dream of phantoms. In this shadow world of dreams there're are awakened shadows and non-awakened shadows. Awakened ones need unawakened ones otherwise they would not be special. It's like an agreement, you play the unawakened one and I play the awakened one and then we have a party. I play my part, you play your part. Just for fun I'm unenlightened today.

You pretend not to know what you are, just for fun. But after a while the fun becomes serious. Then you're in trouble. It's like Shiva plays with the puppets – just for fun with his so-called creation. But after a while he forgets that he was not even the creator. Then he forgets himself that he's never part of the creator or the creation. In that self-forgetfulness he becomes a puppet of himself. Then the Self wants to be Shiva again and from then on whatever he does is futile. He cannot become what he is. But then he has ideas about being bigger cosmic consciousness. Maybe if I accept everything as it is then maybe I become Shiva, maybe, maybe, maybe. From then on whatever he does is futile. But he tries because it's unbearable not to be Shiva. By love for himself he tries to become Shiva again but he never lost his nature in the first place. He just did it for fun but then fun became fucking serious!

Q: So, he just has to remember?

K: But remembering doesn't work because what you are cannot be remembered because you have never forgotten. You can only remember what you have forgotten. But you haven't forgotten that you exist. So, how can you remember? There's no need for remembering, come on! But if you want to remember, you become a member again. Member of society of awakened ones. Then the new earth waits for you. The new Eckhart Tolle, the new earth. You become a soldier for peace. Peace Off!

Q: It appears that people like Robert Adams and Adyashanti have come to some kind of resolution...

K: That's the problem. They have arrived at some kind of resolution. And then?

Q: It appears to be very alluring...

K: Then you're attracted. And then? You get a role model and you believe that if I would be like them, I would be fine. So, now you have a role model. Then you only are your natural self when you are like them. Then you have this illusion. It's like a golden cow, they just make an ideal. They are all ideals, expecting if I would be like them. They made it and I want to make it too. Why not? Whatever attracts you is what? A fiction. What else can it be? It's fiction!

Q: Even Karl attracts me...

K: Fiction! This is a fictive Karl. But I do my very best to not be attractive. [Laughter]

Q [Another visitor]: But the more you do, the more it becomes attractive...

K: I cannot help it. But if you ask me I would pretend to be the biggest chauvinist asshole and still people would look at me with those eyes...

Q [Another visitor]: Because they see carelessness...

K: Nothing is more attractive than that carelessness, what doesn't have any resolution of anything. The one who gives a fuck about whatever, of resolution or no resolution, of awakening or non-awakening. The one who talks to you 'I' to 'I' and there's no expectation from you. From one asshole to the other. [Laughter]

Q [Another visitor]: That's good!

K: [Laughter] That feels good. Dr. Feelgood. Where you can be as you are because everyone knows that they are the biggest assholes on earth and always try that no one knows it, pretending to be good. Imagine you are enlightened and you have to behave like one. What a bullshit! Permanent effort. Then they're always exhausted.

Q: But there must be something in it for them...

K: Of course! Attention, attention, attention. The phantom needs attention. And an enlightened one gets the biggest attention. If you have five hundred thousand disciples everyone gives their attention. Even if you pay for it by being tired, you like it because you get attention. You work your ass off for attention. Like a rock star, if no one comes anymore you kill yourself. You're so depending on the fact that people love you. Woah! I like it when people hate me. That's the same attention. I try my best but it's really hard that people hate me.

Q: But we don't know that aspect of the story that they feel exhausted after all that story...

K: I met Eckhart Tolle in 2002. It's all show business. You have to ask their girlfriends.

Q [Another visitor]: Then they close the doors at night and behind the doors they say fuck you all...

K: I say that while I'm still here. [Laughter] I don't need closed doors. If you ask me what's natural, when there's hate there's hate, when there's love there's love. If you're exhausted that doesn't make you exhausted. It's just another experience. Who cares if the body is exhausted or the nervous system is fragile or anything? It happens. But does that make you less if you appear exhausted or something? That's the main question, what makes you less and what makes you more?

Q: It feels like...

K: Who?

Q: We, me...

K: We and me comes together. So what to do with we and me?

Q [Another visitor]: As you said when you're tired, you're tired. The only problem seems to be when there's a judgement about it...

K: If you're an enlightened one and you are exhausted after every ten minutes then maybe after a while you don't have any disciple anymore. So you need to be fresh and shining like a flower with a little help from your friends, like a picture of Papaji or Ramana and your lineage somewhere. It always pumps you up. Then there's a story of 'my' awakening and you repeat it all the time, what happened then and then. My guru had that experience with Ramana. You keep it alive otherwise no one would be interested. You have to repeat it all the time otherwise even you would forget it. Who would you be then without your story?

The enlightened one needs the same story as you need your story for being unenlightened. Phantom stories.

Q: A few years ago I met Shri Shri Ravi Shankar and I asked him how to be continuously happy naturally, he said for that you have to become a teacher... [Laughter]

K: He threatened you.

Q: Then in the hotel he distributed sweets to everyone and after a while everyone had to leave so that he can rest in his own suite...

K: To eat his own sweets. [Laughter] He didn't want to share it anymore.

Q: And everything was covered in white sheets...

K: What a shit!

Q: But there was nothing of essence that was spoken. It was just chit chat...

K: That's the Pied Piper on tour, catching rats to have a big disciple group. That's just collecting disciples and making yourself attractive so that the disciples follow you. It's like an advertisement tour. Come to me and I'll make you happy. There are many in India, look at Sadguru. He's part of the infamous group of five. [Laughter]

Q: He went on about his enlightenment story...

K: Oh God! Like Osho's enlightenment story. [Mocking] After hundreds of years of meditating about truth, then I just gave up my search and I sat somewhere and then suddenly God came to me and then I was shining and everything was... whoa! After hundreds of years of intensely seeking myself and giving up. That's all part of collecting disciples, come on! And then they say if you're around me that may happen too because you're in a good company of an enlightened one, the Buddha field makes it easier for you to realize yourself and all that blah, blah, blah. Before you were an asshole and later you become an enlightened one.

No business like show business. Do you think spiritual business is different than rock music or any other business? There's always one showing off his story and another one believes in it. You create believers. Jesus walked on water and if you can't walk on water you have to swim... poor you.

Q: That was symbolic story...

K: He just could not swim. [Laughter] There's nothing symbolic about it. Then getting Lazarus back from the dead, what an asshole! He was happily dead and then came Jesus. Then he had to wake up from the dead – fuck you! Just to prove that you have some bloody siddhis you wake me up here? Now I have five years more in front of me. Now I have to please my mother and my wife, fuck it. I was so happily dead. [Laughter] Jesus was part of show business. He had to show that he had some special powers otherwise they would not follow him. Bloody Christ consciousness, it's a crisis consciousness. It's a permanent crisis.

Believe it! Consciousness in a permanent crisis to prove its existence. That's a consciousness crisis because a phantom consciousness has to prove his fucking existence permanently. It always shows off with something. That's part of show business, consciousness playing its bloody game. And you cannot stop it. You try to stop it but you fail. Consciousness will always try to penetrate itself.

Q: I went to one church in Berlin and I saw a woman had the wrong place for stigmata...

K: Every butcher knows that, it's all wrong. There are only three churches in the world that have the correct place for the nails. Ninety nine percent of the churches have the Jesus hanging with the wrong position of the nail. That's crazy!

Q [Another visitor]: If you were sitting in the company of the five ones...

K: I was in Holland with the bloody fucking enlightened ones. I made the opening speech in that conference and they destroyed the video later. I just stood there and asked what do you think you would get from these assholes? They cannot even help themselves; do you really think they can help you? In the next morning at six in the morning, I was gone. Then somehow there was an accident with the video. [Laughter] I'm quite proud about that. After that I was not invited anymore. The organizers in San Francisco always organized the talks and requested me to come. Stephen Wolinsky said you may be the only original one and you have to come, the rest we can forget.

I always said before whoever goes for the meetings for enlightenment for sure is not. But then I had to go anyway, to prove that I'm not enlightened. In that way I'm a party pooper. Everyone is sitting on the table saying, 'Oh, I always wanted to meet you. I like your books so much.' And I was like help me God what have I done to be here? There was a scientist before who spoke about time. He was a disciple of Shivananda, he liked me. So, at least one liked me. You do your best to be disliked but there're always some who cannot avoid liking it. When I saw Ranjit Maharaj in Bombay he said, that what gives the light is running you. There's no difference.

Okay! Thank you for going. [Laughter]

20th July 2018 Talk 2

Ladakh

Yama permanently tells you that nothing is permanent
∿

Q: You said something about the assembly point...

K: That's the montage point where the world gets montaged, that's your point of perception. That's where *nagual* hits the *tonal*[1] and then you go through all the possibilities of perception. Then you're fucked forever. You see all the possible reference points in one strike and then you're gone. Then you slowly come back to this little 'me' point where you normally rest in. But then you cannot rest in it anymore. This is in shamanism. Then you lose your ego. Ego simply means a resting point, like a ball resting in a hole. Normally you have a whole variety of possibilities of perception whatever can be perceived from different reference points. But you only look from this point because you're conditioned in it. It's like your mother kept hitting on that point and then you rest on that as a person. And then you make a story out of it. Then *nagual* hits you and you see all the possibilities at once and then slowly you come back to the reference point of the 'me'. After that it's never the same anymore. This is just one out of infinite.

Q: You can hit us now...

K: I don't hit anyone. I have no necessity of it. And what you are doesn't need that but it is part of consciousness playing, shamanism and all of that. I know that but in Reality it's not needed. It's just part of the

1 *The terms* tonal *and* nagual *were used in the esoteric School of don Juan Matus described in the books of Carlos Castaneda. These terms denote two "parallel" worlds that comprise the universe – the world of material objects* (tonal) *and the non-material world* (nagual).

play but it's not like you gain something by that. You are as much in the hole as in... whatever, what you are. Having a personal experience or an impersonal experience doesn't make you different. There's no gaining and no losing in all of that. So you may rest here or anywhere else or not rest, it doesn't make what you are any different. But this 'me' is like a hunter – hunting for differences, better places that would be maybe better because I have the possibility of being everywhere and blah, blah, blah.

Then they say but you went there. Then I say, okay believe it or not. Go to Shamans, do it, have unlimited *ayahuasca* sessions, just do it. It's not because of necessity. But if it's meant for you, it will happen. If it's not, it will not work anyway. But I say the shortcut is just being that what is now and in the absence what it is. That's a shortcut. But if you want to make it the longer way, I have nothing against it. But it may take a while, quite a long time actually. Lifetimes after lifetimes of *ayahuasca*. It doesn't matter when it happens, it will happen anyway. It is not a question of when, it will happen. You cannot avoid it, that's all. Now you try to avoid it. The fear does not allow it. This fear will be overridden by existence sooner or later anyway and you will drop out of it, just by accident and not by you wanting it. You cannot want That, no one can want that.

Q: Why?

K: You want to survive because you fear nothing more than That. You fear yourself more than anything else in the world.

Q: But why will we anyway be That?

K: Because what came will be gone.

Q: And nothing changes?

K: Nothing is changing now. For what you are nothing ever changed. There's no change. Nothing ever changed for what you are. But this imaginary construct of 'me' came and whatever came will go; sooner or later it's gone. But who cares when? For who does it have to go? But everyone still thinks that something has to go; something has to be solved. For what you are nothing has to go, there's nothing to go, nothing to come. In coming nothing came and in going nothing goes. The going will happen but in going nothing will go.

Q: The dream machine is not any more...

K: For who? The dream machine continues.

Q: For who?

K: The one who's here right now. For the Absolute Parabrahman, the dreamer; for That nothing ever happened. A dream object appears and disappears, who fucking cares? You think the Parabrahman cares about you, if you exist or not? You think it makes it more or less if you realize your fucking self? There's a permanent carelessness; it was and it will be there. No one was ever relevant enough for the Parabrahman that it would care about him. There is no fucking grace. The grace surely doesn't know you and has no need to get rid of you. You're not too much. Only for you, you're too much and not for What Is.

It's crazy. Everyone thinks he's too fucking important, that he's too much for existence, that something has to change. 'I have to go otherwise existence cannot enjoy itself.' 'I'm so fucking important that existence minds me.' Fuck it! Existence doesn't care an inch about you. If you exist or not exist it would not make anything more or less. But this is relaxing. If you're enlightened or not enlightened who fucking cares about it? But everyone thinks that he's relevant for existence. I have to be happy so that existence can be happy. Ha, ha, ha! There is no psychotherapy of existence. [Laughter]

Q [Another visitor]: Many of the so-called masters talk about the acceptance of surrender and you say may it be as it is. What is the difference?

K: The difference is that I don't have to accept anything to be what I am. I don't have to accept, I don't have any idea about acceptance. For acceptance it needs two, the one who accepts that something has to be accepted. But for me there's no two, that's all. So I don't need any acceptance.

Q: So may it be as it is includes non-acceptance as well?

K: Whatever! I have no idea! It is as it is anyway. So, may it be as it is. It's a wish that's actually fulfilled the moment you wish for it. There's a total fulfilment in the wish already inside the wish – 'May it be as it is.' It's a fulfilment of what you are. You don't have to accept anything for it.

Q [Another visitor]: It sounds like surrendering...

K: It's not a surrendering. It's just an 'Aha! Nothing has to be surrendered.' You surrender the surrenderer. The idea of surrendering gets surrendered. It's a renunciation of the renouncer because nothing has to be renounced for you to be what you are. Nothing has to come, nothing has to go for what you are, that's all. But it's not an acceptance, it is just reality. Maybe acceptance may bring you to a point that you have an idea about it. Ramesh Balsekar used to say that you can only accept that you can never accept. There'll never be any acceptance for you. Your acceptance will never be good enough for what you are. So, no acceptance will bring you to that what you are. And I like it, that's the best. What to do?

Q: But it brings the peace of mind...

K: Who fucking needs it? Only a junkie who thinks by acceptance he becomes sober.

Q: As long as...

K: As long, as long, as long... But we're not as long here. We are short here. We only have six more days. [Laughter] Always these excuses... but as long, as long. It will take eternity because nothing will happen. You will always look at consciousness inquiring about itself. It will never stop seeking itself. The seeking will never stop. It will never stop because it never started. So, there's no 'as long'. The longing of consciousness about itself will never stop. So you better don't wait for it. As long – it never stopped for anyone. Not even for bloody Mooji or Adyashanti or Eckhart Tolle. So many names! [Laughter] It never stopped for anybody, there was no one ever for whom anything stopped. 'I called off the search'... feels like a vomit! It's like a call of the Church. Even great masters like Papaji telling people that you have to call off the searching, pointing to it and in the last two years resigning all of that. Then he was real and not while having this transmission bullshit. Mama mia.

I don't doubt anyone's experiences and realization but they never lead you anywhere. It's just a false bullshit, especially the realized ones they are the most fake ones.

Q: So what is the 'aha' that you mention?

K: *Aha* is a split second. The splitting of the second by being what you are, that's *aha*. It's not even in time, you don't even pronounce it, it's just *aha*!

Q: So it seems like there's you who has this *aha*...

K: It was always there, this *aha* is always there. It was, it is, and it will be. This is the flat line, the one sound of what you are that's uninterrupted. It always was, is and will be. Nothing ever happened there, this is *aha*. It's not as if you realize your fucking true nature and then you have a better life – bullshit. Then you teach your people that you have to wake up. Nothing has to wake up. This is uninterrupted what it is. There's no waking up in it or falling asleep. It's neither falling asleep nor awake or anything. You cannot make anything out of it. Bloody awakened ones, shoot them all; I mean it! It's like a carrot sitting somewhere and telling that I'm better off now and you become a donkey running after the carrot all the time. They all should ca*rrot* in hell. [Laughter]

Q [Another visitor]: In traditional yoga they talk about the eight-fold path...

K: I would say the eight false paths. Maybe they just translated it wrong – the eight false paths. [Laughter] You never know who translated it – blue jeans or genes that was the translation.

Q: In Buddhism also they talk about the eight steps...

K: And Buddha says there are no steps. So, who's right? Buddha or Buddhism? Who would you trust more? Christ or the Church? The Church needs followers and Buddhism needs followers, it needs technique otherwise no one would follow that. Who would you trust?

Q: So, is that added by other people?

K: Bent. Little changes make it totally different. It was such a long time ago, it's all hear-say. It's like a silent post. Have you ever played the game as a child called silent post? One says something into the ear of the second and no one else hears it. Then this travels to others and finally the last one pronounces what was said. It comes out as total bullshit. That's like Buddhism or Christianity. Fuck it all! So, whom do you trust? Is there anyone to trust? Can you entrust yourself? Tell me!

Q: What?

K: You didn't even listen? [Laughter] Can you even trust yourself? Or you're angry that it puts you in a position of being a person. Is there something in it, that you're still angry? That you have to experience yourself as this person? If you'd meet yourself, you'd kill yourself; I tell you because you're so angry about yourself. And you don't trust yourself anymore because it puts you in a position that you never liked – in total discomfort. So, whoever is seeking the Self is not for embracing the Self. You want to kill yourself if you meet yourself. But the problem is you will never meet yourself. So it will take a long time to kill yourself because you'll never meet yourself.

Q [Another visitor]: Then what to do?

K: Many people tried to kill the body but it doesn't help. You have already tried it many times, I see it. Everyone who sits here committed suicide so many times. Even going to war is a suicide, driving a bike in India is a suicide or being a pedestrian in Bombay. [Laughter] All suicide attempts! Eating in India is not to be healthy. It's a slow suicide but it is suicide. Living in a city like Delhi is a suicide. Whatever you do is trying to get out of this bullshit. And I say, no way out! This is the way you realize yourself as ignorance, as shit, whatever you call it.

If I say all what you experience is shit, I mean it. Knowledge can never be experienced. Whatever you experience is shit – ignorance. But you cannot not realize yourself in anything else and I say be happy that you cannot know knowledge because if you would know knowledge, that would be two. You would be different to it. So be happy that you can only experience shit. When I say sat-shit-ananda, I mean it. Shit, shit, shit, shit... and only shit happens.

Q [Another visitor]: Is it possible to stop believing in this me?

K: No. You cannot stop believing. If you stop believing, you believe in not believing. You always believe.

Q: Can we get rid of this bullshit story?

K: You cannot get rid of bullshit because you realize yourself as bullshit. The realization of *chit* is shit. You have to say that the nature of ignorance is knowledge. The heart of ignorance and heart of knowledge is not different. The essence of ignorance is the same as the essence of knowledge. So, there's nothing wrong about ignorance.

Q: The thoughts of 'me' always change...

K: That's why I say you cannot trust yourself.

Q: But I still believe in this 'me'...

K: Why not? Love is your issue. You don't believe in this 'me', you love this 'me'. You fall in love with this image of yourself. That's the root of all suffering that you're in love with yourself. And because you love yourself, you believe in yourself. It's all me, me, me. You cannot help it. How can you not love yourself? Try. Why would you not love yourself? Because you have an idea that not loving yourself is better than loving yourself. But then trying to not love yourself is again out of love because you always want the best for yourself.

Q: I don't care...

K: But to not care, you have to care that you don't care. You think not caring is better than caring. You now try the technique of not caring to see if not caring works. But even not caring doesn't work because you still care about yourself. You cannot escape the love relationship with yourself, by whatever you try.

Q: Ramana said you cannot get rid of the root thought 'I'...

K: You cannot kill the phantom. You're in spite of the phantom and not because that the phantom is gone.

Q: It seems like a strong idea...

K: It's not strong. You cannot kill it because it has no existence. If it would really exist, it would be easy to kill. But its strength is that it doesn't even exist.

Q: I understand it but...

K: It doesn't help, thank God! And I'm not here to help you. I talk to what I am that doesn't need any help. I don't want to help you, not even by a single sentence. Fuck you! [Laughter] I have no interest. What would be my interest? Now she's shifted from personal perception to the impersonal perception. Oh God! I'm a good teacher. I transmitted some energy and now she's able to understand a bit more. Ha, ha, ha!

Q: But you just need it...

K: Who needs it?

Q: I don't know but it happens...

K: Always this needy bastard inside that always needs something. It's never enough, it's never satisfied, it's never high enough, the truth is never true enough, the realization is never real enough. It's always doubting. This doubtful 'I' will always doubt whatever you realize, whatever you achieve. It's never enough. This hungry bullshit 'me' can never be satisfied by anything.

Q: You see 'me'; can't you stop it?

K: But I'm not talking to this 'me'. You can only stop it when you are what you are. But not by me helping you. Bullshit! Fucking 'me'. She still wants an advantage as a person, having no 'me' and I give a fuck about the 'me'. From a person with 'me', I want to be a person without the 'me', the no-me. Then you maybe give a *satsang*. [Laughter] "There's no 'me', I overcame my 'me', I overcame my ego, there's no 'me', I saw that clearly. I went into the absence into the void and there was no 'me'." But who saw that there was no 'me'? "I saw it!" That's the hidden 'me'.

Q: Again 'I'?

K: Yeah. You cannot get rid of that phantom bullshitter. He will always bullshit you. In India there's a story. At first there's a thief and then he pretends to be a policeman who says he'll take care of the thief. That's like this little consciousness bullshit. It becomes a guru who tells you that I can help you, I will take your ego away. The no 'me' is the biggest 'me'. It's a hidden 'me'. Very well hidden. It's bigger than the other me's. [Laughter]

I put you into the ruthlessness and carelessness of what you are by being careless with you – total carelessness talking to carelessness and not by trying to help this bullshit 'me' inside you who's always suffering and needy sucking on the tits of existence. This little sucker there. Then he thinks maybe if I don't suck then the sucker may go away by itself. Ha, ha, ha! 'Now I'm on a diet. I don't go to *satsang* anymore. I accept as it is, I don't suck anymore. The non-sucking sucker. It sounds always good. I don't need anything anymore. I don't suck anymore, I don't need any tit.' It's always a tit for tat. Then I go to *atithi* ashram.

Q: I'm not satisfied with your answer...

K: Do you think I care? Listen to that arrogance. 'I'm not satisfied!'

Q: Where is the way out?

K: How many time I have said that there's no way out. How many times did I say that? More than anything else I say that there's no way out. And the only Absolute way out by seeing no way out is by being what you are and you cannot leave what you are. There's no way out of being what you are and you are That. What else can you be? That's the best you cannot get. Being that what is, you cannot leave that what is – that's all. You are Reality that cannot leave Reality. You're that what is nature who cannot leave nature and nature is realizing itself in this artificial bullshit. It cannot realize itself as Nature. It can only realize itself as artificial bullshit. The art you are can only experience itself artificially. It's all artificial. But the art you are is Heart but the heart can only artificially experience itself. But never itself as art or heart. Mama mia...

Where is the way out? Take a pill! [Laughter]

Q [Another visitor]: They say that realization is Self realizing itself as Itself?

K: But who needs that? Even that's a fake carrot. The realized one is realizing itself as the real Self? Blargh... The only pointer is to know yourself as you know yourself in deep-deep sleep in the absolute absence of any presence of anyone who's realized or not realized. Everything else is bullshit. All these words of trying to make it sound nice, blah, blah, blah. It's like the praying mill that the Buddhists turn all the time... repeating bullshit. Whatever can be written is bullshit, that's what it's good for. And you believe in that shit. So, you're self-guilty. You cannot blame anyone else because you believed in that written shit. And where does all this written shit go to? To a lie-bury because all the books belong to lie-bury – buried into lies. It never helped anyone. Only the liar is hungry for lies believing into lies, always relying on lies... online, on lies.

Q [Another visitor]: There's somebody who believes...

K: The liar needs lies because without lies the liar cannot survive. So you believe in lies. The believer needs to believe in lies because Reality would kill him. So he always creates lies and then relies on the lies. And all that what sounds good, all these beautiful words of lies are beautiful bullshit. You are the Self itself, blah, blah, blah.

Just this one pointer: 'You are as you are in presence as you are in absence' – finished! The rest is all bullshit. And this experience you have every night, it's so natural. But you want to have it special for you. It has to be a special fucking experience. 'On the 9th of September 1993, I had this deep insight and my despair was so much that I went so deep into the pain that the pain disappeared and the one who had the pain disappeared and since them I'm happy.' Ha, ha, ha. Then everyone says, 'I want the same. How do I not feel the pain as much like him? Maybe I have to suffer more. I have to have more bullshit relationships that I suffer more. More love pain or something. Maybe I didn't suffer enough.' Mea Culpa, beating yourself up like hell and all the techniques of the Church and all the bullshit that people tell each other. Then listening to someone who made it. Fuck! [Laughing]

Q [Another visitor]: It's not just the contemporary teachers talking about before and after. Ramana too seems to talk about the before and after. Even though he always says that you are the Self, he talks about the time when he was in his Uncle's room where the death experience happened. That gives an impression that there's a before and after...

K: That's why I always say that there are some things that I do not agree with him. It's *by* the way and not *because* of the way. It always sounds like there was a way that he went into some circumstance, he looked at death and how would it be. It sounds like he opened himself to that experience and that it was just an experience and nothing ever happened to him, blah, blah, blah. It sounds like step-by-step. This *aha* is more like by the way and not *because* of anything. Not even because of the death experience.

Q: The death experience itself is not it...

K: No. It's just like having a sip of coffee. It's not worth more than a sip of coffee or any experience. There's no experience that's higher or lower. They're just all artificial experiences. Even the death experience is an artificial experience because whoever gets something out of it, has an advantage. It's relative. But for what you are which is, was and will be, it's just by the way and not because of the way. It's by accident, not meant to happen. It's not a happening at all. It's not because of anything. It's not because that suddenly I had this experience.

Q: I get that it's *aha*. I've had these *aha's* like there's no such thing as birth and death...

K: Those are the small *aha's*. That what is the *aha*, there's no coming back from that because no one was ever there. No one ever went there, there's no fear left to go back from there. There's a fearlessness which was always there which is not depending upon any experience, not on any *aha*. In this uninterrupted Absolute existence which was always in spite of anything, there's no fear because there was never anyone who could fear anything. Then there's no fear to go back or come because there's no ownership in it. Without ownership where's the fear to lose or gain anything? There's no loser or gainer possible. Ownership is the main problem – ownership. This 'me', this 'mine'. If you could just drop it, it would be fine. But you cannot. You would be fine forever but that what you are is fine in spite of presence and absence of the ownership.

There'll always be an owner owning something, lover loving the beloved. You cannot get rid of this trinity.

Q: So, even after the minor *aha's*, the ownership stays...

K: Of course! Because it becomes *your* aha. But that *aha* has no owner. There's no ownership in the *aha* that I'm pointing at. But there are always these minor *aha's*, there are so many insights. In that *aha* there's no insight because that what-you-are is neither in-sight nor out-sight. There's no inside nor outside for what you are. So, you cannot have any insight. There are no insiders or outsiders. This is just what is. There's no fear of losing it because there's no one who owns something, never was, because this knowledge is not depending on any whatever.

That's why they call it *moksha* – the independency of knowledge which is independent of the presence or absence of a knower. There's no knower of knowledge in Knowledge. It's absolutely independent of one who knows or doesn't know.

Q: Sometimes they talk about the knower of the knower...

K: You cannot find anyone there. That what is that Knowledge is realizing itself as a knower. But you cannot put any knower in Knowledge. That's impossible. Reality is realizing itself as a realizer. But you cannot put any realizer in Reality. There's no Self in Self. How can there be a Self in the Self? The Self doesn't know any Self.

Q: Is it an impersonal Self?

K: There's neither a personal nor an impersonal Self. It's just a word, come on! Call it Knowledge – Knowledge realizing itself as the knower, knowing what can be known. But Knowledge is not the knower, not the knowing and not what can be known. It is that what is realizing itself and the realization of Reality is not different. You are That. You are the heart of the knower, the heart of the knowing and heart of what is known, you are that what is. And you cannot get out of that. You are the lover, the loving and the beloved, so what? It's bullshit, yes. But you cannot otherwise exist because in existing there's 'one' existing, experiencing existing. A seer seeing what can be seen. An owner owning what can be owned. It's all the same, always this trinity. The father, the spirit and the son.

What did Jesus say? I'm not the father, I'm not the spirit and I'm not the son. I'm that what is the father, I'm that what is the spirit and I'm that what is the son but I'm not the father and I'm not the spirit and I'm not the son. But in nature there's no difference. But he's not the father which is Awareness, he's not the spirit which is I Amness and he's not what comes out of it, it's not Adam, it's not Eve. You cannot divide it but it is not as it appears. It's not the phenomenal; it's the noumenon which appears as phenomenal as 'me'. But it never becomes the phenomenal. You never became the 'me', you never became the 'knower'. You experience a knower but that what experiences itself as a knower can never be experienced. There's nothing personal nor impersonal. You cannot name it, you cannot give any attribute to that what you are.

Q [Another visitor]: But...

K: I'm not 'but' here. Always these butts here. Everyone who has a butt has a but.

Q: Talking about realization, isn't there a separation?

K: Why not? What is wrong with separation?

Q: It's just Reality...

K: Separation is not real, it's just the way Reality is realizing itself.

Q: In that...

K: There's no 'in that'. You will not understand it anyway so I give a shit.

Q: I don't want to understand it...

K: Ha, ha, ha! That's a true liar. 'I don't want to understand, just for fun I have a question here.' [Laughter] 'I have nothing else to do so I sit here and I ask a question. I give a shit if you answer me anyway, I just have a question.' Okay, I don't answer any more. If you don't want to know, I don't answer. [Laughter] It's very tricky. It's like a man says I don't need sex and then the woman asks, why not?

Q: But there's still separation...

K: I'm happy that I'm separated from you. I'm very happy that I'm very separated to many of you, actually to all of you. I love separation – I love it! You never thought about it. Imagine, if you'd be one with all the assholes around you! [Laughter]

Q: Reality and realization…

K: …is not two. There's no link and there's no bridge.

Q: If there's just Reality, why do we talk about realization?

K: Because you experience yourself right now, or not? You experience yourself right now. And how can you experience yourself without separation? That is called realization.

Q: But this is the point that I want to understand…

K: Suddenly she wants to understand again!

Q: It's all just words, there's just Reality?

K: Then why are you sitting here? If you've come to the total understanding that all is Reality, why are you sitting here? Why are you asking a bloody question?

Q: Why not?

K: From now on, I only say why not. If you have a question, I'd say why not. [Laughter] I'll just put up a sign here, 'Why not?' and go home and watch television, but only for her. [Laughing]

Q: I'm speaking truly…

K: You're a fucking liar. The one who says he's speaking truly is the biggest liar. 'I speak truly, it comes from my fucking heart. I open my fucking heart to you.' You can go to Mooji but don't come here. Fucking depths of my heart! As if the heart has a fucking depth. The deeper, deeper, deeper bullshit.

Q: You ask me why you are here. That's because it's nice to be here…

K: Then just shut up!

Q: But sometimes it's not so nice here… [Laughter]

K: I tell you it feels like a rape if you like it or not. It's a permanent rape and you're the rapist, the raping and that what's raped. Of course you're raped by yourself. Then you always complain to yourself, it always feels like a rape. You always have to do something you don't like. What to do? Do you think I like to sit here, listening to you? Even you don't like listening to you, why should I listen to you? It's all a rape but you're raped by yourself. Who else can rape you? Who else can put this trap in front of you that you step into it? No one else. Only love is the biggest trap and you're raped by love. It's a permanent rape.

Q [Another visitor]: What's the difference between us and disciples?

K: Between an ass and a disciple? Disciples have an ass. [Laughter] [Pointing to another visitor] Suddenly she likes it again. Disciples have a soft ass so that they can sit for a long time, like a cushion.

Q: I want another answer... [Laughter]

K: Why do you want to be different? Yes, there's a difference but it doesn't make one. Yes, always everything is different but it doesn't make anything different. What you are doesn't become different by experiencing itself differently, that's all. You realize yourself differently but your Reality is always unaffected. Nothing has a consequence or an effect on it. It's always what you are. Nothing ever affects it, nothing ever changes it. All your so-called trivial experiences, even junkies having experiences with drugs are still what they are. It can never be affected by anything. You can put in heroin and morphine in this body and nothing will happen. What can happen? Your nature will always be in nature what you are; unaffected by all your so-called events of sensational experiences. If this body gets sick or not, what-you-are is never sick or healthy at all. It doesn't have any advantage or disadvantage by anything.

But now who wants to get rid of the 'me' is 'me' but it knows it cannot kill itself. It's so fucking stable because it doesn't exist in Reality. Fuck it! The Absolute no-way-out means you are That, so what? You were That, you are That and you will be That. What will happen? Whatever happens will happen and nothing happens to you. So, there are happenings but by all the happenings nothing ever happened to what you are. That's called happiness. It's not that there's someone who's happy or something, there's just the nature of happiness. But you want to make it your happiness and that will never be owned by anyone. Impossible! The moment you want to own it, by imagination you step out of what you are and then it becomes reality. Then you long to go back but the more you long to go back you confirm that there's someone who needs to be what he is. It's such a perfect trap. It's such a fucker, this self, fucking himself so severely. And no one else can fuck the fucker so severely as the fucker fucking himself. Fantastic! And it always feels like a rape. It feels like it rapes you.

Your wish for wishlessness is so strong but it will never be granted to anyone. Not even to this bastard here. [Pointing to himself] I don't claim anything. I'm not in any way special or different to anyone, in what I am. And I have no advantage in anything otherwise I would not sit here. If it would really bring uninterrupted happiness, I would sit on a beach and watch the whales blowing, whatever!

Q: The waves are coming in...

K: They do a big blow job, especially in boring bay, everyone sitting in the sunset watching the whales. I was in Goa 25 years ago and there were people sitting on the table reading The Times of India. I went there again six years ago, the same guy was sitting there with The Times of India. Then at 6 pm all the Osho people marching in for the sunset. I thought there's really no time. But I make fun about myself... look at what's happening. All these stupid events... sitting here listening to me talking bullshit and no one can help it. Everyone heard it infinite times before and cannot get enough of himself. You can never get enough of what you are. You are always hungry for yourself, fantastic! In all possible ways, because you have no taste. That's the main issue of the Self, he has no taste. He has no discrimination. Fuck it! He takes everything as it is. This tastelessness is such an Absolute taste, such a peace of tastelessness. Does it make difference if there's a taste? No. This tastelessness is so fantastic. Such an ecstasy of tastelessness, selflessness; doesn't even know anything, of knowledgelessness. There's not even knowledge there.

Q [Another visitor]: This sounds like the next carrot...

K: I want to make you a junkie of the drug you are.

Q: We are the drug...

K: No. You're not the drug. It's all blah, blah, blah. There's no 'we' in that bullshit. You're the only drug that can make you satisfied.

Q: But a junkie...

K: There's no junkie in it. You're the junk right now and you want to have the key.

Q: And I'm looking for a way out...

K: How many times should I tell you? You will fuck yourself all the time. By just trying to find the way out, you fuck you, fuck you, fuck you. You fuck you by trying to find a way out. and by that you should suffer. By trying to leave yourself you suffer. That's misery, trying to leave what one is. That's the only misery you can experience, trying to not be what you are. Trying not to exist and by that you suffer. So, you fuck you, you fuck you, you fuck you. You cannot blame anyone else.

Just because you don't want to exist, you suffer. You want to find a way out of existence. Fantastic! And this *aha* is – How can I leave what I am? Without understanding. How can I not *not* be? So, may it be as it is – fuck it! But not 'Where's my fucking way out?' Every drug you take is trying to find a way out because you don't want to exist. Every fuck, every sex, every whatever you do is trying to find a way out of your little misery of existence. What to do?

Q [Another visitor]: Accept... [Laughter]

K: Just another fucking way out.

Q: What else can you do?

K: Just be the fucker, the fucking and the fucked; you cannot be otherwise.

Q: But that's accepting...

K: It's not accepting. It's being the fucker, being the fucking and being the fucked. Be that what is fact. You don't need to be proven. You are the asshole and the ass. [Laughter] When you're the Absolute ass you have infinite assholes. Then it doesn't matter what stinks more or not. All the assholes are there because you're the ass. But you're not the asshole that's different from another asshole. You're the ass itself and you experience yourself through many assholes. It stinks just to be an asshole because then you have a nose because you know something. Then you're the asshole and by being an asshole, it stinks. But if you're the ass, it doesn't smell; it doesn't have a nose. It doesn't mind. But now the asshole wants to find a way out of another ass thinking that another ass is better than this ass.

Q [Another visitor]: You talk about choicelessness...

K: I talk about noselessness, having no nose.

Q: It sounds like something better...

K: It is the best you cannot become because you are That. You are that what is the superior ultimate, call it whatever. You cannot become it because you never left it. But now you want to become it and by trying to become it, you are not That. So, you fuck yourself by trying to become what you already are. Complaints, complaints, complaints, just complain to yourself because you don't fuck yourself right enough. You have to fuck yourself absolutely. You have to be the Absolute fucker, absolute fucking and the absolute fucked and not this little fucker, little fucking and little fucked.

Q [Another visitor]: There's recognition of the beauty of that tastelessness...

K: The first taste is the taster you taste. But that what is tasting the taster you cannot taste. The taster, the tasting, what can be tasted, you can taste. But you can never taste that what is tasting the taster tasting and what can be tasted. All of that is a taste you can taste but not what you are. The seer that can see the seer, is not that what the seer is. You can experience the seeing but you cannot experience that what is experiencing the experience. So, just be that what can never be experienced but it still is what it is. You don't have to give it a name or not. It doesn't matter, you can call it underwear. Out of underwear comes aware. It doesn't come by that. There's a permanent presence of manifestation of what you are, of all possibilities; and the absence of it. Both are permanently there. It's just that your perception shifts from the frame to the non-frame. Then there's absence, like deep sleep. Awake, asleep. But both are permanently there.

Nothing ever came, nothing will ever go. All the moons, all the manifestation is never born, never dies. There's only eternal life. Even this moment is an eternal moment. It never came, it will never go. Every sensation is eternal. Every experience is eternal. That's the nature of silence because in that silence nothing comes nothing goes. There's no birth and there's no death in anything. Nothing can ever die because nothing was ever born. Even this manifestation is never born, it was never created. There's no creation. There's no action. Silence is not something that's prior or behind. This is silence. Whatever is, is silence; eternal life. The dream is in believing that something comes in coming and something goes in going. That's the dream. Nothing ever happened means that nothing ever came up so nothing can ever go. Nothing was ever created so nothing can ever be destroyed. Even this 'me' is eternal. That you cannot take. That scares you, how can this 'me' be eternal? How can I get rid of it? You cannot get rid of it because as you are eternal, your 'me' is eternal. Even the phenomenal sensational 'I' is as eternal as you are.

Q: But is it possible to...

K: Arghhh.... Complaining again. I want to find a way out, a way out, a way out, a way out. Why me? Why me? Why me? Why not you? The only answer to why me is why not you? I'm not better off than you, I tell you.

Q: But something happened to you at the Virupaksha cave...

K: I didn't say that. I said that in Virupaksha there was one insight that the experience of light cannot be what I am, that's all. But nothing ever happened in that. The awareness, the light of Shiva is still an experience, as subtle as it may be. But that what's experiencing the awareness can't be experienced. That's very easy. You're in the presence of the light and in the absence of the light. Nothing is simpler as being what you are. That's why I repeat, be as you are or be what you are because that is what is the Absolute and you cannot not be the Absolute. So what? And this is your Absolute realization, your Absolute experiences. They don't come and they don't go. You are That – finished. This is Nisargadatta's I Am That. And no way out of it and no help from any guru. They cannot even help themselves. Fuck yourself and fuck the gurus and be the Absolute fucker that fucks even the fucker. So, fuck the fucker and don't be the fucked fucker. That's fact.

What else can I tell you? Should I give you some beautiful lies? That all the things that you have done have led you to me, blah, blah, blah. Now you're in front of me and now I'll give you the last hit and then you'll be a hit. All these beautiful words are traps. I'm not into that. It's all by accident. It's all by the way. But it's so natural and it was always there, you just always overlook what you are. Because without the Absolute presence or pre-sense you are, there's no presence and no absence possible.

You always look at what moves and what does not move but never to that which has to be there before even something can happen. That's the basic ground of existence. That you have to exist so that you can even have one who can have an experience of existence. It's so fucking easy but you want to make it complicated. You want to be entertained by it because you cannot show it off to your friends. If everyone is it anyway and nothing has to be done or needs to be done, how to tell your friends that you have a special experience? If it's not in any way special that you are. You are, I am and we are not different in nature. But that would never even say that. So, even that is like a blah, blah, blah.

That's why these guys say that you better be quiet. But look I cannot even help talking about it. But it still doesn't disturb that what I am. So, I'm silent in talking. I never say anything. I never add anything to anything. I never take anything away from anything. It's just empty words. Jesus called them living words, which is just life living without any intention of any understanding or anything. And that's called good company – life living. No advantage or disadvantage to be here or not to be here. And not selling something in the presence of someone who doesn't want to sell you anything. And you don't have to buy anything and then suddenly you may just disappear into whatever you don't know because it is not something that you can know. Suddenly there is... It's actually permanently there but it was always covered by something. You give attention to something else. So, attention to Attention, awareness to Awareness. But Awareness doesn't know any awareness, Attention doesn't know any attention. There's no *giving* attention. By *being* Attention, by being that what is Awareness but doesn't know any awareness, there's no ownership of Awareness, it's not *my* awareness, not *my* beingness, not *my* spirit.

Be the blue and whatever comes out of the blue, you are not. There's no coming out of the blue. That's why the colour of Krishna and Shiva is always blue; dark blue. But now you have blues. That I don't want to help anyone here may be the biggest help I can offer. That I don't want to change anyone here; everyone can be as stupid as he is. I have no idea what's wrong with that. Now you're in love with knowing yourself. You have to fall in love with not knowing yourself; just a little shift. Now you're in a fucking misery because you don't know yourself and you want to know yourself. But just fall in love with not knowing yourself and enjoy the silence in it and enjoy the ecstasy of not knowing yourself. That's enjoying yourself. Enjoy yourself, by not knowing yourself and not knowing what's ecstasy and not knowing what's peace and not knowing what's... whatever. There's a joy of not knowing.

In that way I try to make you fall in love with that what you are which doesn't know itself because now by knowing yourself, you're in misery. Any moment you know yourself, you're a miserable bastard of time.

Q [Another visitor]: What does it mean to not know yourself?

K: You don't know what you are and what you are not – that's not knowing yourself because there's no knower left. The absence of the knower doesn't know what the knower is and what's not. So it's not for *you*! There's no grasping it, there's no compensating it. There's no ownership in it.

Q: But...

K: But, but, but... But what shall I do with it? Nothing! You cannot do anything with it. You cannot sell it, you cannot buy it. That's the beauty of it. No one can sell it and no one can buy it from anyone.

Q: When I wake up in the morning, I know that I like porridge for breakfast. I know *me*...

K: That's what I say; you're fucked by knowing yourself.

Q: But I don't think that...

K: Of course! But you don't think that you are how he is. You're just firm in your taste – I like porridge, I don't like that, blah, blah, blah. Always defining yourself. This bloody definer is such an asshole who defines his asshole all the time. I shit this way and not that way.

Q: When you are at the breakfast bar...

K: I just take eggs. [Laughter]

Q: Okay! That's the difference, porridge and eggs... [Laughing]

K: But it doesn't make a difference because it becomes shit anyway, that you should know from the beginning.

Q: We are off topic now...

K: No. It's not off topic. One eats porridge and other eats eggs, but what comes out of it? That's why it's called a shit factory. It doesn't matter what you put in, shit comes out. That's the same with your brain. It's a shit factory, preference doesn't matter. What comes out is shit.

Q: I'm trying to get a handle on this knowing...

K: Why should you put it in the hand? You have to take it by a knife and a fork. [Laughter]

Q: I eat porridge, so I'd need a spoon...

K: Try with a fork. That's an *Ayurvedic* diet – having a clear soup with a fork. [Laughter] You cannot kill this bastard who has the conditioned preferences from all the ancestors before. Who could decide what tongue one has? Where did it come from? What you hear, what colours you see, what you like? It's not by your choice. It's all given by all your ancestors before. All the events that happened before decide what you like. It's not your liking. It's from all the likes and dislikes before. It doesn't belong to you. It's not your fucking taste – porridge or not. It's always for the poor and for the rich.

Q: But I don't have much sense of...

K: You have no sense at all. [Laughter] No one has sense. Sense cannot be owned.

Q: Knowing myself...

K: You don't know yourself.

Q: That's what I mean...

K: Be happy about it. That's happiness – not knowing yourself. The moment you know yourself, who you are, where you come from, you're fucked. You come out of fucking.

Q: Thanks for that! It's a little late to get this knowledge now... [Laughter]

K: Everyone wants to kill their parents before they meet so that they don't get born. That's why we have rebirthing techniques – just to meet their parents and kill them before they can make you. Not this time – Incarnation prevention. Everyone who sits here would rather be not born. He would rather not exist; it's amazing. Then trying all the techniques to get rid of that what exists now. Whatever you try is futile. You cannot change any event of existence. Whatever is meant to happen, happens – will happen – do whatever you like. No one can control existence. That's pure beauty, there's no control of existence. No one can control his tongue or thought. The question is always who thinks the thinker? Then the thinker just claims that it was just his thinking. But there was never any thinker who had any thought. It's amazing.

Q: From where does personality come from?

K: Don't ask me, I don't need to know.

Q: Do you have a personality?

K: I don't know! Some say it's quite strong. [Laughter] If you ask me, it's not about having one; it's just there.

Q: It's a German personality...

K: I could not get rid of the germ, I'm infected. Germs and germs and germs. It's all about ownership. What you are doesn't own anything; what-you-are is whatever is. There's no ownership in that. You're the Absolute owner of existence because you are existence. But you don't have to know that. Just by being what you are, you are that what owns everything because you are everything and nothing. You are the presence, you are the absence, you are that what is prior, you are that what is beyond. You are That – finished! Just that there is a being and there's no second being. That's all, that's non-duality.

As you exist, you are that what is existence. As there's no second edition of existence, you are that what is existence – finished. It's easiest to understand, come on. That you cannot take it. You want to be special and by that you have to suffer and you're meant to suffer by trying to be special, to be apart, very apart. Because I'm unenlightened, I'm special because there's someone else who's enlightened. You live from differences. I'm suffering more than you. I'm in a competition of sufferers and my *guru* is better than yours.

Q: Is that personality?

K: That's competition – competing with yourself. It's like an Olympic games, who's sicker than the other one? Who seeks deeper? Who's seeking the right thing? Who's seeking truth and who's seeking Mercedes Benz? The seeker of truth is very arrogant – You seek matter, I seek spirit. You cannot find more arrogant people as in seekers.

Q: And my teaching is the highest...

K: And my *guru* is the highest and there's so much *shakti* and there's so much *shanti* – holy shit! Competing all the time. Even the gurus compete! Who's more realized? Awakening is the beginning, then comes enlightenment. There are even steps of gurus. Then there's sadguru who's beyond realization. Oooh... Ramana Sadguru. There are even levels. There's a school teacher, then mother, then high school, then comes the guru; the last door of your true being. What fun! Isn't it fun?

That's why I say when the religious persons go up there then they look back and start laughing about all the steps. When they're up there they know that they're already there what's up there even before they started. But maybe you still have to go up there. What you are never changed as being up there as being down here. This little *aha*. But even that will go away again. You know that game. It's like pulling up the stone of enlightenment up the mountain. You pull the stone up the mountain and then you relax. Then automatically the stone rolls down. So he goes down and says I'll pull it back up with all my effort. When I'm up there, I don't enjoy myself and I just try to keep the stone up there. That's like staying in awareness in *vipasanna*. 'I will stay in awareness, I will stay in awareness, I will not give up, I will not be sluggish, I will just keep the awareness alive. Vigilance, alertness is in my being.' Then one moment without alertness and the stone rolls down again. You fail again. That's the nature of failing.

The Taoists say, you can reach awareness for a very long time because there's not even time in awareness. By whatever intention, you would end up in this market place of life. And no time passes during that; you are as thirsty as before. Then you start again, step by step, shifting your perception to the first, to the second, to the third and to the fourth, to the *samadhi*.

Yama is the teacher. Yama tells you permanently that nothing is permanent. That's the teaching of Yama – the god of death. The permanent teaching of the impermanent. But does it help? No.

Q [Another visitor]: Then you're back in effort...

K: You cannot help it. Out of love you focus again, you put the stone up again. You think when I put it up, I fulfil my duty and I would be satisfied by what I've done. So, you try to satisfy yourself by rolling up the stone. When I make it up there then I'm satisfied with myself. But there's still a self. That's the way this movie is made – up and down the hill. You cannot help it; you want to please yourself. Out of love for yourself you want to please yourself. The biggest pleasing yourself is realizing yourself. But you will never realize yourself because there are no two selves. But out of trying to please yourself, you try all your best and you cannot stop it. That's consciousness, trying to please itself – permanently. But it will never be a final pleasing. You will never realize your true nature. That what is the Self will never know the Self, but you try. How can you not try to please yourself – out of love for yourself – permanently? You will fail. Buddha failed, Ramana failed, all failures.

As I said, the so-called masters fail permanently and the students fail sometimes. And they enjoy the failing. That's why I tell you enjoy the failing, enjoy the not knowing. You will never enjoy the success. You will never succeed otherwise you become a successor who sucks on its success. All the people who claim that they made it, that they realized their fucking true nature. They are suckers for successes – I made it!

A *jñāni* who knows to be a *jñāni* is for sure not a *jñāni*. The nature of *jñāni is jñāna* – knowledge. In knowledge there's no owner. And a *jñāni* who knows himself as *jñāni* is not a *jñāni*. The realized one who knows himself as a realized one for sure is not real.

Q [Another visitor]: There's a story that you knock the door and you realize that you're already in...

K: It's like a hotel with a revolving door. It's not going to the other side; it's going in and out again. You go around and you're back in, that's called rebirth.

There's a nice story about a Ku Klux Klan member from Texas who dies and reaches heaven and he finds that Peter is a black person. [Laughter] What would he do? What would you say? Would he go to heaven in spite of meeting the black person? Can he take it?

Q: When I visit the monasteries, I have a sympathetic feeling towards it...

K: All the monks are now in the internet café, not in monasteries any more. [Laughter] Twenty-five years ago the monasteries used to be full; there were people in yellow robes, red robes, black robes. Now it's just an empty theatre. There's just a monk selling tickets. Already ten years ago it had changed to monks selling tickets for the museums. That's everywhere; even the church is the same. I think that's a good sign. You have to be what you are in any circumstance and for that it doesn't need any effort. You can do your dishes, you can watch television, all of that is meditation. You don't need any special place or silence for that. So, maybe something is changing. Then you're back to the other side, like a pendulum.

It will not change anything but it will just become different. And if you like me as Karl, I like it because I like to watch television. I don't like to clean the floors of the monastery. That's called personality and I don't mind it actually. It's as good or as bad as everything and nothing has to change for you to be what you are, that's the beauty of it. Nothing has to go, no acceptance is needed, nothing needs to be done, no intention has to go, none of whatever you can imagine has to change in any way for you to be what you are. That's the beauty itself, come on! The beauty that needs attention or caring is just bullshit. It's not beauty; it's ugly in its nature. The nature of beauty you will never know and the beauty you can know and the beauty you can define, is ugly. So, be the beauty but don't know beauty. And don't be beautiful because then you're fooled by beauty.

We were talking about effort. It's a doingless doing and the doinglessness. What you are never lifted one finger. There was never any effort in what you are – never ever. The laziest bastard you are. The laziness of laziness, never did anything. It's like a dream. Just as you cannot say that you did something in the dream, you cannot say that you did something here. Can you claim that you have done something in the dream? You can create a whole different world, an entire universe in the dream by no effort. Can you claim that it was by effort? Then you have some action in that dream. That's why they call it waking up from that. That you have an effort, that the dream is real or something. The dream changes all the time out of your dream effort. Parabrahman doesn't need any effort in this dream, just as in night you don't need any effort to dream a totally different character, totally different world, totally different personality. Sometimes you dream the whole drama, whole world and nothing happens. Then you wake up and say, 'Thank

God it was only a dream.' That's waking up. This is the same; it's just that no one wakes up from this dream.

The one that wakes up in an insight will fall asleep again. It's a relative insight and the one who has a relative insight, goes back to sleep. The deepest insight is not good enough. Nothing is ever good enough for what you are. Whatever you experience will never ever give you the experience of what you are. It's all futile. It will all come and go.

Q [Another visitor]: Even in the deep sleep...

K: There is no 'in' deep sleep. Do you know when there's deep sleep there's 'one' in deep sleep?

Q: The brain cells are still working...

K: That's just deep sleep. But is there any one in deep sleep? The body functioning continues from outside but for the one who's gone, is there still an experience of the body? Tell me. Someone can tell you afterwards that there was a body movement. Then the scientists measure the bloody brain cell movements. Then they say I proved existence – there's still something going on there. There's brain activity and the brain is now dreaming. The brain is not dreaming anything; it's still part of the dream. How can that which is still part of the dream, dream? Scientists are the most stupid people on earth. There are no more ignorant and stupid persons one earth than scientists. If you want to find the most ignorant persons, go to a scientific convention. And if you really want to find the unenlightened ones go to an enlightenment convention.

Q [Another visitor]: Now there will be evidence-based medicine...

K: Bullshit medicine. If you find a good doctor he will say I never healed anyone. Just by accident he recovered.

Q: They heal...

K: No. The doctors never healed anyone.

Q: If he's a good doctor...

K: There're no good doctors. They are only bad, there's only bad medicine. They get good money for bad medicine. I talk to many doctors and if you find a doctor who agrees that they're bad, they'll tell you that they never know how they heal someone. It's just a miracle; suddenly they were fine.

Q [Another visitor]: In spite of the doctor they get healed... [Laughter]

K: In spite of the guru, someone is what he is – not because.

Q [Another visitor]: The belief in the doctor makes people...

K: To get sick. [Laughter]

Q: If he believes he can help him, he will be helped...

K: Fuck you! You just like to be sick, that's all. And you only go to the doctor who tells you that you're sick otherwise you don't like the doctor. If the doctor tells you that you're not sick, you go to another one until you find one who tells you that you're sick. You're a sick seeker. You seek sickness.

Q: It works like a placebo...

K: It's not placebo; you like to be sick. You like to be junkie, admit it. You love every moment of it.

Q: Not every moment... [Laughter]

K: I just see joy enjoying itself – everywhere. Even as a junkie in pain there's existence enjoying itself in everything. There's no exception. Joy can only enjoy joy because the nature of existence is joy. There's nothing but joy. There's nothing but Shanti. Shanti, Shanti, Shanti... there's only peace. There's no second because without a second, there's no fight. That's the nature of peace. There's only joy of existence and existence is enjoying itself in all possible and impossible ways. What you are enjoys every fucking and non-fucking moment of the fucking junkiness. Why should I disturb you in that? Why should I heal you for that what you enjoy? Why should I take your enjoyment away because you enjoy to be sick? No one enjoys to be healthy because healthy means you don't feel anything. Then you see health that's why it's called health-see. Boring!

Why should one interfere with the joy of existence? Oh, you're seeking, having fun. Oh, you're miserable today. Aren't you enjoying it to the maximum? You always enjoy yourself to the maximum, in whatever you experience. Fantastic! Even misery is part of enjoyment. Why should I have interest in anyone's misery getting away? No interest. Why should I spoil the fun? What can one do?

When you really go to that point which was enjoying every fucking moment, that what enjoys all the bad and good, there's an Absolute never mind. Not having any preference. Enjoying every fucking moment because there's the tastelessness of what you are, which was always there. It was there, it is there and it will be there. This joy, this ecstasy is not something new. It's always present. But it's so silent that it doesn't move and you only give attention to that what's changing and not to that what's ever present. What to do?

From there comes, what to do? Why should I do something against myself? If I would see you as a sick person and would want to heal you, I'd spoil all the fun. Doctors are the worst. They always destroy all the fun. [Laughter] People who have dengue fever have experiences. It's such an immense bone breaking disease, such intense pain. But there's a moment of disconnecting of what you are from the body and the whole universe… there's infinite peace and not minding anything. So, you're already dead – never minding anything. You could even die the next moment. Everyone has this experience once in a while. There's who cares? This carelessness of living or dying, that's what you are. It was always there before even being connected. But then being disconnected because of this intensity of pain, this glue goes away and then you're fine. Now you're glued to this body because you're the owner of this fucking body. Then you're in mind and then you want only comfort. Health is just an idea of comfort because the body doesn't bother you, that's all. If I don't feel my body, so I'm happy. If I feel my body, I'm sick. When I'm hungry, I eat because I don't want to feel my body. You do everything not to feel your body. Then they fast just to say that even if I'm fasting, it doesn't matter. I just don't care. But it doesn't work.

This loving caring about your body is a natural thing because your intention is comfort. And it's right because your nature is comfort. But the comfort you are cannot be disturbed. But the comfort that you get out of an undisturbed body is not comfort. It's a fleeting, fragile, absence of disturbance. Acceptance is so overrated. It just confirms that there's one who needs to accept. It's a total joke, a total trap. Fuck it! These little advantages that come out of it, you always need one who has them. Then he's confirmed in this needy little 'me'. What to do with it? 'I get an advantage, don't tell me anything. Otherwise I could not survive.' But who cares if you survive or not?

No. It's all fine. I talk to everyone and not to *you*. [Laughing] You fail – be happy! You will fail again and again. There'll always be a neighbour or a circumstance that you cannot accept and all your acceptance will be gone in one click.

Q [Another visitor]: Then maybe you just don't fight against it...

K: Then you fight against fighting. What's the advantage of that? Just fight! Who wants you not to fight? You're spoiling all the fun again. I try to fight with you. I'd like to fight with you. I like to fight. That's why I'm sitting here; I like to fight. Come on! Fight with me. And if you convince me then maybe I agree with you. But I'll never agree with you. Even if I said something five minutes ago and you repeat, I'll just say the opposite.

Q [Another visitor]: Exactly! You're the winner!

K: I always win, even if I lose. I win especially when I lose. Especially when I talk so much bullshit, everyone knows its bullshit and no one says anything. [Laughter] I just keep a balance; I just say as much bullshit as the so-called tra, la, la. And for me there's no difference in nature. Who's afraid of talking bullshit? I'm in the lowest and in the highest what I am. And the highest doesn't make me higher and the lowest doesn't make me lower. So, what's the problem with talking low? It comes out anyway even without me having any control. I hate beautiful words but sometimes even they come out! [Laughter] I hate them all. I hate them more than the bloody bullshit words. That's my nature. But sometimes I cannot help it.

Presenting that indifference is all I can show you. This carelessness, this total indifference! What else can I do? I cannot teach what you are. Come on! You may resonate with the carelessness, that's the only good company you can be in and not resonate with statements and truth and always fighting against something. Irrelevance you cannot avoid because it penetrates everything because it's already everywhere. You cannot have any defence system against irrelevance. It's already inside and outside and everywhere. So, your armour doesn't work. Normally you have an armour around you, your concepts.

You cannot defend yourself in that. Total irrelevance, defenselessness which penetrates everything because that's the nature of existence. So, what to do? Just be as you are – irrelevant, absolutely irrelevant. Whatever you do is absolutely irrelevant. No consequence at all. Where's the fear in it? I present you the fearlessness and in fearlessness you cannot have an armour. It just penetrates everything, naturally. That's why they call it Buddha field. Whatever it is. I would not call it anything.

I'm not a teacher and you have nothing to learn here. Come on! Nothing to take away. This is not a take away for junk food and then repeat something. And I never experienced anyone who could repeat what I've said; never – impossible. The moment they try it, it's gone. No one can *be* carelessness.

Q: I can't even remember what you say...

K: Yes. But there are some things they remember but when they start repeating it; it's all wrong. I don't even have to remember; I just have to listen to him. Maybe you can repeat 'Be what you cannot not be'... but when they say it, it's not the same. Ha, ha, ha...

Q [Another visitor]: I came here because I want my mind to leave my body alone...

K: So you think your mind is different from your body?

Q: When I sleep my body feels really good...

K: Because you don't feel it.

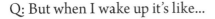

Q: But when I wake up it's like...

K: Fuck! You're not alone here. [Laughter] There's always something wrong. It's fine when you're asleep but when you wake up, out of fine comes not fine. Absence is good, presence is bad. Actually you just want to go back to sleep, if you could. But maybe your bladder is under pressure and then you go to the toilet. Then you come to the mirror and look at your face – fuck! Then you need a coffee and you try to make it bearable. The whole day you try to make it bearable that what is unbearable; to have a body. Permanently trying to make it bearable that there's a body. Then like a junkie, trying to make it bearable in your own way.

It's unbearable, I agree. It's totally unbearable. But what to do? If this body is gone, then another bullshit comes. But the moment you try to bear it then it really becomes unbearable because then there's one who wants to bear it. Then you suffer about it. But if it's really unbearable, you don't even try to bear it. What is there to bear? You're not a bear. Maybe if you'd be a bear you could bear it. But since you're not a bear, it's hard.

Papaji would say, 'Wake up and roar.' I always say imagine you're a sheep and you always believed to be a lion. Then you wake up and say Meah... Many believe they're lions but they're sheep. At first you're like a sheep who tries to roar. Then you start crying, 'I cannot wake up and I cannot roar, poor me.' Then there's more misery in his world than ever before. Otherwise there's always something to do, 'I have to wake up, wake up, wake up.' You permanently feel like an underdog, whining and howling; poor me. But that's still fun because there's still someone who enjoys it.

That one who's enjoyed cannot enjoy it. But that one who is enjoying the non-enjoyer sometimes enjoys more that there's someone not enjoying himself than one who claims that he enjoys everything because he made sure that one who's enjoying everything would not enjoy it again. Such a bastard! Because there's more fun in non-enjoyment than enjoyment and we all know that by heart. The moment everything is harmonic and everything is calm, it gets boring. Then something wakes up in you who wants to destroy it. The worst for what you are is boredom and you want to destroy it by all means. It could be war, killing your partner, divorce, fucking with the neighbour. Something has to be done. [Laughter]

Q [Another visitor]: Drama...

K: When Rama is awake he needs drama. That's his battlefield. There's no Rama without drama. There's no way! Only when Rama doesn't know Rama, there's Shanti. But when Rama is present, there's drama because there's separation and an attempt to end separation at all costs. For that it fights permanently. That's Ramayana. It's always about fighting. Then they go home and enjoy themselves because the warrior can only sleep well if he has had a war. If a warrior doesn't do anything and only chants Shanti, Shanti, Shanti he gets really angry. Then the beast comes out.

That's why when I talk I really try to offend people by poking them. The beast wakes up, this Rama inside. This beast is in everyone. This is Papaji's wake up and roar. Don't hide the beast in the back-room. When what-you-are is awake, that's the beast and it's very beastly and angry. You know this angry beast inside; everyone knows that. Why do you cover that bullshit? Just be angry. [Laughing] Some are mice, some are rats and some are bigger beasts. The size of beast varies but the beast is present even in the little ant or in a mouse or rabbit. In every being there's this beast. What's wrong with this beast? All this aggression. Without that you cannot survive anyway. This Kali inside, that's the beast. It's here to chop and it goes chopping. Where are the heads? Then comes Shiva, not so much, don't destroy everything.

All these are the tendencies of the Self. All the Gods of India are the tendencies of what you are. All presenting what you are in different variations and frequencies of tendencies. Why do you limit yourself? All of that is you. [Pointing to a visitor] Even doctors have tendencies.

Q: No! [Laughter]

K: Tendencies of making money. 'How much do I get out of it? Which sickness will help with most expensive pills and treatments?' You have to buy a ring for your wife and then the next patient has to pay for it. Then you think, 'What disease should I tell him?'

Q [Another visitor]: In Chinese philosophy, there's *yin-yang*. There's power when there are both...

K: I always say you are the Shanti who has to wake up as a beast. In nature you are Shanti, there's no warrior but when you wake up you have to play a warrior. What can you do? Then you worry about yourself; loving, caring is worrying about what you are – naturally. As what you are there's nothing to worry about, the absence of the warrior. But the moment you're present, there are worries... there's a worrior. Then you have relatives and then the fighting starts. Then you really have to fight for your right to exist in the family. Then comes the heritage sooner or later. You have to fight for your position. Everything is to fight for. You have to fight for relationship. You have to work on everything. Your wife will tell you that we have to work on our relationship. If she doesn't then you really have a problem, you know that. You have to fight for your right to sit down and watch television. [Laughter] You have to find the remote control because it's always hidden. You become a true seeker. How to make a realized one a seeker? Hide his remote control.

A realized one is lazy; you can never get him out of his sofa. He feels like a couch potato. He needs the remote control and the food next to him. That's why it's called *seva*. They always have disciples around them doing *seva*. They say when you serve the guru then you serve the Self. Then you collect the points of your *seva*, of the selfless service. Does it help? Fuck! It didn't work.

21st July 2018 Talk 1
Ladakh

No one can claim – I Am That!

Q: I don't know what's right and what's not and it happens more often...

K: That's failing to know oneself. It should be permanent. You're on the right track. If it happens more often then it's already in the right direction. You falsely signed-in to this life and now you sign-out. The signing in is to know and then you get fed up of knowing yourself because it's unbearable and then you sign out – you re-sign. The last is that the resigner gets resigned. The substrator gets substrated and then the substratum remains. It was, it will always be the way. You falsely signed into this universal learning system of trying to know yourself. Then you get fed up totally and you resign out of that tendency of trying to know yourself. The resigner resigns. Then the last step is, what-you-are resigns even the resigner: that's renouncing the renouncing. But before there's a renouncer who renounces everything. And the last can only be done by the Self, by grace; renouncing even the renouncer or devoting the devoter. Earlier you devote everything and at the last the devoter gets devoted. But it cannot be done by himself. That's why they call it grace. By grace only the Self gives up the Self; to be the Self.

What to do? And all happens by itself. By itself you sign in by falling in love with yourself by knowing yourself. Then it seems like the love for your self gets sour. You get fed up. The misery is more than the joy in knowing your self and then you resign again. The way you go out, the same way you go back again. It seems like you forgot yourself but in forgetting you don't forget and in remembering you don't remember because all the time you were as you are. That what-you-are was always there. It never forgot itself. It's a dream-like forgetting and a dreamlike remembering. But it's all dream-like. It all happens in time but it's always certain that what went out will go back.

Q [Another visitor]: And then?

K: Nothing.

Q: The body goes inside...

K: It has nothing to do with the body my dear.

Q: I know...

K: You don't know.

Q: When Karl is buried one day...

K: Karl will never buried, I will be burnt. [Laughing]

Q: As you said, the game continues...

K: Reality is trying to know itself; there's no end to it. You start to re-love yourself. You drop the lover, the loving and the beloved. And then by whatever, you start again to be the lover, the loving and the beloved. There's no 'final' in it.

Q: And does consciousness again...

K: It will always be stupid enough to fall in love with itself again.

Q: And the whole suffering starts...

K: There's no suffering. There was never any suffering, that's the problem. That which was never there cannot stop. There was never any suffering; it was just Reality realizing itself. There was never any suffer, no suffering and nothing to suffer about. All there was and all there will be is always that Absolute itself and the Self without a second Self cannot suffer. There's no suffering. It's a dream of suffering. How can something stop what was never there? There's only joy enjoying itself. Then enjoying itself in the circus of falling in love and out again but nothing ever happened. There was never any suffering, no sufferer, no suffering, nothing to be suffered about. What can end?

Q: The reason why people want to go home is because they're fed up with life...

K: Yeah. And that what-you-are is enjoying it, moment-by-moment. So what can end?

Q: So everybody can be it...

K: There's no everybody. There's only joy, only Self. Your former teacher really didn't do a good job, I tell you. [Laughter] That's the whole problem that there was never any problem. And you try to create one but you cannot create one. You try very hard to make a problem because you need a problem but you cannot make one.

That's why they call it a dream – a dream sufferer and a dream suffering doesn't exist. It's just fiction. How to get rid of the fiction? If you try to get rid of the fiction by your attention it becomes real but there was never any reality in the sufferer or suffering or what he's suffering about. It never existed, just like a dream.

Q: You say suffering doesn't exist...

K: I say there are dream sensations but there's no Reality. They are but they're not. I don't say there's no experience of it. I just say that the experience of the sufferer is not real. Whatever exists, is not real. That what-you-are doesn't need to exist to exist and that what needs to exist doesn't have any reality. So what?

Q: This body we live in...

K: This body was never there. It's just a cluster of energy.

Q: This cluster of energy...

K: It never came. It just transformed into some other bullshit. Where's the body? It's just a cluster of energetic atoms becoming something else. There's nothing that dies, it's never born, this bullshit. How can it die? So what? The worms have a party with you, that's all. 'Oh, my little finger, I'm so in love with you. I miss you so much already because one day you'll be gone. Whoa! I miss you so much.' Everyone is so much in love with his little finger. 'What happens when my body is gone?' [Laughing] What will happen? Nothing happens.

Q: Once you said that the dream goes on...

K: The dream cannot stop because there's not even a dream. [Laughter] He agreed with me that there's Self and nothing but the Self and the Self is never born and never dies but he still says, 'What about the dream?' Where's the dream if only Self is? Where's this bloody dream? What about the dream which is not?

Q: I give up... [Laughter]

K: Life goes on. What would Byron Katie say? Can that really be true? You need to work it out. [Laughter] The barren Katie.

Q: She has four kids...

K: She was never a mother of any kid. The kids have a barren women as their mother. Nothing ever came out of anything.

Q [Another visitor]: She woke up with a cockroach...

K: That's one profound master – 'I' to 'I' with the cockroach. Then she saw that 'me' and the cockroach are one. I cannot escape the cockroach. [Laughter] She was totally fucked up by drugs and weighed over a hundred kilos and then the cockroach looked at her and said, 'Hello!' Then she realized herself as a cockroach, herself. Not being different to a cockroach. Then she stopped eating, stopped drinking. These are the nice stories.

Q: There's a before and an after...

K: Again. After seeing the cockroach she wanted to become a supermodel again.

Q [Another visitor]: Is perception a trap?

K: It's already part of the dream which is not. Without perception, there's no perceiver, no perceiving and nothing to perceive. So, it's the first and last. But the nature of perception you will never know. The 'I' of the God is the last we can talk about. That is never an idea, never a concept. Whatever you say, it's not. That's why they say that the perception is the first and the last. You just go back to the perception which is prior to the perceiver. You're perception that perceives the perceiver, perceiving and what is perceived. By that you will not know the nature of perception. The Absolute not knowing what is perception, that's the first and the last because that's perception. Without the perception of Parabrahman, the dream cannot be.

So, what is real? Is it something we can talk about? Or is it something that doesn't know itself? Perception would still be different from a perceiver but still perception is, with and without a perceiver. So, in a way it's more real than the perceiver but it's still not Reality. The best thing is to be quiet and to not know at all.

Q [Another visitor]: That's the only point you can abstract to as a concept...

K: You cannot abstract any further than going to the perception. It's the abstraction of the abstraction where the perception is perceived, the first and the last.

Q: And you say being silent is the only way and there's no concept...

K: But even no-concept is a concept. You fail even there. When you just pronounce it, you cannot not be. It's the end of all that you can reduce. It's the substratum where the abstraction is finished. The substratum that doesn't know any substratum. Being that what it cannot not be. There's no way out because there's not even a way in. Whatever you imagine doesn't fit but still you are. That's why when UG Krishnamurti says no way out, I agree. For that what you are there's no way out of being as you cannot not be. You cannot not be and the rest is the rest. There's no way to get out of whatever it is and it is not. If this is a dream or not a dream, it's all irrelevant. The main thing is that you cannot not be. That's the final neti-neti – You cannot not be. You are in any way of presence or any way of absence of whatever is and is not. None of that can unmake you. So what is there to do?

What can death or birth do to you? Nothing can change what you are. All the ideas and changes, they may be or maybe not. That's the final 'Who cares?' It cannot unmake you. As it cannot make you, it cannot unmake you. Total resignation... but there's no resigner. Then it still continues. But what to do? And no one can claim that. No one can claim – I Am That! No ownership possible. And there's no advantage of being That. As there's no advantage, there's no disadvantage. That's the Absolute advantage.

Q: Sometime you try not to run away from it...

K: The phantom 'me' will always try to run away. It's a worst-case scenario. You cannot take it. You can take suffering, you can take misery, you can take anything. But not to know what you are, you cannot take as a 'me'. That's killing the fake self.

Q: And you cannot try to stay close to that...

K: There's no closeness. That's why it's non-duality. There's no closeness. How can there be closeness if there are no two? From who to what? What can be closer or not closer? As you cannot be closer to it, you cannot go further away. Then whatever is, you are That; as you cannot not be That. This little 'me', this little seeker, always wants to be closer and complain that he's so far away so that it can survive. Being close or not close, being advanced.

Q: It's unbearable but you do everything to bear it...

K: And you will see that you cannot bear it. For what you are there was nothing ever to bear.

Q: What does it mean that you cannot take it?

K: There's not even nothing what can be taken. You cannot take That what doesn't exist because that what-you-are doesn't need to exist to be. So, how can you take that? How can you claim That? Who can claim to be That? So, it's better to be quiet about it.

Q: UG says, if you knew what it is, you'd run away from it...

K: That's what I say, you will run away. By trying to become it, you run away. You claim that you want to have it. By wanting to go there, you run away. You cannot otherwise because you want to survive there. No phantom can survive where no one can be – impossible! So whatever you try to become, is trying to run away from it. All your sincere truth seeking is all fake! You will be dropped. That's why it's called grace; you will be dropped but not because you want it. You want to claim it.

You want to have it, your beloved Self. But you can never claim it, you can never marry it, you can never put it in your pocket. You can never make anything with it. But you may try; it doesn't mind.

All these truth seekers, the ones who think they're advanced who say I only long to be That, is all false. You always run away from it. By intuition you know that you cannot survive there. So you do everything against it. By looking for it you are very safe because you make it an object. And by making it an object, you become very safe. By whatever you do or don't do, or by meditation it's always trying to survive. But grace shows no mercy. It will drop you because it doesn't even know you. For grace you don't even exist. There's nothing even to drop. What is there to drop? It doesn't need you to go because it doesn't even know you. It has no necessity at all of any change because it doesn't know anything what could change. Absolutely no need of anything. No one is too much or too less. That's why it's called satisfaction by nature because there's never too much or never too less.

That's joy because it doesn't need joy. It doesn't need to enjoy itself to be what it is and that's the nature of joy and not an already enjoyed phantom. What do you want to be? Do you want to be the one who realized his fucking self which is an idea? Or do you want to be that what never needed anything? It was never born nor not born nor does it have any idea about dreaming or not dreaming. It never needs any explanation or anything. It never needs to understand if it is or is not. What can be done or not done? Because all the doings and not doings are fiction. How can anything that's fiction lead you to that what's not a fiction? If even awareness is fiction, what is there to do?

Fiction, fiction, fiction! Enjoy the fiction and know that the fiction cannot give you anything nor can it take anything away from you. You can never get less than you are by anything. How can a fiction give you that what you're looking for? And only *you* can be what you are, no one else can be it for you. I just repeat it. Don't hope for anyone outside or inside you who can help you. No fucking guru could ever help anyone. Be happy about it that you're totally independent of anything. And I'm not here to help you, for sure not. Maybe the opposite, if at all.

Q [Another visitor]: This happening of not knowing...

K: It doesn't happen, it's permanent.

Q: But there's a knowing that comes out here...

K: Yeah. Because there's nothing else to do. They asked Ramana the same question. Why do you talk if it's not necessary to talk anyway? To be quiet is the best, so why do you still talk? He said, just sport. What else to do? No expectation of anything coming out of it. No one who teaches anyone. It's just for fun.

Q: This not knowing...

K: Doesn't come out. Out of the not-knowing comes knowing. It's complete in nature. It's knowledge in nature. Not knowing is knowledge. Knowledge doesn't know knowledge. Knowledge not knowing knowledge doesn't care what comes out of it. It always sounds quite profound. If there's something, the certainty which cannot be earned by anything comes with it. You cannot get it from anywhere. You have to be the certainty; the certainty what cannot give anything nor cannot take anything from anyone. That certainty cannot be transmitted – never! You cannot learn it. You cannot become it by understanding. This certainty is unshakeable. And the words are loaded by certainty, that's all what comes. The words you don't dare to hear anymore, it's just the certainty which is the resonance. The rest is fiction anyway. But it's a certain fiction. [Laughing]

Only this is good company where there is this certainty. Jesus called it 'living words' where life is living and life is speaking, without any necessity, without anyone wanting to change something. Just by prrrrr.... What to do? There's not even accepting it. There's no acceptance or anything. It's just.... prrrrr. [Laughing]

Q: Then there are times where you need to download...

K: That's what Nisargadatta said. You drink and then your bladder gets full. When the knowing gets full, it's just a joy of releasing the pee. Otherwise you feel a bit... arghh. That's the only reason I talk anyway otherwise maybe I cannot sleep if the energy is too much. So I'd rather freely release it into the blue. But not because I'm here to be a messiah who wants to change the world and save someone or whatever. I have no idea about creating a new earth or something. Waking people up? Whoa. How far can it get?

It's more like I wake you up from the idea of waking up. Just showing you that even waking up is just a concept or an idea. So you may wake up from the idea that you have to wake up, but not to anything. So, wake up from waking up. Wake up but without a call.

Q: I was overhearing some monks talking in the coffee shop discussing about their teacher. The lama told them that suffering is the master of the individual self...

K: Sounds like a religion. Religion needs sufferers; *mea culpa*. The Christians, the Buddhists... all need sufferers. Without sufferers there would be no believers. There would be no followers. Only for the one who suffers, they can promise to end suffering. One needs the other; it's like a SM mission – slave and master. Masters needs slaves and slaves need masters.

Q [Another visitor]: But is it also vice versa?

K: Master needs slaves and slaves need masters. It's a conspiracy. Each one confirms the other one. Both are phantoms that need confirmation and suffering is always the best confirmation.

Q: But it's also a belief...

K: Believers need someone to tell them to believe in something.

Q: But there's no suffering either...

K: Even with a believer there's no suffering. What are you talking about?

Q: You have to believe...

K: Now you create a religion again. You have to believe that you don't have to believe. In believing you suffer and in not believing you don't suffer. So, that's another religion. So, not believing is better than believing. That's religion – my God is bigger and my truth is more true than your truth, all those things come together.

I was laughing when I heard someone say, 'I am nothing'. But nothing is the opposite to something so you're still something. But maybe it's more comfortable to be nothing. But who needs that bloody comfort to be nothing? You're nothing, I'm nothing, can we be nothing together? [Laughing] We are *two*gether, we're both guessing that we're nothing. And we two know that we're not separated. *Two*gether we're not separated. What an oneness, nice! Then we hug each other like hell. I hate huggers, this bloody oneness bullshit. Especially the sannyasin bullshit, these Osho huggers. They hug as long as something relaxes in them, then they move to the next one for this orgasmic oneness.

Q [Another visitor]: Have you been having all these experiences?

K: No. I avoided it all the time but some tried. Sometimes it's unavoidable and then you know what you don't want. I don't say there's something wrong or right with it. It's just for fun. But sometimes it's too much fun. It's too funny. Have fun, come on. Enjoy yourself, come on. If you don't enjoy yourself, there's no other self who would enjoy you, I tell you. Enjoy that you don't have to enjoy yourself, so enjoy yourself. And no one can give it to you, no one can teach you that – especially not the huggers.

Q [Another visitor]: So hugging would be oneness and not hugging would be separation?

K: It's like what the hug is going on? The huggers and the non-huggers. It's like a smoker and a non-smoker. When the non-smokers smoke, it's not nice and it doesn't taste good. But if you not smoke as a smoker, then it again doesn't work. When you're a smoker, smoke; when you're a drinker, drink; when you're an addict take your bloody drug. If you don't do it, you suffer. If you're a lover, love; if you're a hater, hate. Nothing is more or less as the other one. If existence wants to enjoy you like that just be that so that it enjoys itself like it. Just be a tool of enjoyment and don't fight against it because that makes you suffer. Just be a smoker, be smoked. Be piped, all the smokers smoke a pipe. So, I know I'm not a hugger.

Q: But you can change...

K: No. [Laughter] That's too late. After so many years one knows that one is not a hugger. And it was really bad when Mooji hugged me. That was too much, since then I hate him. [Laughter] This feeling I really didn't like. Someone comes to you and doesn't even ask if he wants to hug you, 'Ah I always wanted to meet you' and then hugging. I was like, fuck it, what do you want here? He raped me. [Laughter]

[Group]: #MeToo... [Laughter]

When I now watch these videos from satsangs where people are in a corner so that nobody could touch them and he especially goes to them and hugs them. I feel for them. I have full compassion for them. Mooji hugging one who doesn't want to be hugged. Fuck it!

Q [Another visitor]: In Zen Buddhism there's a sutra which says that with hugging you feel the discomfort of being two and you want to destroy it...

K: What to do? If someone comes and just does it then you hate him for the rest of his life. Milarepa never did that; he was killing people with black magic. He was a very bad guy, for that I really like him.

Q [Another visitor]: Once I was in Poona and I counted the hugs and most of them lasted about fourteen seconds. They were very long hugs...

K: Until this bloody oneness happens.

Q: You look at someone and you know they're going to hug you and then you run to the other side. [Laughter]

K: If you have the possibility to run away. Here I was cornered in a little cafe, there was no way out. [Laughter]

Q [Another visitor]: Don't you like hugging?

K: I have to eat, that's already enough. I hug them but secretly. [Laughter] And I don't hug people who don't want to be hugged. Sometimes they try and sometimes I cannot say no.

Q: For some it's like an addiction, they have to do it...

K: A hug-habit, like Mooji. He has to hug. He's a junkie. When I see him, he's a total hug junkie. Absolute junkie for hugging. He cannot

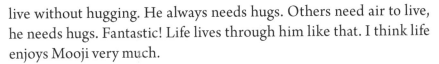

live without hugging. He always needs hugs. Others need air to live, he needs hugs. Fantastic! Life lives through him like that. I think life enjoys Mooji very much.

Q [Another visitor]: Ammachi is a hugging vampire...

K: Huggers are always vampires you know that. They always want the best from you; that you love them. I love you and then they hug you. It's not my family constipation; it's my guru constipation – being hugged by Mooji. Now I need to have a guru constellation. [Laughing]

Once I really annoyed Ganga, the wife of Papaji. There was a party in Tiruvannamalai. She said she met a man who had problems with sex. He was always thinking about it. 'Then I hugged him and for three months there were no sexual tendencies anymore'. Like success story. [Laughter] And I just said, after all these years you still don't know to take it. After one hour someone came and they said there's not enough food here and we may have to leave before the lunch. She was really angry with me for two years. She thought her energy can take away some tendencies and I just made a joke about it. That was too much for her. But after that she came for the talks and it was okay. At one point she really had a pride in *my* energy and I just made a little click. If someone is proud about his bloody energy, of what he can do. That's with Mooji too when he runs around with his so-called energetic field. He's quite proud about it that some people cannot take it. It's crazy. Then it really gets funny. I cannot help it. I smell this pride – *my* energy, *my* Buddha-field. What to do?

But that I feel everywhere. Only when I went to Ranjit Maharaj and UG Krishnamurti. UG was funny, he was not proud; he just played to be proud. He was playing with his hair for a photo session but there was no pride, it was just a play nothing serious. There was no fucking importance – 'I'm fucking important and I will change your life' – bullshit. So if someone said he's like a barking dog, I like that more than someone saying listen to my words they are being simultaneously translated into eight languages. Then tears came from his eyes and he was so proud about it. He said, that can happen. Oh my goodness! And then his crowd is very proud that they're serving a very big guru with many many flies around him. [Laughter] I like Upanishads. It says the biggest guru is shit because so many flies cannot be wrong.

Q [Another visitor]: But this is not said in the Upanishads...

K: You have to read what is before and after. [Laughter] They never read the preface; they already go to the end. What is the end of it? What is the solution? But they never read the preface. The first page, the empty page, everything is already there.

Q: In eight languages...

K: In all languages! It doesn't need any translation. The first empty page never needs any translation. It's totally clear and blank. Then starts the bullshit. You should only remember the first page which is blank. Then you know enough. You don't need to know anymore. Blank, blank, blank...

Q [Another visitor]: You're saying no one wants to read the first page...

K: They cannot read that. You only read the black letters and no one sees where these black letters appear on which is always uninterrupted what is blank. Everyone is interested in these bloody black lies appearing on the pages. What to do? To be what you are you don't have to read, you don't need to learn or anything. But now that you can read you only see the words but not where the words appear.

Q: People look for solutions and they don't want to get into the problem. In Zen meditation [Pointing to picture of Buddha]...

K: He's not meditating. That's a false image of meditation. Buddha never had any face, Buddha never had any form; he never meditated. All the pictures you see about meditation are fake pictures. Do you think Buddha looked like him? He looks more like her. In Buddhism they say women can never get realized... but men neither. That they always forget to mention. They always say women can never get enlightened but there's this little next sentence... and neither can men. They never mention that. They stop there but that's the most important thing – neither: *neti-neti*. Neither men nor women can ever... or *as* woman or *as* man – never. Then there are Lamas and Rinpoches. There are not so many Rinpochinas. Maybe in China. [Laughter] Even Hinduism is similar. [Asking a visitor] Can women get enlightened?

Q: I have never come across any such reference...

K: Was Anandamayi maa enlightened?

Q: Yes, and Meerabai...

K: Okay. So even women can get enlightened in Hinduism. But there are not so many, there are infinite men... all kinds of *anandas*. I always give spiritual names to people but no one wants them. Someone asked for a name and I gave him a name – *duschananda* and sometimes *nichtalibiananda*. [Laughter] Sometimes I say you're *mahatma-mahatmanicht*. Till now no one took the name I gave them. I succeeded. But it's all *ananda*.

Q [Another visitor]: Is *ananda* a solution or a problem?

K: The idea of *ananda* is a problem. When *ananda* is your nature then you don't know *ananda*. Then you are *ananda*, that's not a problem. Having an idea that you have to reach *ananda*, then you have a problem. That's the same with Self, when you are the Self – no problem. When you want to realize the Self, then it's a problem.

Q: Is experiencing problems as problems...

K: A problem? No. [Laughter]

Q: In Zen when you look at Buddha, he's supposed to be a solution and then you sit for a solution but all you see is infinite problems...

K: You have to look at the infinite problems because that's the nature of Zen. You always meditate on the boredom of eternity. Zen means 'to see', and then and then and then... Never-ending then. No one can take that. You can only be a person if there's a beginning and an end. But if there's then and then and then... eternal then, you cannot take it. That kills you. That's why Zen meditation is looking into the eternal boredom. And no one can take that, but for what you are – no problem. What you are has no problem with eternal boredom, that nothing ever happened. But that what needs something to happen, cannot take it. You can only kill yourself by eternal boredom.

In that way, that no one can take it, you get killed because what-you-are has nothing to take. It has no problem with eternal boredom because for what-you-are nothing needs to happen. But for that what is living by happenings, by coming and going, being born and dying, that cannot take it. So you have to meditate on boredom and that is Zen. Then and then and then and then. That's why they sit in front of the wall for hours and days just to be confronted with the eternal boredom. Then a *satori* happens because when that what-you-are disconnects from any intention of getting there and there's a resignation, then perception disconnects from everything. That's called a *satori*. But by whatever intention you come back. It connects again to this and hope starts again and things. There's no end of it. You go out and in again. You cannot help it. It's like helplessness. You cannot remain where there's comfort. That's the comfort zone – the absence of any time or no-time. It would be very comfortable but no one can stay there because the one who disappeared will appear again. Then the body is there and everything is back and you have to work and you have to eat. All the bullshit happens again. So, no way out!

When you see that there's no way out, that you cannot stay there where it's very comfortable, you always come back here, then you're here what you are and you are there what you are. Here – what can happen to you? Nothing can happen. You are in any circumstance what you are and you don't need any special circumstance to have comfort, because the comfort of your being is not depending on an experience of comfort or no-comfort. There's an independence of any circumstance that can give or take anything away from you. This discomfort cannot bring you discomfort and the comfort of absence doesn't bring you comfort because the comfort of your nature is independent of comfort and discomfort. They're just two different experiences that cannot give you anything or take anything away from what you are. You are Absolute in the discomfort as you are Absolute in the comfort. There's nothing to achieve in it. That's called Zen meditation; and I like it. You fail. You fail to stay there and in failing you know – Okay. You're okay in not okay and you're okay in okay. So, you're okie-dokie anyway.

I have nothing against meditation. I always tell people to meditate by twenty-four-seven. Maybe you start by one hour but then you have to extend the time. You have to be in meditation while working, while washing your dishes, while watching television. It has to be a permanent meditation.

Q [Another visitor]: Meditation on what?

K: On nothing! Didn't you listen to me? Doctors don't listen; they only want a dream to come out of it. I said before that you have to meditate on eternal boredom, that nothing ever happened. Did you not listen?

Q: Yes...

K: So I told you already. Now I become angry here. The most studied and more intellectual people are the most stupid in that case. Sometimes I talk to some helpers in shops. They just listen for ten minutes and they are okay and then they leave and continue their work again. But these so-called advanced seekers they're the most stupid. They carry so much knowledge and are loaded with all these ideas and concepts of awakening and blah, blah, blah, how should it happen and how it should be. They are so blocked by bloody knowing something. Fuck them! And I have to talk to them.

Then there are left-overs from the *guru* before. Then I have to first destroy the *guru* before I can even talk to them because they're loaded with all the ideas and concepts of the *guru* before. All this guru-shopping. In that shop I got it like that and it was no nicely decorated in that shop. I had hugging with him in that shop and here... Nothing! You give me nothing. There's a joke. There are two Mullahs praying in the mosque 'Oh, Allah, I'm nothing.' Then the cleaner prays as well 'Oh Allah, I'm nothing' over which the Mullahs say 'Look, who thinks he's nothing!'

Q [Another visitor]: I know nothing...

K: I'd say I'm *blödsinn*(dumb). I was *blöd*, I am *blöd* and I will be *blöd*. I'm dumb, dumber and dumbest. You realize yourself as dumb. At first is dumb – Awareness. Then comes dumber – Spirit. Then comes the dumbest – Body. It's always dumb, dumber, dumbest. Knowledge realizes itself as dumb, dumber and the dumbest. Then you have to crucify it.

Q: And how does that happen?

K: At first the dumbest body gets pierced, then the dumber spirit gets pierced and then the dumb awareness gets pierced because even awareness disappears. That's crucifixion. That's why it's called crucifixion. You hang on this cross. Jesus was crucified. This is a symbolism that everything that you experience is fiction. The horizontal time, the vertical spirit and the centre of Awareness, the Heart, where both meet. All is fiction. So, it's cruci*fiction*. And when everything went away he went to the absence which is the dead zone where nothing ever happens. From there he came back resurrected as Christ. Before he was Jesus, a teacher, a Messiah. Then he came back as Christ. So, Jesus died, the fiction died and Reality remained. That's the crucifixion. And you are sitting here to be crucified.

Q [Another visitor]: 'The cross of golden altar cannot give you salvation if it's not built in what you are...'

K: I'd say you have to hang on to the cross for a while. You have to be nailed. You have to go through the passion; you have to see the fiction yourself. The cross is just a symbol of Christ. It will not give you salvation by just looking at it. That's what it means. The symbols cannot give you salvation. You have to look at it yourself and you have to crucify yourself into that because there's no one else around. But when you're lucky there's someone who crucifies you; like your husband or your wife. [Laughter]

Q: This is a quote from Saint Augustus...

K: It's a pointer to that.

Q: I always wondered what it meant to be crucified in oneself...

K: There is no 'oneself'. You will be crucified by Existence, you cannot do it yourself. Only grace can crucify you. You cannot do anything. It will not be yours. It is not in your hands. It will crucify you. It will kill the fiction you are. Who pierces the spear of destiny through the heart? This cannot be done by yourself.

Q: When it happens, I will ask you to do that...

K: No. I will not be there. [Laughter]

Q: The last phone call...

K: 'Come Karl, come with a spear.' [Laughter] Normally people want to be spared but you want to be speared, penetrated by grace. If grace fucks you, that will be the last you can experience.

Talking about Christianity, imagine you have to nail Kali! That would be a real *seva*. [Laughter] It would be everything but not a cross. She would chop your head before you can crucify her. When Kali goes chopping, watch out.

Q [Another visitor]: My experience is that I'm alive and I exist and I know that wouldn't exist and I know that crucifixion is the way out...

K: Jesus shows you that what you are cannot die on the cross. Nothing can kill you. Even being crucified cannot kill that what-you-are because that what is the nature of Jesus cannot be crucified. So, even by trying to kill him, by piercing the spear, that what-you-are cannot be killed. So you go to the land of the dead. It cannot kill you. Wherever you go to, even the absence of the presence of life, you come back to that what is Life. So what is not born, your nature, that what is living this life, your nature, what you are never depended on the experience of the body or anything. It is with and without experiences. With and without presence or absence or anything. This *neti-neti* is more like you are with and without.

Q: You mentioned that this crucifixion wouldn't be something that you enjoy at all...

K: Some enjoy it. In Philippines people always volunteer for being crucified. Then one gets crucified and everyone else is suffering not being crucified because 'Take me' gives very good attention. They're always ready for that, running around Mea Culpa. They feel happy with all the pain. You may say it's a bit stupid to hurt yourself but it gives attention. It's like you go to a meeting and you have the best story of your disease. My suffering is deeper than yours. There's a competition and if you're the biggest sufferer, everyone looks at you. Then one sits there and says I was raped and the other one says me too but five times!

It's always a competition of who's suffering more. Then if the goal is no suffering then the competition becomes, 'I am suffering only a little bit' and the other one says 'I don't suffer at all, I never suffered'. If the goal is not knowing then someone says, 'I never knew anything. I know less than you.' The competition will never stop. You always compete with yourself. That's the way you realize yourself. The Olympic Games comes from the same origin, who's stronger? Who's winning? Who's losing? But who's fighting?

You're right that the fiction is the hope, this idea that you may die. No one is afraid to die everyone is more afraid that he doesn't die when dying happens. That's your biggest fear that it will continue. There's no fear of death there's only a fear of not dying.

Q [Another visitor]: Where does this fear come from?

K: Because you are fed up with yourself to be and you fear that it will continue. That's where it comes from.

Q [Another visitor]: When people say I want to die before I die...

K: Pfff... They are dead anyway. 'My ego died, now I have a no-*me*.' [Applauding] 'Bravo! I have a thousand me's in me. When I wake up, I don't know who's up. I'm so schizophrenic that I can just choose who I am today, just as everyone. If I have to go to the government or to the tax persons, I'm a totally different person. If I have to go to another meeting, I'm a totally different person. If I need to have a joyful dinner or a party, a different one goes there. I don't even know. It chooses by itself. I just have to see what happens.' No one can define what he is, it's always different. It's fantastic! Sometimes you go to a party when they were supposed to go to the tax persons. Then they're boring. They're sitting around and are afraid what may happen.

I grew up in a village in a pub where they came for a party. Then you see them, very boring. Then they have one beer, another beer. They see their neighbour and they don't like each other and think what is he doing here? But after ten beers, they are laughing and cheerful. Suddenly there's such oneness in space... a drunken oneness. Then after twenty beers they start fighting because when they're so drunk they don't fear the consequences. [Laughter] It's amazing how people really change by drinking or whatever they do. You just give them some schnapps and they are a totally different person. Then their synapses work totally differently.

I try to do the same. I try to make you drunk by an invisible beer. That's why they say that Jesus made them drunk just by talking to them. By the living words you get drunk from yourself. You feel drunk and jolly.

Q [Another visitor]: But do you try to give us twenty beers?

K: I give you one litre of rum right away. [Laughter] Do you think I can wait until you have twenty beers?

Q: Is that where the fearlessness comes from?

K: Yes. Fearlessness feels like being drunk – totally drunk. No drug can give you that. Maybe it can get close but never to that. That's why you take *hero*-in or more-*fine*. But it's never fine enough. It's like meditation when there's a meditator. He gets some peace but then peace goes away again. That's just another drug. Nothing what you can achieve can give you the drunkenness of yourself, this ecstasy of what you are. But you try everything.

Q: What attracted me most in spirituality was always the fearlessness because I'm so fearful...

K: I know. Even in Bombay he was shaking because they wanted to kill him in Brazil. Even I would be fearful, I wouldn't even go to Brazil. Since I heard you, I have no intention to go to Brazil. His boss paid an assassin to kill him.

Q: No, he was the assassin...

K: And then he invites me to come to Brazil. [Laughter] It's crazy! Thank God that I don't have to prove that I'm fearless otherwise it's such a bullshit that you have to prove that you have no fear.

Q: It would be nice to not care about the consequences...

K: But that's not what I'm talking about. Then you want to own it. But you cannot own fearlessness. There was someone who fears and then there's someone who doesn't fear. Fearlessness is not it. In fearlessness, there's no ownership in it. It will never be your fearlessness. You may not fear the consequences but still you fear because what-you-are needs fear. Without fear you don't exist as a phantom. There's no phantom existing without fear. You need an existential fear that you remain as a phantom. Without the existential fear you cannot exist as a phantom.

Q: But if you create an artificial fearlessness...

K: If, if, if, if... If Easter and Christmas fall together then we can talk again. [Laughter]

Q [Another visitor]: Fearlessness is the same as freedom?

K: No. There's no freedom in fearlessness.

Q: What's the difference?

K: Freedom is just another idea. You are doomed by the idea of freedom. What would you be free from?

Q: From fear...

K: Then you're different from fear. So there are two.

Q: Duality again...

K: All those free people, God oh God. The moment you have an idea of freedom, you're free doomed. Doomed by the idea that you need to be free. Who needs to be free from what? When you are That what is, how can you be free from something? It always needs separation, it always needs something else to be free from... or love. Whatever you call it, is what?

Q: I am nothing...

K: But nothing wants to know something now. What nothing would know that it's nothing? I'm always surprised that someone says I'm nothing or you're nothing. What nothing knows that it's nothing? It's crazy! If you really look at the word and what comes out of it, it's madness. And everyone sucks these words in and says 'Yeah!' What craziness! It's a total madhouse, total bullshit. Nothing knows that it's nothing. Then it makes two nothings. If someone says 'I'm emptiness', what emptiness knows emptiness? Even to call it something there must be someone. That someone is always one too many.

Q [Another visitor]: I have a notion that crucifixion is a very bitter medicine. Is this just a delusion?

K: You have to ask Dr. Mooji. He always coats the bitter medicine in sugar. My mother used to do it like that. She used to coat bitter medicine with sugar. Beautiful words need some very ugly truth. I'm not into sugar-coating. You have to swallow it as it is. [Laughter]

Some really like it extra bitter. Sweet chocolate is bad. Some sugar-coat it because otherwise you cannot take it. They show compassion, they give you some sweet words so that you can swallow it. Then they hug you so that you may feel safe and at home. It's all fine, it's not so bad. No. I sit here and say it's worse. It's worse than you can ever imagine. Then you start laughing. There's a joy in it – 'Yeah, I cannot take it!' This cannot be taken, it's so bitter. You don't have to swallow anything to be what you are. The sweetness of your nature is that you don't know any sweetness. It can never be bitter or anything. Bitter for you is not bitter and sweet is not sweet. What you are is the sweetness that cannot be tasted. And nothing is sweeter than that sweetness you are. Compared to that it's all bitter anyway. Even the sweetest words are bitter. Fuck! No one can taste the sweetness of silence.

Q [Another visitor]: Is arrogance a really bad thing?

K: It's very bad. It's worse.

Q: In spiritual circles you can make a lot of mistakes but you can't be arrogant...

K: Yeah. It's very bad. And I'm arrogant like hell. I'm so arrogant that I don't know where the arrogance starts and where it ends. I'm so fucking arrogant and I like it. So, I'm not spiritual, thank God. If I would be spiritual, I'd be fucked like hell. Imagine I'd be spiritual, or even worse, esoteric!

Whatever has a circle, whatever has a group or a flock, flocking together, making rules of what you have to be – what a bullshit! Even a meeting of atheists is a religion. Then they say only the atheists are the real ones. The non-believers are the real believers. Blah, blah, blah... Help me God! And all the rules of how it has to be. They asked Ramana if you have to practice a *sattvic* life? He asked, who makes the standard? Just ignorance makes standards and dimensions of how it has to be. Truth never asked anything from you. It never asked you to change one little inch of what you are or what you are not. It never asked anything. It doesn't want anything from you. It totally leaves you as you are. That they call acceptance but it's not acceptance. It leaves you because it doesn't know you. It's very easy to leave you as you are because it doesn't know you.

Q: Then they say Lucifer is an archangel...

K: Every guru is Lucifer you know that. It's always the devil who wants you to change. It gives you hope and everything.

Q: There are two devils Satan and Ariman...

K: One is the grandma and the other one is the grandson. The devil is only afraid with his grandma. [Laughter] He is not afraid of anything, only his grandma. Hell's kitchen is the worst place for him.

Lucifer is the one who wants to enlighten you. Lucifer – the light, who wants to bring you to the knowledge of yourself. It promises you something and gives you hope. Every guru promises you something. If you follow me then you will be enlightened. You can realize by my presence, by my whatever, by my grace. It's all Lucifer, the devil who creates hell – separation. It promises you something. It's always promissing. You miss yourself by that but you want to believe. You're so full of hope. All the disciples gather around where there's hope. It's like football; a hundred thousand disciples looking at the Lucifer ball and having a ball and then being fascinated by it. In India they say every guru is a Lucifer who wants to enlighten you. It's like bringing you to the light you are. That's already a joke.

Why do I talk so much about shit? Just to get rid of the Mooji disciples. It happened in Tiruvannamalai. Mooji had a break for a day and then all these girls came for talks and sat there and I was like 'Fuck what's going on here?' For ten minutes I started talking about so much shit and then one by one they left. Someone said he just talks about shit. I just had to make it unbearable for them. No beautiful words, no welcome to satsang, no silence, no whatever, no introduction, no pre-play. You'll never make it. You are all leftovers. No-one of you will ever wake up and get enlightened – forget it. You failures! Leftovers!

Q [Another visitor]: What about shadow work?

K: You want to bury your shadow, that's shadow work. Your dark side.

Q: Once someone told me that you need to do a bit more shadow work...

K: I agree. [Laughter] There's a famous story in India about the one who wants to bury his shadow because there should only be light. He dug deeper and deeper and finally he saw his shadow down there. Then he closed his eyes and closed the grave and then he opens his eyes. And what was there? Shadow. Fuck! That's called shadow work. It's like the Sisyphus work of rolling up the stone; all futile.

Q: The light workers...

K: They are shadow workers because they want to bring the light everywhere. They want to kill the shadow. They are very bad. I hate light workers. And positive people – fuck them all! [Laughter] The one who thinks he's positive is the most negative because he creates negativity by being positive. It's crazy. Good people create bad people. Bad people don't create good people; they kill them. Positive thinking is the worst thinking you can do. How can there be positive thinking? Can you imagine positive thinking? Or is every thinking bad? And positive thinking is the worst. Someone who's bad tries to be good. The devil who appears like an angel. These esoteric people always find what's wrong with you. You never thought about it and then they tell you. I never thought about it but maybe you're right. There must be something wrong with me. I don't feel good all the time, something must be wrong with me. [Laughter]

Q [Another visitor]: If there's a Buddhist that doesn't suffer, that would be quite something...

K: He would be suffocated... under water. If you push a Buddhist under water for ten minutes he doesn't suffer anymore. He will be suffocated. [Laughter] It's very easy to kill the sufferer. If you don't want to suffer, go under water for ten minutes. Then you meet the flipper and you flip away. Then you can ask the corpse 'What are you? A Buddhist or a Christian?' Does the corpse answer? Now you're dead. What was your religion? Silence, silence, silence. They say the corpse is stiff for a temporary period of time. After a while, it relaxes again.

Q [Another visitor]: I like Barry Long...

K: He was the guru of Eckhart Tolle. He invented the concept of 'now' and Eckhart Tolle just copied from him. Eckhart admitted it on Australian television that he was a student of Barry Long. He just stole everything. He also changed his name because he liked Meister Eckhart. Meister Eckhart spoke about the 'now of the now'. It was not the power of the now, it was the essence of the now. But calling it the power of now is good selling.

Q [Another visitor]: What is the bitterest thing?

K: The most bitter pill is that in dying you don't die. That you cannot take. That all what you have done in this life was for nothing. Didn't work. As if nothing ever happened, because in dying you don't die. You believe that you prepared yourself for dying and you will not come back, you will not be reborn. All what you have done was futile and it was for nothing. Because with this body everything is gone, all the precious insights and understandings and realizations are just gone with the wind as if they mean nothing. They are just connected to this body storage like a hard disk and with this hard disk all the bloody precious information of all kinds, all your insights, all your gurus, all your shakti experiences, all your peace and shanti is all.... Brrrrrr – Bang! As if it was never there. Then comes the next – and then and then and then and then. And nothing ever happened. This shit factory is collecting shit and with this shit factory this shit goes too. So, what to do? Be happy about it that this collection of shit will be gone and you will be fresh as you are, always were, always will be and there was never any spot on your nature. Then something else will happen, whatever happens. This is as fleeting as everything else. So why care about the ignorance you collect? Knowledge cannot be collected; only ignorance can be collected. All your insights and all your understandings is just ignorance. All your precious acceptance and deep insights and end of suffering and all the events of blissful, tra la la that came… all gone.

Q: You just said Knowledge cannot be collected only ignorance can be collected...

K: Because the collector is already false. And the knowledge you collect, what is that? Ignorance… because the collector is already a fake one. Therefore false can only collect falsity. False, false, false. It starts false and it ends false and whatever the false produces is false. False, false, false, false. UG would say, shit, shit, shit, shit. And I say – ha, ha, ha.

That is the hardest for the owner who is very proud that his collection is very pure and now I made it! All these awakenings are gone in one... psssst. All the insights and all the enlightenment is gone as... pssst. As if nothing ever happened, because only phantoms need to be enlightened and only phantoms need to wake up. And the phantom comes with this body and with this body this phantom is gone with the name and form. So who fucking cares if this is enlightened or awakened or stupid or anything? Just be that what cannot gain anything by any unenlightened or enlightened bullshit corpse. Only corpses can get enlightened. Waking up – all a fart in the wind. It stinks for a little while and then it's gone. And what you are remains what it is; as it always was.

21st July 2018 Talk 2
Ladakh

The whole exercise is an exercise of helplessness

～

Q: While coming here I saw a monk who looked just like you. He had similar eyes...

K: Since seventies I was a fan of Milarepa. I like that out of the bad comes neither good nor bad. In India most of the times the bad guys, assassins became the biggest saints of India. The good ones never make it. Good people are too good to be true. They have too much to do to be good. Bad is easy.

Q: So, out of the good and bad comes bad?

K: Out of the bad comes good and out of the good it becomes bad. [Laughing] Nothing comes out. But it's just to point out that you can never be bad enough to not be what you are because you cannot prevent to be what you are. Even by being totally bad. Even by being Trump, you are what you are. That's very fascinating. Even Trump is what he is – fantastic! But you would never expect that even Trump is what he was or Hitler is what he was. There's no exception. That's quite hard.

Q [Another visitor]: Some different schools talk about 'pure' consciousness which is unchanging...

K: That's the dirtiest consciousness, which is never changing – the pure consciousness.

Q: As I was walking around I just saw consciousness becoming the sound, becoming the light. There is no independent consciousness independent of the object. Consciousness always takes the shape of its object. Can you help me understand the nature of consciousness and its relation to objects?

K: There's no relationship in consciousness: then there would be two consciousnesses. Then they call it pure consciousness because there are no two consciousness. It cannot be dirty because it has no second. When you are one with your surroundings, when there's no difference, no separation, then they call it pure consciousness because the perceiver and what is perceived is not different. Then there's no sense of separation left. It can happen in art too. When you look at the painting, the perceiver and the perceived disappear and art remains. That they call as pure consciousness; the experience of what you are without a sense of separation. In that sense when you walk in nature, you become one with nature because there's no sense of separation. Then you resonate in the way of the spirit, the clean way. The other way is the dirty one if you have to define how nature has to be. In that there's a definer. But without the definer you're just one with nature. Otherwise you say nature is only when there's green and wood but you can have the same experience in the city or the dirtiest place, the biggest red light district. You just get lost. The sense of separation disappears and there's no why.

From the horizontal, separate story and concepts, a definer *me*, it becomes the non-defining *me* and you disappear in the oneness. Then many say this is better than the other one, more clean, more pure. But for me that's not the case. As I always say, the idea of purity is the dirtiest idea because then you make a difference between separation and non-separation and non-separation is better than separation. But for who? That's always the question. For who is separation bad and oneness good? And who feels better in oneness and not so good in separation? Who has more comfort in oneness than in separation? It's a dependency. You just create a dependency of your so-called comfortable life of feeling good because in oneness you feel better than in separation.

Q: So, it's exactly the same as presence and absence?

K: No. That's part of the presence. Absence-presence is more extreme.

In presence there are three different ways of experiencing yourself. In personal way, day by day defining who you are and having friends and enemies and all what comes with it. Then the oneness way, where you're one with your surroundings, like formless spirit. Then the awareness way, where you're just a screen where the oneness and separation dances on. So, there are three different ways of perceiving yourself. And you may shift every day, many times between them, infinite times. Most of the times you don't even realize that you're in oneness and awareness. More than eighty percent is the awareness, the screen, and fifteen percent oneness. Maybe only five percent is separation experience. There are these shifts. Then the whole training of vipassana is to be aware of these shifts. That you don't change and you're just aware that shift happens but you have no preference. The separation experience is just different from the oneness. The experience should be that you experience helplessness; the shifts happen by themselves and not by anyone wanting them. They just happen.

And they are always there. The moment there's oneness, there's separation – always there. Then there are even four more states of absence. In the first three you realize because there's one who makes a memory out of it. The fourth is already out of presence. About the fifth, sixth and seventh, one cannot talk in a horizontal way. But the first three are personal. A personal experiencer experiencing himself as separate, then oneness and then screen? Where you cannot make any difference. By differences, there are memory effects, there's a story. You can make a story out of all of that. The fourth is already out of story. No story can be made out of that what is prior and out of impersonal awareness no story can be made. Out of impersonal awareness, the sixth, there can be no story. For the seventh, for sure not. Even the impersonal-person, the Absolute-person has no story. But about the first three we can talk as a personal because there are stories. That you can learn something. The fourth is the last because you cannot exercise that. About the first three you can exercise. Even that exercise is out of an accident. It happens by itself.

And you always try to stay in the oneness and then in Awareness, but by no effort you can stay there. You try to land there but you will always depart again. There's no way to stay there. Even in the 'prior' you cannot stay because there's no one who could stay because there cannot be any effort anyway. Even awareness needs a very subtle silence; you have to be quiet. There's a dependency that for awareness you have to be quiet... totally quiet, don't move. A slightest intention and you're out of it. That comes naturally; you cannot avoid it. Something happens that makes you just get out of it and then you're fucked.

So, the whole exercise is an exercise of helplessness: that whatever happens is not in your hands. Then you relax in that helplessness... and then you may just slip away because there's no one who has any advantage or disadvantage because you cannot control it. The controller dies out because the idea of control cannot stay in that controlessness and helplessness. That's why these techniques of vipassana and all of that are all there to experience helplessness and not that you start to control yourself. You try to control yourself but you fail. By failing to control, there's a relaxation then maybe the perception easily travels between the presence states and maybe even goes to the absence. The fourth state is the Samadhi, where no one can be, but still you are.

The idea of purity comes only in the horizontal. Already in the oneness there's no idea of purity. Only later when you come out of the oneness, you call it pure. But in that what is oneness, you would not call it oneness. There's no one who calls it oneness. There's an absence of separation. But who defines something as pure and something else as impure? Only in the impure, in the horizontal, in the first state, there's a concept of something possible. What to do? All the memories are in the first state. It's rare that people have any memory of even oneness. Then rarer is awareness. It's impossible to go to the fourth state because no one went there. No one ever, because no one can be there. The teachers talk from the oneness, the second state. The realized masters talk from Awareness. But no 'one' talks from the fourth state... there's talking without a talker. There are only masters of oneness or awareness.

Q [Another visitor]: When you are talking, the intellect tends to go into abeyance. I have to make an effort to try to understand what you are saying. Something goes into abeyance and I don't really seem to understand. Some things have an impact and some don't. So, I'm wondering should I try to use my intellect more because it doesn't work anyway...

K: What is happening is for whenever I talk and for as long as I talk you can be quiet, that's all. I'm not important. This being quiet is the highest that you can be. Being quiet is the only way. Normally you need an effort to be quiet. So, I'm just a little helper to be quiet because as long as I talk, you cannot think, because you cannot follow. And as you cannot follow, you can relax. You give up following and be quiet. It's not a technique, it's just the living words you cannot follow because you cannot grasp it with your intellect and then you stay where no intellect can be. That's what is quiet, that's all it is. I'm not here to teach anything. I just talk so much so that you can be quiet. And whatever I say doesn't matter actually. It's just that you can be quiet.

These words are full of silence because silence cannot be grasped. They are empty, they have no teaching, they have no learning inside. So, they are just living, but not giving you anything. You try to get something out of it but there's nothing to get. After a while you give up trying to get something and then you just be quiet. That's the nature of meditation. I can talk and talk but still I meditate because I talk out of meditation. I'm not talking out of a teacher or someone who knows more. This is meditation for me – talking meditation. And you just fall into that because it's without some learning and achieving something or controlling something. By my words you cannot control anything. It's not about knowing something more than someone else. In that sense, what to do?

Q: Being quiet...

K: But there's no contradiction in it. Being quiet and talking is not a contradiction. That what is quiet doesn't need to be quiet and that what needs to be quiet to be quiet is artificial. It's always an artificial silence. The silence that has to be silent is not silence. And the knowledge that has to know, for sure is not knowledge. I like purity because no one needs it. I like dirt. I can be a dirty bastard and still I am what I am. If I would have to become a saint or something, a pure heart bullshit, then I really would be fucked, fucked forever, because there was never anyone who was pure enough for himself. Nothing was ever pure enough for what you are. No knowledge of any knower was ever knowledgeable enough for that what is knowledge. No intellect could reach that what is intellect. No way!

Q [Another visitor]: I'm bored...

K: You are a woman. [Laughter]

Q: I was just thinking there still so many days to go... [Laughter]

K: You can try to go every day.

Q: I came all the way here...

K: But it doesn't make any difference. If you think you have to go, you go. It's like 'I paid so much for this body, I cannot let it go.' [Laughter] There's a businessman inside. 'I came so far and now I have to stay.' She's a mother and home it's always busy and there's no time to be bored. But now she comes here and then she's bored. She needs action. That's why mothers have kids because they have to be busy. They have no time to be bored. If you have a busy life, you're always in working meditation and you try never to get a pause because that's boredom. You always try to fill the void because the void is unbearable. The void is boredom, you know that – the emptiness; and you always try to avoid it. And now you find a reason to go because you want some action... because the void is unbearable for you, you know that.

Q: I'm not used to it anymore...

K: As a mother you are so spoilt. [Laughter] Self guilty. But the void always waits for you, you know that. Sooner or later the void is there. If you don't face it now, you have to face it a bit later when the kids leave. Circumstances change and the void waits for you. The void has infinite time. It's just waiting for you to look at it again. You will be raped for that, you know that. Now you maybe found a way to avoid it for a while. Then it comes back again. So, as long as you can avoid it, bye-bye. See you next time, where there's no time.

But it's always like 'I'm so bored,' as if someone else is guilty that one is bored. Always looking for someone who's guilty if one is bored. Existence is guilty or husband is guilty or family is guilty. Someone has to be guilty that I'm bored. And then they say, do something I'm bored.

The final thing is sooner or later you have to go into that and you have to face it. That's called meditation. You have to look into the boredom of the void. But if it's not the time now, it will be later. But there's no escape, no escape for anyone. Some become junkies because they want to avoid the void by taking drugs. Either they work all the time or drugs. Everything what a person does is to try to avoid the void. Whatever you do. You can have schnapps. Alcohol is good against the void because you become alcoholistic... the hole of the whole.

The whole humanity is permanently day by day trying to avoid the void. Having kids, having a family, doing a job is all trying to avoid the void. That's called humanity. That's called being a human, trying to avoid because the person cannot face the void. In the void you cannot exist. Your little existential fear always puts you into some action to avoid the void. It's like a defence system, survival system, because the void will swallow you, you know that. If you allow the void to be there, it swallows you and you don't know if you still exist if the void swallows you. It's like jumping into the abyss and seeing if you still survive. This little fear, 'Let's do something, let's party, let's have something to do, jogging or something. What can we do?' So, what to do?

Void is just another name for boredom because something inside knows this will never end. That nothing will ever end, you fear more than anything else. You do not fear to die. Dying is not a problem but in dying nothing happens. That this continues is what you fear. If you really would be sure that you would die by dying, everyone would've already killed himself. It's more the fear of not dying, that it doesn't help, because you tried it so often already. After dying something else happens, and then, and then... Now there's a little hope that maybe this time I can die. Maybe in enlightenment I can die, maybe if I realize myself I can die. But even that doesn't help.

The realization of what you are is realizing that you never die. This is eternal life. As you were never born, how can you die? The moment you're born, you're bored, you know that. You kill yourself the moment you believe you're born; you're dead and then you're bored, deadly bored. You're in a cemetery of life. You're a walking corpse. You only meet shadows, tombstones walking everywhere. Every tombstone already has a 'rest in peace written' on it, on his forehead like a tattoo. He thought he was born and then he didn't die. Walking tombstones and then resting tombstones, always wanting to be stoned.

No! No way out. But the amazing thing is what-you-are is never bored by anything. It doesn't know any boredom. It doesn't even know itself. That's the beauty of not knowing yourself. By being what-you-are not knowing yourself, there's not even an idea of boredom. This idea of boredom and void is only there when you know yourself as a body or someone. Then there's a permanent boredom. You permanently try to avoid boredom and the void. Self-guilty. Be bored, I have nothing against it.

Q: When you are the absence in presence?

K: When you are neither absence nor presence. When you absolutely don't know what you are and what you are not. If you only know what you are not, then you have a problem. When you know what you are you still have a problem. You absolutely have to know what you are and what you are not. Then it's just, what to do? You are then what is the absolute nothing and absolute everything. The absolute presence and the absolute absence. So, you're the absolute and then you are That. There's no boredom in that. How can there be a boredom because there's no one who could be bored? But now that you're born, you're always bored. Since childhood, even as a baby – bored. Always trying to fill up the time. But for what-you-are there's neither time nor no-time. There's just silence. How can there be boredom? For who? But this little belief system of me is the misery of boredom. And I agree that this punishment is justified.

You punish yourself instantly when you are not what you are. You get punished by what you are by not being what you are. You cannot even say that God is punishing or existence is punishing. You punish yourself. No one else can punish you. You punish yourself by not being what you are. Fantastic! Then you look for someone who's guilty. Just look for this asshole who's guilty for everything. If you want to complain, complain to whatever is this... because you fall in love with an image of yourself and no one else can do that. And only you can fall out of that love. No one can fall out of it for you. This self has to die. But it cannot die, that's the problem. It never had any existence. It's just another phantom.

I understand this. Since childhood everyone has this boredom. Every child is playing all the time, always trying to do something, always active. Even dogs do that and if nothing happens, they get sad.

Q: It never stops...

K: It never stops anywhere. The horizontal plane of humanity in this world is boredom.

Q: The kids they wake up so happy and so early...

K: And then they're bored. Then they go to the mother and say, 'I'm bored. You promised me that you will take care of my boredom. I want to go to the zoo, I want to go to the movies, McDonalds, Coca-Cola.' Everything about them is, I want to lick on something. As long as my tongue is busy I'm not bored. Then you get these overfed American people, they are fed due to boredom. Even mama's in Spain, they overeat out of boredom because they think, 'Now I have a husband and a kid and nothing can happen to me anymore. I can eat as much as I can because the longer I eat, something happens. As long as I chew, the brain is quiet and talking about food all the time, everywhere.' Around the world everyone talks about the food. How to do it right and then they eat. And then while eating they will add, my mother did it this way. Oh God! Fantastic! The French are the worst. I always wonder if there's any time left to eat. They just talk about it.

Having a body is boredom you know that. Even being spirit is boredom. Having ownership is just boredom. Any ownership is boredom because ownership means there's something that's born. 'I am the owner and I can lose something.' I'm painting a dark picture today just to make it so unbearable that the interest drops. The idea that the world can ever make you satisfied is just bullshit. It's just empty, sensational farting in the wind. All the beauty of all the paintings. That's why the Buddhists make the sand paintings so that they can destroy it again. All of it is fake. As beautiful as it seems to be and as entertaining as it seems to be, you can never get satisfied because you're hunting for the next entertainment; the next movie maybe is better than the one before. Personal misery! And it's justified. You just fight for entertainment and it's never good enough.

Q: So, you never get bored because you're never there?

K: I'm always there. I cannot leave what I am. I am not afraid of boredom. When there's boredom, there's boredom, when not, then not. If the boredom doesn't leave you anyway, you're not interested anymore. You're now interested in boredom because you have the idea that one day it will stop. It will never stop. When I experience myself as Karl, it's total boredom. The saint of Kanchi always sat there yawning and looking completely bored. Expressions of boredom… he's even too lazy to hide. He was walking throughout India all the time; wanderlust, just out of boredom. Like UG Krishnamurti, he went somewhere and then he had to go somewhere else. They are like gypsies, homeless people. They become a nomad. You ask a wandering monk, are you bored? Yes, I'm wandering it away. [Laughter]

We are talking now about why you came here. What is pulling you here? You're sitting here because boredom placed you here. Nothing else can get you out of your slumber of the drama of a person. You're fed up with yourself. In a way, you cannot avoid the void anymore. The boredom is already after you. Boredom is grace, I tell you. Grace is licking on you and you're leaking already. [Laughter]

In that sense when I see people who are bored, boredom is what makes them meditate because they tried everything before. All drugs, working away and all the techniques that can get them out, and nothing worked. Then they are ripe to be quiet because they have no energy to run away anymore from themselves because the void is what you are.

You can run away for a while but not forever. Sooner or later it gets you. Then you get angry about yourself. [Laughing] But grace is what you are because the Self is fed up with the Self and then by whatever means it catches you. Because wherever you go, the Self is. It will not let you go. It will drop you one day and it just makes you ready for it. So, what to do?

In that sense if someone becomes a junkie after trying everything, grace is already after you; it's already a preparation for facing yourself. The absolute void. The total absence of any end or beginning because the void has no beginning and no end and you always try to avoid that. There's no beginning and no end. You have a little hope that you find a beginning and for that you can find an end. No way. What to do?

Q [Another visitor]: Is spirit the content of consciousness?

K: Or is consciousness the content of the spirit?

Q: It seem that you make a difference between the spirit and the consciousness...

K: It's not different. Spirit is one resonant field of consciousness. The formless consciousness is the spirit and the information of consciousness is this world. This body is the information of consciousness, the formless will be the spirit and the formlessness will be awareness. So, there are three levels of consciousness, three ways of consciousness, but all of that is consciousness. It's consciousness as pure consciousness, the superior consciousness as awareness, the pure as spirit and the impure as the body or separation. But for me all of that is consciousness. You just experience yourself as the father, the spirit and the son but in nature it's all consciousness just showing itself as different. But showing itself in differences doesn't make it different. You just see that there's no second consciousness.

You are consciousness but consciousness doesn't know consciousness. The moment you know consciousness, there's one knower too many. The moment consciousness calls itself consciousness, there are two consciousnesses, the two imaginary consciousnesses. Only when consciousness doesn't know itself absolutely, by neither knowing nor not knowing itself, just by being that what it is, there's not even consciousness. But it shows itself as the father, the spirit and the son. This trinity is the way you realize yourself. But you're not the way you realize yourself. You are That what is realizing itself. You're not the realizer, you're not the realizing and you're not that what is being realized. You are that what is the heart of it and the Heart is never bored. Maybe the realizer gets bored with my creation because there's a creator and this is his creation. Then he wants to change his creation and tries to control his creation. Because maybe he has an idea of how his creation has to be. Then he becomes a Hitler or Tolle. It's the same. Wanting to have a new earth, a new creation. But the Heart has no idea of how his creation is. There's no need of any change or anything. What is there to change? Only Heart is. And Heart doesn't know heart. Heart doesn't know what is Heart and what is not Heart. But the moment you have a Heart, you are fucked. Ownership is always the main issue and in ownership there's boredom. Then you want to control your beloved. There's a lover and a beloved. The lover wants to own his beloved totally. I want to know myself, totally. I want to realize myself. And before I know myself in and out, I cannot really be quiet. Totally fucked up. So, you have to know yourself as that who never needs to know itself as that what is consciousness. There's nothing to gain or to lose in it by being that. And this little gainer one believes to be, this businessman, cannot take that because there's nothing to gain. Why should I be what I am? What will come out of it? There's nothing to gain, even in the spiritual way. In no way there's anything to gain. There's no gaining, neither in the material or spirit or whatever.

There's no advantage in anything. Who can take that? No one. Whatever you do is business and trying to get an advantage out of it. Even vipassana, meditation, you always try to get something out of it. More peace, more understanding, being more content, being more satisfied. Always having an idea of some gain. You do it out of pressure not out of freewill. But then you just say, I give in, I devote, I surrender. 'Maybe when I surrender, I am more in peace with existence. So, I surrender, I don't resist existence, then I'm more with the flow. I go with the flow because when I go with the flow then I am...'

So, this businessman, this business self, does everything for advantage. There's no other way. The idea that you are better off in anyone of these seven states needs a businessman. It needs one who has an idea that one dimension or one state is better than the other. There are advantages for this little one, that's the problem. When you're drunk you don't feel yourself. Drinking or having drugs has this advantage in the material world. But the advantage turns into a disadvantage because you're always depending on that. And you are unbearable that you are not free from that. You want to be free but you depend all the time. So, your little comfort depends on circumstances or drugs. Then you feel like a slave. But you want to become the master, but by trying to become a master, you become the slave of the master. Whatever you do is a carrot for this little donkey. So, what to do? You're always in an S-M business – slave and master. And the master is as much slave as the slave. The one who wants to help you is as enslaved as you are. It's all slavery. Even the masters are slaves – unbelievable! All of them are slaves. And I tell you, who has to be slave of oneself? I have nothing against it. I am a slave of my self, I am in service of my self, absolutely. It's always self-service. What to do?

But I know that if you're only the slave, you really feel fucked, even as a master. But if you are enslaved by what you are, who cares being imprisoned by what one is? Yes, you feel being in a prison but being by being imprisoned by what you are, what's the problem? You are the guard, the prison and the prisoner – all of that. You don't even have to know that. You just are that and you cannot not be that. That's all. So, where' the boredom in it? There's only boredom when you see that this will never end. There's only boredom because there's an idea of ending... A beginning and an end, then there's boredom. There's no one in the never ending. There can only be a one when there's a beginning and an end. But without a beginning and an end, there's no one who can be bored – come on! Very simple.

When you are born, then comes boredom. Born into boredom. If you believe to be born, you're one who's bored. Because you come from fucking you are one who's fucked. Then you keep fucking to produce some other *fucker.* Then you hope that the next fuck would be better than the fuck before. Keep fucking! The whole humanity lives by this idea that maybe the next generation would be better than me. All parents say that 'I only work so that my kids get it better than me. I am a slave and I work my ass off and I punish myself and go through this misery only for my kids. The only reason is that my kids get it better and then their kids do the same.' Like a hamster in the wheel, running and running and thinking that if I run faster I may get out of it.

Q [Another visitor]: If you don't have to feel bored, if you're happy or sad or depressed you're always running...

K: You always want to avoid it. You even want to avoid happiness, that's worse – especially *you,* because in happiness you cannot be. So, everyone is happy not to be happy. You try permanently to avoid happiness because happiness is the worst-case scenario. In happiness you cannot exist because happiness is the nature of the void and you cannot take happiness. No one can take happiness. Unhappiness or misery is easy. You are a master of suffering but no one can master happiness. There's no master in happiness. There are only masters in misery.

Q: Misery is comfortable...

K: It's not comfortable; it's safe. You play safe. Comfort you cannot take. Only in discomfort you can exist. You maintain the discomfort because you're afraid of the comfort. When comfort comes, you instantly fall asleep. That's playing safe. Then the comfort is there but you are not and then you wake up, ha, ha, ha discomfort again. It's safe again. You wake up in misery because that's what you need. When you say it like that everyone says, but I want happiness. But by trying to want happiness, you try to avoid it. You say you want to be happy but by *wanting* to be happy, it's always far away. You always make it a future happiness. It's always somewhere else, when this and this and this happens. It has to be harmonic, in peace, maybe then... You always live from then. Eternal now you cannot take.

Q [Another visitor]: Can the 'I' stay only in the state of desire?

K: In*tension*.

Q [Another visitor]: But we all do the same...

K: Wherever there's a *we*, there's *mesery*. *Wesery-mesery*. The moment you say *we*, there's a *me* because without *me* there's no *we*. When there's a 'W', then there's a double-you. [Laughter] That's the nature of the phantom. It cannot remain in the absence. It needs presence of differences. 'Differences' is separation and separation is misery. Then you cannot decide what you are because the one who wants to decide is a phantom. That what you are is always undecided and it cannot decide what he decides.

Boredom is always a good subject. But knowing how it works doesn't help. That's the problem. That would be another hope. 'Now I know how it functions and I will not step into that trap again.' Ha, ha, ha! It's just the next trap. 'If I know how it works, I'm out of it. I called off the search.' Ha, ha, ha! 'I don't get into that trap anymore', that's just the next trap! It's so subtle, such a bastard; yourself. It always puts itself in the next trap, just for fun. That bastard I tell you, don't trust it. Whatever it shows you is so promising. Then you step into it and you're fucked again. But who cares being fucked by oneself? Who fucking cares?

And you are that Absolute trapper, the trapping and the trapped. It's all your trap. What can you do? Trying not to step into it is just the next trap. You are so fucking intellectual and you are so clever. And you will always find something that was missing. 'Yes, I want that and the next *guru* and the next *guru* and this experience and the *shakti* and peace experience.' Or, 'I want the absence of it. I don't want to experience anything anymore. I am nothing.' [Laughter] That's a master trap I tell you. 'I am nothing. I don't desire anything anymore. There's no *me* because there's no desire.' Ha, ha, ha. Trap after trap.

Q [Another visitor]: Is there a problem in taking drugs? [Laughter]

K: Taking a drug is not a problem but that there's one who needs it is the problem. Otherwise air is a drug, oxygen is a drug. You need all these substances to survive. Food is a drug. What you call drugs is just one drug that keeps your brain a bit different, that's all. Otherwise you're always drugging yourself. Breathing is a drug, digestion, having farts. Drinking is a drug. This body cannot live without drugs. You only eat what makes you happy; it's a drug. You don't eat what makes you miserable. So, you choose and choosing is a drug. What is not a drug?

Q: In Manali I thought I should just get some hash instead of coming here...

K: I would be happy too if you permanently go. [Laughter] Why not?

Q: I think that was something coming from boredom...

K: Take belladonna. So, what to do? What comes next? I can only tell you that there's a Zen and Zen. Zen is just another word for Self. Zen means existence. There's Zen and Zen, never- ending Zen. Zen never began and Zen will never start. You can never escape the Zen because you *are* the Zen. But you want to be the centre of something, the heart. By trying to become the heart, you're fucked already. You will never reach the heart. And it will not reach you because when Heart is, you are not. And when you are, it seems like Heart is not. But still Heart is.

In Tiruvannamalai there's a Mukupudi Swami. Then everyone runs to him there and then he lies down at Sheshadri Ashram where all the saints are. Then he doesn't care if he is or he is not and everyone is like, there's a carelessness and I want to be like him. It's fantastic! Before I came, I went there and thought this was unbelievable. He was in Ramana Ashram and then everyone was around him. Then they throw money towards him. Five hundred rupees, doesn't work. Two thousand, doesn't work. Such carelessness! Then everyone adores him. His energy is such careless. He doesn't react to me. Then when he reacts like crazy, they all feel blessed. [Pointing to visitors] They went there too. I was just talking about them. [Laughter]

Q [Another visitor]: She was hit with a stick...

K: And she felt so blessed. She was happy and then she couldn't think for one week. That's because she had a trauma. It's unbelievable, such a circus. And the most advanced seekers who went through Nisargadatta in the 70's and Papaji, still looking for that stick. He was just, 'Fuck off, and leave me alone!' What to do?

We started with boredom, how to fill up the time which is not there. Not unlike me, I entertain you and I'm also part of the show, I'm not better. In Tiruvannamalai when I talk, they come there because during morning hours they have nothing else to do. Then they sit there and then in afternoon another one and in evening a Papaji video or drinking. Just filling up the time. But I don't mind to be the clown of the circus, it's fun, I don't mind to entertain myself. What to do?

Q [Another visitor]: I'm wondering what he's got that everyone wants to sit around him…

K: I always tell people that you just go to the next mad house and you'll meet a hundred of them, going around like Mukupudi Swami. In Tiruvannamalai the circus is unbelievable; shiva-shakti… tra, la, la. Going around unknotting the *karmic* knots. There are ash babas and hash babas rolling around the mountain. Existence has many faces. It's like going to the zoo. Ramana sitting in the middle and being the snake charmer, just by being quiet.

We talked about boredom, what comes next?

Q [Another visitor]: Loneliness…

K: That's part of boredom. You feel lonely because you're bored, you need company. The lonely boredom. What else? Dissatisfaction? Boredom.

Q: Usually action comes after boredom…

K: No. The avoidance of boredom is action. Boredom is always there but action you don't see. There's an uninterrupted boredom. Boredom is ever present. The void is ever present, come on. You just get your attention away from it by some action. But the moment the attention gets tired then you cannot avoid it. Then the void waits for you, all the time. It's always there. Then you would like to fall asleep because then you can bear it. Then you wake up fresh.

Q [Another visitor]: I don't enjoy boredom because I think there's something that I should do…

K: No one can enjoy boredom. Didn't you listen to me? No one listens to me. No one can take boredom. In boredom you cannot exist. You fight for your little existence.

Q: Isn't that what keeps us existing?

K: That's what I just say, it keeps you being an American from San Francisco having red hair going to a hair dresser; out of boredom. Many reasons to do something.

Q: If I thought that there's nothing that I need to do...

K: Then by doing nothing you fill up boredom. Then you call it meditation. But even in meditation you try to avoid the boredom. 'I'm doing nothing, I'm meditating, I don't exist, I'm nothing.' [Laughter] Another hiding behind something, trying to avoid the void. 'You cannot catch me, I'm nothing.'

Q: I like meditation because it takes the guilt away...

K: You see. You try to avoid the boredom of feeling guilty. You're just running away. You're just an escape artist. Everyone is an escape artist. And you're so perfect in your escapes. As perfect as you are, as perfect is your nature. Always running away from yourself until you're out of steam. Then the moment you're quiet, *you're* there too; then there's no distance anymore. Before there's an imaginary distance. You are in an imaginary thing, running after you. Then it's instantly there. But then you get air for some seconds and you run again. The time you sleep is when you're exhausted from running. You're the roadrunner and the other self is the coyote Karl. [Laughter] Coyote Karl running after the roadrunner. He tries to find all possible ways of bombing him, killing him, trying to destroy him. That's like the Self running after the Self trying to kill the Self. But it cannot kill the fucking Self. For years I was enjoying that cartoon. Trying to run a truck over him, dynamite over there and always the coyote was blown up and not the roadrunner.

If you see that, it's all Self running after the Self. It's all self-made. And I was fascinated by Kung Fu fighting. All this black and white wisdom coming out of the television. Those were times, that one hour on Saturday was the time when you had all the entertainment. Now you have it all the time; it's so boring. Nothing to look forward to. You can watch YouTube all the time. You can Netflix whenever you like. Everything is available all the time. [Yawning] When you go to the shopping market, everything is already there. You don't have to wait for anything. You just go shopping. It's so boring. You just shop for a moment of peace and then you go home with all the bullshit.

There's a famous picture of a woman standing in front of a long wardrobe looking at all the clothes and then saying, 'I have nothing to wear.' [Laughter] A thousand shoes but they don't fit anymore. And men have many excuses to go to the next bar. They have to get a packet of cigarette and that takes five hours.

Q [Another visitor]: I'm not sure if I understand boredom...

K: Boredom is never-ending eternal now which no one can take. Boredom means there's no end. There's no beginning, no end. But that's called meditation; you face yourself. Looking at that boredom, into the eternity, into this eternal now. That's called meditation without a meditator because after some time if you can really not avoid it anymore, the meditator disappears. Then there's just meditation left and there's no boredom in it. Then all your fear was for nothing. You fear you cannot take it but if you really just go for it, after awhile the meditator is not there and there's absolutely no boredom in that – the opposite actually. Silence in nature is ecstasy itself!

These masters want to make you a junkie for yourself, of that void which is that ecstasy, a drug that doesn't give you a hangover. Where there's no consequence, no side effects, which is just that what you are.

Q: So boredom is like someone resisting...

K: No, I would still call it boredom if there's someone who's *not* resisting. That's just another technique to control boredom – not resisting. There's no 'as long'. [Laughing] I like this 'as long as someone is resisting'. Then if he's not resisting then there's no boredom? Ha, ha, ha! That's still boredom but there's no one who minds. What to do? There's boredom, so what? It doesn't have to end for anyone. This idea of enlightenment or realization is that for you it will end and then there'll be no boredom anymore because there's permanent excitement. Ha, ha, ha! Keep dreaming. That's a dream that keeps the seeker seeking. That there'll be a moment when the boredom ends for him because he wants to have it; the end of boredom and a permanent excitement afterwards. After enlightenment, I'm permanently happy – *me*! Ha, ha, ha. Wonderful! Keep dreaming.

Whenever there's *me* there's misery whether you like it or not. Even the no-me is too much misery. Dependency. Only when there's no-me, I can be a little bit satisfied. With a *me*, never, but without a *me*, the *me* is better off. But the *me* who's off is still a *me*. Then the *me* comes back, very strong. So, you better be with and without the *me* what you are. The rest is fiction anyway.

Something else that's 'as long'? Who is longing 'as long'? She had a master called Barry Long and now he's buried along. He has been a long time buried.

Q [Another visitor]: Should we seek out boredom?

K: No. Just be quiet, then there's no boredom. The only remedy that helps you get over boredom is being quiet, being what you are. There's no other medicine against boredom. Whatever you do otherwise only makes it stronger. You depend on an end of boredom. But by being what you are there was never any boredom. That's the only medicine for everything. For whatever you complain, the only way to kill the complainer is being what you are because that what-you-are is satisfaction and there cannot be any boredom. So, be quiet.

Q: But the way to quietness...

K: There's no way to quietness. No way!

Q: I was just thinking of a technique of finding the most boring things to do...

K: Just be yourself. [Laughter] It's easy to be bored. You don't have to do anything else, just be yourself. That's silly enough and then you're bored. Don't think anyone else is better off than you. There's no such thing that there's anyone else better than you. There's no so-called master or saint or bloody guru that's better off than you. Never was, never will be.

Q [Another visitor]: With regards to being cold, people want to climb Mount Everest...

K: The Mountain is called Everest because they think they can ever rest up there.

Q [Another visitor]: And a lot of them do... [Laughter]

K: It's like the Everglades in America. Many go there and hope that crocodiles come and eat them so that they are forever ever glad.

Q [Another visitor]: People climb Everest during summer but...

K: I will tell them to climb in winter because the possibility of ever rest is better. [Laughter] They found out that the easiest way to die is freezing to death after drinking a bottle of vodka. That's a very common way to commit suicide in Russia and Siberia. You just slip away and they find you mummified by ice and they don't mind. People look at you and you just smile because vodka makes you smile and you're in a good mood. You die in a good mood. [Laughter] Maybe it's the best way not to come back – going in a good mood. Just trying that I'm fed up with life before dying, this drama is too much. Just freeze to death. But that's too hard in India.

Q: When something is in Absolute zero...

K: Still you exist. Existence still exists in Absolute zero. You cannot be killed even by the total zero. There's just total silence there. Zero doesn't allow any movement of any atom. There's no movement possible, that's zero point. But still you are. But from that zero point all the movements, all the frequencies come. But still you cannot be killed by the Absolute zero. They never reach that point. It's just a theoretical point. Maybe they are afraid that if they reach that point the whole world will be gone. They may just create a black hole where no one can exist. Theoretically it's a number but no one will ever reach it. They stop maybe one degree before. And you don't have to reach it because you are the zero point. You are that silence, the zero point – zero-zero. And even that cannot kill you.

This is all hell. What to do? No matter. What would you do without matter if nothing matters? All the famous tra-la-la's before. All the so-called persons who were in different dimensions, being where no dimension can be, the Absolute zero where no dimension can exist – and still you are. That's called 'no way out'.

Q [Another visitor]: In Hinduism they talk about Karma moving from one life to another. But how does it move?

K: It's just a good trick to keep them moving. In Christianity they say if you do good, you go to heaven. It's just so that people behave, that's all. In India they have a technique that if you don't behave you will be born as a dog and if you behave then you become a saint. But it's just so that people don't kill each other right away. Otherwise they'd kill each other right away. If there would be no consequences after life, there would just be murder. This is the only way to tame them. By lies they are civiliezed. It's all lies but with lies you get civilized – consequences. Like a mother telling a child if you don't behave then the boogie man will come.

Q: No television...

K: That's the worst. Then you're really fucked. One week no television, that's really hell. If there would be no limits for you, no consequences for your actions, you would just kill. You have this aggression inside. This beast which is always present. This six-six-six beast of Aleister Crawley who is fed up and hates himself. There's so much hate inside. It's just Kali running wild. It just goes chopping, all is too much. Everyone has this Kali, this Shiva, this Vishnu inside. They are all there and you never know who plays today. All these gods are inside.

You are Shiva with all these tendencies. The one who creates, the one who destroys, the one who conserves it. It's all there. The beast is there too, the destroyer, the killer, and religion is a technique to tame the beast. So that humanity can survive... but now the surviving humanity becomes a bigger problem than the beast because now there are too many survivors. So maybe now they will find another way of having a war and cleaning up a bit. Consciousness will find a way to make it bearable. When there was AIDS disease they said this will clean up the earth a bit. The fundamental Christians in America said that this is the revenge of God for the sins of the gays. Now all the gays will be gone and God will be happy. There's so much hate and killer instinct inside. Then there's radical Islam. If they just get a reason to kill, they kill. If there's a good excuse to kill, you kill. You just need a good excuse like war, fighting for your country, for your mother, for your wife. Then you kill and become a hero for the same act that they would have hanged you as a criminal if you hadn't done it for your country. What a fuck! My grandma was really funny. She just said that Hitler is a revenge because Jews nailed Jesus. And with that little excuse she could take it; otherwise it was impossible to take it. They killed our beloved Jesus and that was a reason enough to do what Hitler did. Fantastic!

And that beast is inside everyone and sometimes it comes out, especially when you are in a restaurant or a pub and you drink than this beast comes. If the funny one comes, then you are more funny but when this aggressive beast comes, there's no one there anymore. Just the beast.

Q [Another visitor]: There's a story about meditation that is like polishing the mirror that's already polished. What is the use of polishing the mirror?

K: It's just like working on your awareness. The mirror will never be clear enough to show what's not there.

Q: Then it continues, but you should sit in meditation. There is no way to get around meditation...

K: I would agree. You are the Absolute meditator and you cannot *not* meditate about yourself. You have to meditate and meditating about yourself is realizing yourself. This is meditation. Living is meditating. Life has to live life. Life living life is life meditating about life... Life experiencing life. And there are infinite ways to do that. So, meditation is unavoidable. There are two ways of meditation: one with meditator and one without meditator. The meditation with meditator is misery because there's an expectation in it, there are tendencies. When meditation is life just living in its nature, just meditating, then there's no problem. Knowledge knowing is the same. Knowledge knowing but without a knower. Life living but without one who is alive. Being, being: the Absolute being without an Absolute being. It's just being.

But still these differences. You even have to be in meditation with a meditator as the meditation without a meditator. Both are the ways you meditate. You cannot avoid one of them. You have to be what you are *with* the meditator even if the meditation without a meditator is more comfortable. You cannot have one side without the other. Both have to be there, and both are equal, it's not as if one is better or worse. It's just two ways that life lives – *with* one who's alive and without one who's alive. For life it doesn't make any difference. It has no preference. So, there was never any problem. It's just that the difference doesn't make any difference, that's all. There are two different ways of meditating but the different ways are always the Self meditating... with Self and without Self. But normally one self wants to kill the other self and thinks that without the self is better than *with* the Self. Then there's a personal self who has tendencies, but even that is unavoidable. Otherwise it would not be there. If we could avoid it, it would not exist. All of that is... what to do?

That's why I say, you have to meditate in whatever way: personal, impersonal, with and without. All is meditation but maybe you can say that there are seven different ways of meditating about yourself. And none of them is better, it's just different but they make no difference for what you are. There's no difference in quality; they are all the quality of life. Life living in seven different ways. But the differences don't make any difference. Everyone says this is the lowest and that is the highest. What to do?

Even boredom belongs to that. Even action, non-action and all of that, is just life living itself. Even that you get bored is life living itself in boredom. For life it has no problem if she's [Pointing to a visitor] it's bored or not, life doesn't mind. And life doesn't need her *not* to be bored. You can be bored forever and life wouldn't mind. That's the beauty about life; it never minds. It doesn't make life better or worse. Life would not have any advantage if she would not be bored. Life enjoys itself infinitely in whatever is. Even in her boredom life is enjoying life. There's no moment without life enjoying life. But this idea that life wants you not to be bored... Life has no intention. Life doesn't want anything. There's no need or necessity for change. It has no idea of good or bad; of what is good life or bad life; of what is good meditation or bad meditation. All of that is what? Just *lie*braries – full of bullshit. And who knows how life has to be lived? 'Me!' And by that you suffer because you think you know how life has to be. By that arrogance inside, this feeling of being special, you suffer and that is totally justified.

Q: Seeded meditation is very painful...

K: But that's how it's meant to be, because perception needs to disconnect from the body. Normally you're glued just by an idea. If it becomes unbearable, you disconnect. It's like falling asleep, but aware. You disconnect from the body and then you are the space, the spirit, the formless. From being glued to the form, the perception shifts from being the formless. In the formless there's already no pain because you disconnect from the body. That's why Osho took the laughing gas so much because the laughing gas disconnects the perception from the body. Then you're just the space-like spirit. You have no reference point from where you look because it's just space. But still there's a perception without a perceiver. And the body is part of the whole environment but there's no ownership anymore. That's quite relaxing. So, I understand why Osho took laughing gas. When I took laughing gas, I was always out watching the dentist pulling my teeth and having fun. And I always wanted to go to the dentist. But then they changed everything, only injections.

Q: When you talk about twenty-four-seven meditation, do you mean that there should be no preference twenty-four-seven?

K: No. It's just twenty-four-seven being quiet. It's not about having no preferences. That's still one too many who has no preference. No preference is still having a preference of having no preference. It's too much. Just being quiet is meditation. In whatever action or no action, whatever you do or not, being quiet. That's meditation. But it doesn't mean that you have to sit down and be quiet. You can do it while watching television, making dishes or driving a car or working. It's effortlessness, without any effort. But having no preference is still an effort. To be what you are doesn't need any effort. It doesn't need any change, nothing has to come and go for it. That's called meditation. This twenty-four-seven meditation no one can do. That's the problem. There's no meditator in it. The meditator needs a special time for two-three hours sitting down and meditating about peace or absence, 'I am nothing, I am nothing' or whatever. But there's not even nothing. There is a not-knowing of what you are and what you are not. That's being just quiet.

Q: My understanding of Zen meditation is that there is no good or bad meditation...

K: But that's still trying to get an advantage. It's okay. I don't mind any good or bad meditation because maybe then you become indifferent. But the one who is indifferent is still different to the one who is different. No way out!

Q: The experience that this moment is perfect...

K: Needs an idea that there's something else which is not perfect. Perfection is an idea that instantly creates an idea of imperfection. Peace instantly creates war. Whatever you give a name, there's always polarity. Light-darkness, good-bad. Even if you become indifferent, it's still different. Any experience needs differences. But that absolute experiencer you are doesn't need any experience. So, there cannot be any difference. But everything else is different. Every experience needs a difference. Only the Absolute-experiencer-you-are is without a difference. To be that what-you-are is without any difference. But every other experience with an experiencer needs differences. Without an experiencer there's no experience possible.

Q: So, does being what-you-are includes all the misery?

K: To be what-you-are includes nothing. There's no misery possible. Only by being not what-you-are, there's misery. But by being what-you-are there was never any misery and there never will be.

Q: Does it include enjoying?

K: There is no including! Including and excluding is only in time and when there is *me*. The idea of including and excluding and out and in, is only in time. But what you are is neither in time nor no time nor not even in timelessness. All of that trinity is not what you are. And the question always is who needs to include anything? If all what is, is what you are, there is no one who includes or excludes anything. There's not even an idea of in and out. You can say that in the dream everything is, but in Reality not. In Reality there's not even Reality because there is no *in* Reality and no *out* of Reality.

Q: For the dream to be a dream, does it have to be without a preference?

K: No. The dream means preferences. There is no dream without a preference. There is no dream without intentions. There is no dream without forms.

Q: To avoid anything in dream would be to deny it as a dream...

K: To avoid anything in the dream is trying to survive as a phantom. The phantom needs to avoid the void otherwise the phantom cannot exist. It's his job to fight for his life because it's not alive. That what doesn't exist has to fight for existence, permanently; it's in a permanent existential crisis. It always has to fight for its existence. It always needs attention. And the suffering is the best you can get because suffering is permanently there and it confirms that you exist as a sufferer. So, you permanently take care about the suffering. Misery is your field because without misery you cannot exist. So, you really take care about misery. What can you do? It's a survival tendency. Even if you try to kill yourself, you survive because by trying to kill yourself, you confirm that there's someone who can kill himself. This game is really fantastic. What a trap!

What I'm doing here is showing that all those tricks cannot help you. The tricks are infinite and the traps are infinite. Whatever comes next is the next trap. You cannot escape the traps. What can you do? The only thing is hopelessness. You cannot help yourself. You cannot help realizing yourself in separation. So, what can you do? Parabrahman can only dream himself in separation because this dream is a dream of separation. And what can keep you going is the hope that one day this would be over. And I sit here and tell you that the dream has no beginning as you have no beginning and no end. The only dream is that one day this dream will end because you believe that you have a beginning! But what you are has no beginning and no end, as life has no beginning and no end. What can you do?

But who can take that? That's the question. Try to take that you have no end. It seems like the only way out is that there's no way out. That's the *koan*, the paradox. You are only interested because you believe in a way out, but if there's no way out, there's no interest. Then you are quiet. But who knows? This becomes another hope.

23rd July 2018 Talk 1
Ladakh

The truth you have to fight for is
not worth fighting for

∽

Q: You say that in waking up no one wakes up...

K: There's an experience of waking up but in the experience no one wakes up. There's one but there's no 'one' waking up.

Q [Another visitor]: What's the difference between deep sleep and deep-deep sleep?

K: Deep-deep sleep is the nature of deep sleep. Deep sleep is just on the surface and deep-deep sleep is the nature of deep sleep. It's like the nature of the presence and the nature of the absence.

Q [Another visitor]: Is consciousness already there?

K: No. You can say that the deep sleep is the absence but the nature of that is the deep-deep sleep. Waking up is the presence. You're awake and asleep. The awakeness of awakeness, that's the nature of awakeness. The nature of presence and the nature of absence is...

Q: Consciousness?

K: No. It's that what you are. Then to know yourself as that what is in deep-deep sleep. Deep-deep sleep is awakeness of the awakeness. But it's not the awakeness that's different from deep sleep. You harvest yourself in two different ways; in awakeness and in deep sleep. But the harvester is never known in the presence and in the absence.

Q: In the morning when you wake up, you cannot differentiate if you had a deep sleep or a deep-deep sleep...

K: No one had deep-deep sleep. You cannot find anyone there. In deep sleep you can still say there was a deep sleep. The doctors can tell you that there was a deep sleep or if there's awakeness. But they can never find the nature of deep-deep sleep: it cannot be sensed by any scientist or by any apparatus. There cannot be any recording of it. It's like energy cannot be known. You can only know the effects of energy but never the energy. Matter in nature cannot be found. What you can find is an expression of matter. You can always find the expressions of matter but matter in nature cannot be found. No one ever knew what electricity is. You can have its effects that it starts the bulb. You can talk about the effects and the differences but never what is electricity. No one knows what it is but everyone is using it.

The same is with knowledge. No one will ever know what is knowledge. You can always know the effects of knowledge – the knower, the knowing and what can be known but not that what is knowledge. For all of that it needs differences. The nature of nature knows no difference. Nature already is an idea of nature and no-nature. Even nature has an opposite of no-nature. But the nature of nature is the same as the nature of no-nature. There's no difference. It shows itself as difference but in nature it's not different. If you call it self then there's no-self. If there's something, there's nothing... but that what is something and that what is nothing in nature is not different. But if you call yourself nothing then you are again fucked because then you make it an opposite to something. And that what you are is defining itself in everything but it can never be defined. It defines itself in everything but it can never be defined. It defines itself as a definer or the non-definer, as the knower or the not-knower. But the knowledge of what-you-are is never defined by that. It's so simple. It's such a common knowledge but you want to have it complicated.

Then they asked Ramana why do you still talk? Why do you still explain Vedas and things? And Ramana said, what else to do? It's just sport. No one needs it. Not because someone helps someone by anything or it has any effect or purpose. But that's the fun of it. That's the joy; it doesn't need any purpose. Life doesn't need a purpose to live itself. Thank God it doesn't make any sense. Imagine it would make sense. Imagine you could end suffering by understanding. What a controller would that be! By what? Then life could be controlled by someone, by understanding. What kind of life would it be that you can control? Bullshit! A bullshit life, a relative life that could be controlled by a relative controller. Do you want to be that? The controller or the controlled? And for control it needs two, that's the problem.

Q [Another visitor]: So it's complete no sense, no purpose...

K: I didn't say it has no purpose, I didn't say *it* has no purpose. [Laughter] Maybe it is the absolute purpose that it doesn't need any purpose. It's purple rain.

Q [Another visitor]: Is it like a fire of Awareness or Reality that can burn anything?

K: You can say that Awareness is already the effect of the fire; it's not the fire. The light you see is not that what is light. The awareness you can experience is not that what is life. It's the beginning and the end but what has a beginning and an end is not that what is the nature of it.

Q: You talked earlier about The Lord of the Rings where the ring of fire goes back to the fires of Mordor...

K: It has to go back to the fire of Awareness but no one can throw it because everyone is too much in love with that. Your precious love for your body cannot be thrown away by you. Grace will kill you but you cannot do it. It happens by accident but not by your intention. The ring falls into the fire by accident and then it's gone. No one ever can drop it. You are too much in love with your body, your life, your awareness. The Self cannot drop the Self. It drops by the way like an accident. That's a good pointer in The Lord of the Rings. Even Frodo – the purest heart, who walked through all that and killings and was always 'yes'. But at the last moment he could not. He wanted to go back and keep it. So, even the purest heart cannot do it. It can never be pure enough so that you can drop your ownership, this love for yourself. I like it; it's a nice pointer.

Q: Nisargadatta's guru told him to stay in the fire of Awareness...

K: He wanted to keep him busy but only by accident it can happen. Who knows what the intention of a guru is, of what is he pointing by it? You never know. But everyone takes it as if because of that something happened. No. There's no cause in anything. It may or may not, who knows? And maybe his guru told this to others and nothing happened. It didn't work. For one it worked but that doesn't mean anything.

[Distinct sound of cows mooing]

They're crying for the milkman: 'Milk me, I'm ready.' It's like a seeker who calls for the Self, 'Please take me I'm ready. I'm full of milk, I know everything. My Milky Way is full. I walked the Milky Way and now I'm ready for you. Open the door, take me in.' Where do you end up? In a discothèque in Amsterdam; Milky Way. [Laughter] Then you get a little joint and you can join everyone – Oneness in Amsterdam. [Pointing to a visitor] Spain?

Q: I don't know...

K: What do you not know? You have to know what you don't know. I want to know what you don't know.

Q: I was thinking about what is being spoken here...

K: What the fuck is going on here?

Q: I don't know...

K: So, what's not going on? You know but you would not tell me.

Q: Whatever I know is intellectual...

K: What's wrong with that? Intellectual can be fun. Intellect trying to understand intellect is fun; always futile and always fun.

Q: I like futility the most...

K: That I like the most, failing, failing, failing. The intellect permanently failing to know itself.

Q: I would like to fail all the time...

K: You already fail all the time, don't worry. You imagine not to fail but even in that you fail. Even in succeeding you fail. You cannot not fail. You're the Absolute failure, I tell you. No one can fail more than you.

Q: Last year I started sharing your teachings with a friend and he said this was not enough. I felt like a clown...

K: Everyone has this experience when you go into Advaita, you think you have found something precious and you want to give it to people and you become a Messiah and you create a total mess. So, better be quiet. Don't talk to anyone. There are already enough Facebook gurus who know better than everyone.

Q: I felt so much resistance from them...

K: I would resist too if someone tries to tell me how it really is. They have to ask you; don't tell anyone anything. Everyone has this experience that no one wants to know what you know.

Q: Then why do they ask?

K: But then you're stupid enough to answer. Look at me; I'm already stupid enough to answer. Answering is stupid. Look at me what I have to do all the time – totally stupid. I'm fucked I tell you.

Q: I'm just stupid to answer...

K: But you're not more stupid than me. We have a competition now. Look at my experience here. I talk to some for twenty-five years and they still come with the same question. What shall I do with that one? They're born with that question and they die with that question. [Laughter] I have no hope I tell you. But I enjoy it. No one ever learnt anything. That's the best for me. Imagine, there's someone who can learn something and really get something out of it. What would he do with it? That would be hell. That you could really learn what you are. That, by studying, after a while you know what you are. Then it would be predictable, like a technique; a technique to control yourself, a technique to know yourself. Thank God none of that is possible. I'm happy that everyone fails and they come back with the same question. So, I don't mind it.

Q: Futility is the best. The crucifixion is already there...

K: It's all crucifixion.

Q: What do you mean when you say be quiet?

K: I said it a hundred times in last few days.

Q: But I don't know...

K: That's confirming what I just said. Being quiet is being what-you-are that never said anything. It doesn't listen, it doesn't ask. It's just that what is quiet. There's no *one* who is quiet. You cannot learn to be quiet. The one who speaks now can never be quiet. It lives from action, from movement. But what-you-are is always quiet. Being quiet is more than easy. It doesn't need anything. For what-you-are-not it always needs an effort, to do something, an effort to exist. Be lazy. Be that what is lazy, that's the nature of that what is quiet – Absolute lazy. In that laziness no one can exist. That's why everyone is active. The actor has to act all the time – 'give me action.' In the morning, this body is like an awakening – action! And at night it goes back... it is tired from all that action.

Q [Another visitor]: What sense does it make in being what you cannot not be, if we anyway cannot be what we are?

K: You cannot not be what you are. But that what tries to become what he is, is not that what you are. It's impossible to *become* what you are.

Q: Because you already *are*?

K: Because that what-you-are doesn't exist so you cannot become that what-you-are. When you become what-you-are you have to become something that exists. But that what you are doesn't even exist. So, you cannot become what-you-are by any effort. Not because you already are what-you-are. That's a bullshit understanding. I'm already what I am. This is so common in Tiruvannamalai. Everyone says, 'I'm already what I am.' It's crazy!

Q: So, by whatever you do...

K: You have never done anything. So, what happens by what you have not done? You can become anything, you can become Awareness, you can have Samadhi, you can become whatever. But whatever you become has to exist and that is not what you are. Maybe you are so powerful that you may become the Almighty. But whatever you can *become* has to exist! But that what is your nature doesn't even exist at all. So, you cannot become what you are. Then there's this answer – 'Because I'm already what I am.' I heard it a thousand times every time I give a talk somewhere.

Q: But you say that...

K: I don't say that. I say you cannot *become* what you are.

Q: But you also say – You are That!

K: No! Be what you cannot not be. You can neither become it nor not become it. There's no becoming at all. But not because you are already what you are. It's just like a phantom repeating something. But you are not something what you can repeat.

Q [Another visitor]: Nisargadatta says, I am That, you are That, That is That...

K: No. That's not Nisargadatta, that's Sailor Bob. I don't know anything but I know what Nisargadatta hadn't said. Adding some slogan to a name doesn't mean anything. I know where it comes from when I hear it. It's all hearsay. That's why I say be quiet and not repeat something. But for that you don't have to be quiet.

This is mentioned in all neo-advaita books that, 'You cannot become what you are because you are *already* what you are. You cannot get enlightened because you are *already* enlightened.' All of that is.... brrrggghhh... repeating something what sounds good. It sounds profound. Then you repeat it because maybe you feel good. 'I am already what I am.' Who says that? Only a phantom would say 'I am already what I am.' Do you think Self would say 'I am already the Self'? So, who says that? And who is already what he is?

Q [Another visitor]: But it is not wrong...

K: It's all wrong. That what is wrong and that what is not wrong, is all wrong. Even that what is not wrong is wrong. Whatever can be pronounced is wrong. That's why I always contradict myself permanently. The only thing I don't contradict is that you are what you are *in* whatever; but it is not *because* what you are.

Q [Another visitor]: There is a kind of freshness...

K: It's just the living words that can never be conserved. You cannot put them in anything. They are just changing permanently. If I would be a teacher, I would have a teaching – 'You cannot become what you are because you are already what you are.' When I say something and you repeat it, I destroy it.

Q [Another visitor]: These contradictions are unbearable for the mind...

K: It's a *koan*. There was a Zen Buddhist lady in Berlin and she was angry and said that you just talk non-sense. Then after half an hour she was overwhelmed and said you are a living *koan*. No one can find out what you say. A living *koan*, permanently producing *koans* where the mind cannot follow. I am so fast so that the mind cannot follow. And I contradict myself so much that no one can say that I said anything, because it's always wrong. Try to catch me if you can. Then they say you are like Teflon, nothing sticks on you. Why should something stick on me?

Q: Because probably you are not afraid of contradicting yourself...

K: I can only present you the fearlessness of being stupid. I don't fear to be stupid. What does that make me? Nothing.

Q: All the masters pay attention to be coherent...

K: They are afraid that someone can catch them with something that's wrong. Fuck them all! I am always wrong. Try to find something that's right. [Laughter]

Q: This is typical of all crazy wise people...

K: That's called crazy wisdom. Wisdom doesn't know wisdom and craziness doesn't know craziness. So, it's crazy wisdom. It's not that someone has some precious knowledge and now becomes a messiah speaking it out. What is there to fear? To be wrong is easy, to be right is impossible. Easy is right. But everyone wants to have a fixed solution to his fixed problem.

Q: Being quiet, playing safe...

K: Yes. 'Now I am quiet and in this I find my home, my space. I place all my furniture, my knowledge and things. Then I feel at home. I just use this tool for that program. I am my own doctor, my own dentist. I always have my little medicine for everything. One slogan for all little problems. Something comes up and I just accept it.' [Laughing] 'The medicine man inside, I control my feelings, I control everything because I have medicine for everything. I just have a library of books that contain all the answers. Then I read one book of Ramana and it's good for all medicines, then this one and that one.'

Q: It's like the freedom of being relative...

K: Not to be afraid to experience yourself in a relative way. But it's not the freedom of being relative. Don't feel free. Does that make sense? [Laughing] Because the one who feels free is imprisoned by freedom. What an idea! So who needs to be free? Again *me* – always me.

Whatever one says, even if one says you cannot find yourself because you never lost yourself. All of that is like that you rest for one moment and don't try to figure things out again. But the moment you repeat it, it's already wrong. So you fail again because you cannot stay in that. No understanding is permanent. It comes and goes, as everything. Empty words, empty understanding, empty deep insights and empty flying high. Blah, blah, blah. And be happy all is empty. There's no need to conserve it or holding on to it. Enjoy it as it comes and enjoy it as it goes. It's like 'Hello' and 'Goodbye' all the time. But everyone is afraid to lose it. Now I stay in that clarity.

I hated when people came from Papaji and said that he gave me this pearl and now I have to maintain it and polish it and not let it go again. And everyone let it go again. Everyone failed. Everyone! Then he was pissed. Then later he said that there was no one here who maintained the pearl as I liked it. They all should rot in hell. No one ever came who got it from me. They are all failures.

Q [Another visitor]: That, he didn't enjoy...

K: I would enjoy it. I would enjoy that I am always surrounded by failures here. But if you are a master or a transmitter transmitting something and you think you have something to transmit, then you have a problem. Then you could be pissed that you gave all your intention, all your energy, all your *shakti*, all your knowledge. You just transmitted everything by some *siddhis* and then you see that he got it. Then after three months they come back losing it totally. Crazy! In that sense I don't even try – too lazy.

It works and that's the problem. When there's this *shakti*, then transmitting it works and someone can get it. There's a sender and a receiver. But whatever can be sent and whatever can be received is bullshit. As much energetic as it feels, the *shakti*, the *shanti*, it's all bullshit. Whatever can be transmitted is all bullshit.

Q: It is okay...

K: It's not okay. It's never okay.

Q: Why not?

K: No! It's bullshit. It's like a man who wants to satisfy his woman – impossible!

Q: But it's fun... [Laughter]

K: It's not fun. Transmitting knowledge. What kind of knowledge would it be that could be transmitted? You just make junkies for that energy transmission.

Q [Another visitor]: It doesn't make a difference what you choose to do...

K: It makes a difference. If you put your money in the wrong bank, it makes a difference. It all makes a difference. Now she wants to say whatever happens for what-I-am nothing happens. But that's an artificial understanding you know that. If that would be a Reality, you wouldn't even talk about it. It's like a lullaby you say to yourself to feel good. It's like a lullaby that you sing to a baby – 'It's all good and nothing will happen and nothing ever happened.' Blah, blah, blah. Does it work?

Q: Maybe if you believe in it...

K: Oh help me God!

Q: It makes you feel better...

K: And what does that mean? You have this distinctive feeling that you can control your life. What the fuck is going on here? [Laughter] It's like I can do this and nothing will happen to me and blah, blah, blah. Who wants to have my job?

[Silence]

No one? Okay. Then I have to continue. [Laughing] Otherwise I'd have to talk like Byron Katie, 'Can that really be true?'

Q [Another visitor]: If transmission is bullshit, what does it mean to be in good company?

K: When there's no transmitter and no receiver, that's good company.

Q [Another visitor]: So are we in bad company?

K: Did I transmit something? Did you hear what I said? Did anyone ever understand what I said? [Laughter] Come on! Now I have to test that.

The meaning of good company is the absence of company, which is the Absolute absence of any presence or absence of that imaginary self. It's not being in good company of someone who realized himself and now he shows-off his realization and someone else claps – Bravo! I want to have that too. I am not here to make slaves, come on! I like Nisargadatta when he said I am here to make gurus. I am not here to enslave anyone with my bloody talking, that you believe that I am the master and you are the disciple – bullshit. I give a shit about disciples or anyone. Fuck it! I like Nisargadatta when he says I am here to talk to the guru you are. Guru means Self – guru to guru, and not a little poor *me* who thinks that maybe now I would repeat that and get some results. A guru doesn't need any result of anything. A guru never did anything. He's the laziest bastard you can be. But not being someone who sings himself a lullaby and falls asleep by that.

It's not about slavery. Otherwise if I try to make slaves, I would become a slave of becoming a master. Disciples, de*votees* – who needs your vote? If I hit on Mr. Mooji it's because they have these bloody photos hanging around and thinking that the bloody lineage of some

Papapa or Ramana-Banana. They always need these little pimps because they are prostitutes who are walking the line; in the lineage of someone. They are all prostitutes of some pimps behind them. [Laughter] Just needing some backups because they cannot stand for themselves, those little bastards. And I mean it. I tell you, this is not a show. That's what I really think about it. [Laughter] All these erection bears and Gangaji's, sperm-ananda's. All these rotten apples from Papaji, I tell you. Madhukar is the worst. If that comes out of a master, then really forget it. Fuck it all! I had to say it.

Q [Another visitor]: At some point they all will be listening to what you said...

K: Why should they listen to that?

Q: Maybe some of the disciples listen to it...

K: No. They don't dare to tell them. Mooji is just repeating what I say sometimes. I can show you some videos where he says something and then he fucks it up totally. He says – Be what you cannot not be, *consciously*. Fuck it! For that I could beat him up right away. [Laughter] I would make his *Rastafari* long. People send me these video clips where he always says these bullshit things there. [Laughter]

But this transmission I like, this transmission of joy, ha, ha, ha. When you beat everything down to nitty-gritty and no master is left. If they repeat, they should repeat it correctly. [Laughter] Not even Shri Shri, H. H. Mooji can repeat it correctly.

Q [Another visitor]: I think they are afraid of copyrights...

K: I would never take a copyright. You have the right to copy I would say. You have the right to copy but if you copy, copy right! [Laughter]

Q [Another visitor]: But that's how I would think as well – Be what you cannot not be, consciously...

K: ...for the phantom. The phantom needs to be consciously what the phantom is. Ha, ha, ha. Fuck it!

I like the last two years of Papaji. In the last two years he resigned from all of that. Then he didn't bother about transmission and things and then he was okay.

Q [Another visitor]: When Papaji didn't want anyone around him, he would say you are ready, go and teach...

K: That was after someone asked him ten times. I would right away say 'go away'... [Laughter]

The fire burns, burning down every master. What would you do without any master? If there would be no word to repeat, if you would never listen to anyone or never read anything, what would you do?

Q [Another visitor]: Look to the night sky...

K: You think you can do that alone? For a minute or two? What did the Stone Age people do? Did they talk about Advaita? Everyone is fishing. Jesus was a fisherman. Everyone fishes for fish and then he wants to sell them. But it stinks because it's an old stinky fish. 'I have something for you, maybe I can help you.'

Q [Another visitor]: That's a very powerful question...

K: If you wake up as a Stone Age person and you have never heard about anything, what would you do? Would there be a problem of Advaita or Self or absence-presence of any bullshit? You would just go fishing. Would it make you different if you would have never heard from any scriptures, Avadhuta Gita and Vedas and all of that? All the questions and answers. Now you are full of it and it doesn't help you either.

Q [Another visitor]: There was a simplicity to life...

K: Now you again make it fucking extra ordinary. Now you are even worse than anyone else. She really believes that having a simple life is better than having a complicated life. You never learnt anything. [Laughter] What are you doing here? I failed again. Now you think that a simple life is better than a complicated life. Close your eyes, take your big stick and try to find your woman but without any moralistic or ethical background. What would you do?

Q: I didn't think about relationship. I was just connecting with nature and sky...

K: You are really bad. First you have to ask nature if it would really like to be connected with you. [Laughter] If I would be nature, I would never connect with you, come on! You have to be like Mooji. You have to first ask, please, thank you, may I? All these esoteric things, going out and connecting with nature and the sky. 'I plug into nature and I get so much energy from nature.' You sucker you! All these suckers going out to nature and sucking nature. That's why nature is so exhausted. [Laughter]

Q: Would the cave man have any concept of happiness?

K: Go there and ask them. You go to Amazon there are still some primitive tribes who never had any contact with civilization. Whenever they are stressed, they just fuck. [Laughter] No concept of happiness.

Of course! Even a baby who doesn't know what a baby is has a tendency to be happy, to be comfortable. Happiness is another word for comfort. If the stomach is hungry and there's some discomfort, it is genetically designed to suck on some tit and for a while it is comfortable because the stomach is full. The mind is the same, what's the difference? Even the Stone Age people would be the same. Whenever they were hungry, they would fish or hunt. Just go into nature, close your eyes and plug in. But sometimes there's a power cut. That's a big problem, especially in India.

All these pointers from Ramana, become like a baby because the baby doesn't know to be a baby and has no concept of happiness or unhappiness or anything. There's just an action and reaction. It's just a cause and effect. The effect is the cause of the next effect. It's just life living without any concept of good or bad or anything; if you can do that. But now it's too late because you know too much and you are too conditioned and you are so filled up with moralistic tra la la... what I should do and what I should not do and how much awareness one needs. If you would never have heard about awareness, you would never have any problem with it. But what to do?

Now you cannot forget it again because by trying to forget it, you remember it. It doesn't work. So, now you have to be *in spite* of whatever but not *because* of babyhood or something. It's all too late. Now it's too late. Is there a pill for that? A pill for dementia? I always think these self-realized masters and if you give them a pill for dementia, they would forget all their so-called deep insights and their realizations of the true self. All of that is instantly gone. What would they do? Would there still be a master?

That what you are doesn't need any memory of anything. No so-called deep insights or self-realization needs to happen for what you are. There's no concept of self-realization of what you are.

Q [Another visitor]: There's a saying in Zen that with no practice and no realization That can be defiled...

K: The idea of purity is corruption. The idea of self is corrupt, happiness is corrupt. All of it corrupts you. Masters are totally corrupt. Milarepa had to give up all his belongings and all that he owned so that nothing is left. Why do you think he had to give up everything? Normally people think that Milarepa thinks that he has nothing to lose anymore. No. It's more like then the guru has nothing to get from him anymore. So that he can be as ruthless as it is needed to be. That there is carelessness in his action and not that he thinks that he still can get something from Milarepa. It is for the guru that you have to be naked that you have nothing to offer anymore. It's not for you that you have nothing to lose... and freedom is just another word that there's nothing left to lose. I always thought I should do the same thing. But I can still be ruthless as I am without that.

Q [Another visitor]: Even in the lineage of Nisargadatta Maharaj this tradition used to be there. That the disciple has to offer everything, his house, his money, everything...

K: Come on, we can continue. Now that you say it like that, maybe lineage is not so bad after all. [Laughter] How much do you have? Your wife you can keep. Did they even have to give up their wife and kids?

Q: No. Only the house and the money...

K: Only the material things. The wife they could keep. That's a good deal. Yeah that's in the old traditions. But it doesn't work anymore. I think these days the disciples are much too miserly and stingy. They just want to have it for free. Go to Tiruvannamalai, all these Papaji disciples keep saying Truth has to be free. How dare you take money for something? We vote for you and now you have to be in service for me. You have to serve me. The traditional system doesn't function anymore – nowhere. The idea of *seva* doesn't work anymore. What to do? These days the master has to pay to you so that you go to him. [Laughter] It's like disciple hunting. You have to rent a hall and make sure that it is filled with disciples and then you are somebody.

Q: Many masters tell their disciples to not go to anybody else otherwise you'd get confused...

K: Ramesh did that.

Q [Another visitor]: Osho did that too...

K: Because he needed your money. I say go to everybody, just leave me alone. [Laughter] Get confused somewhere else. Why not go to everyone? What's the difference?

Q: Good entertainment...

K: No.

Q: I'm used to this entertainment...

K: But you are not the standard here. [Laughter] Hopping from one to another like a bee. So many flowers, I suck everywhere. The honey is everywhere.

Q: Not so much sucking, just... [Laughter]

K: Just plugging, connecting.

Q: Checking them out...

K: You should shake them out. And I'm the unlucky one she comes to regularly. [Laughter] Now there's a competition between Mooji and John de Ruiter about who is the bigger Christ consciousness. Do we want to have a black or a white Jesus on the cross? [Laughter] They will be nailed. It is just unbelievable, another one with Christ consciousness.

Q: The third coming...

K: I think it's the hundredth coming. 'Come to me, come to me. I'm the light, I'm the way. I'm the fiction.' Wonderful! 'I will lead you to salvation and redemption.'

Q [Another visitor]: The suffering is permanent...

K: There's an idea of suffering. If I say there's no suffering, I'd confirm suffering. There's an experience of what you call suffering.

Q: So, does suffering arise in a phantom?

K: It doesn't arise; it's permanently there. There's maybe arising of Jesus as Christ. He rose again, like a rose.

Q: In the Heart Sutra they say that there's no suffering and there's no end of suffering. It's not clear...

K: It's very clear. If there would be suffering, it could end. But try to find the suffering. Try to find the sufferer. Try to find him and then show him to me. You will never find a sufferer and you will never find suffering, you will not find anything. If you really look into it, it's gone. Yes, in imagination it all exists but when you look into it, it's gone. It's like a mirage in the desert, the closer you come you find it doesn't exist. But from distance it looks like there's water. If you really come close and look into it, it's gone; as everything. Nothing remains when you really look into it; it all becomes empty or non-existing. Right now you are half looking into it. If you bring the light into the darkness, there was never any darkness. But before that you think there's darkness.

Q: Would you say it would be like...

K: Face yourself and try to find yourself and you will not find any self. In not finding any self, there was never anyone who lost himself. Even the Self becomes an empty idea. Whatever you look into, it's gone. It has no substance. The wisdom of emptiness was a book from Dalai Lama. It's a wisdom of emptiness, when you look into it it's gone. You cannot find anything. When you look into the universe the universe doesn't exist. If you look into the phantom, the *me*, it's gone. Like the scientists now, they look into the matter and it's gone. They go deeper and deeper and the tools are getting much more defined. It's like the light of Shiva; you cannot find the end of the light of Shiva. If you want to find Buddha, it gets smaller and smaller and smaller and it disappears. It's impossible to find its size, the biggest or the smallest. It disappears into nothing and everything. Minimize yourself to that what you are and that what-you-are is neither nothing nor everything. You are That what is. I minimize you to the maximum or I maximize you to the minimum. But it doesn't work. Even if you stay into that 'I am nothing', it's still too much.

Q: If you really look and find there's nothing, you freak out...

K: No. I have met at least a thousand people who went into emptiness of void and they all say there's no one. I was really there and there was no one. I felt no one, I saw no one, there's no one. Then they come back and tell everyone – there is no one. But they don't count themselves. Crazy! I really realized that there's no one. I went so deep and there was just emptiness. An empty void and there was no one. It sounds always good. Then they tell everyone that there's no one.

That's why Ramana says be quiet because all of what you can find out is ignorance. Whatever you can pronounce or whatever experience you have is dreamlike and is different to something else. That there can be no one there has to be someone.

Q: The Self is not something positive...

K: No. Only from Switzerland come positive people. [Laughter] Positive thinking people are the most negative that you can meet because the idea of positive creates all the negative. You're fucked by positive.

Q [Another visitor]: So I'm just a jukebox really...

K: Everybody is just a jukebox. Where does the trigger come from so that the thinking can happen? Who puts the coin into you? Life is never stingy; it has infinite coins to put into you. Life puts the coin from the top and gets it out from the back. It's always the same coin. After a while it stinks a bit but it's always the same coin.

The question is who thinks the thinker? Did the thinker ever have any thought? Or was the thinker already part of the thinking? That what is thinking the thinker, the thinking and what can be thought of is never part of the thinking. It's not different in nature. That what is living whatever, what to do with it? How can the Parabrahman be exhausted by a dream? Everyone falls in sleep at night and dreams infinite universes and planets without any effort. That's how Parabrahman dreams the whole existence, without any exhaustion. Everyone thinks that he can exhaust himself. That he can exhaust the Parabrahman that the dream stops. No way! You have to wake up from the idea that it will ever end. That you can exhaust the inexhaustible existence. Every night there's a little power cut, the deep-deep sleep.

What do they say? If so much energy goes through you the bulb will explode and life always gives you the right amount of energy so that you don't explode. Otherwise it could not have fun with you anymore. It's always adjusted to what is. Everyone hopes that *kundalini* rises and burns down the house. It always gives you as much *kundalini* as you can take. Then later you have a running *kundalini* and you're proud about it – 'My *kundalini* is now quiet and calm. I am at peace and my body is totally in tune with existence. My Kundalini is fantastic! And I'm great and my rainbow body is shining.' These are all the stories that go on. And if you look into it, it just disappears. It's just another joke of existence. Nothing remains, not even nothing. What do you do when there's not even nothing?

Q: You can't speak about it...

K: I speak all the time about it. You can never be a master of the Self. You can only be a master about an imagination.

Q [Another visitor]: What about the breathing of the universe? When it inhales it becomes nothing and when it exhales it becomes everything...

K: That's the *atma* meditation – *atma* breathing in and breathing out. Breathing into nothing and breathing out into everything – try. I have nothing against it. Maybe it works. Who am I to say anything? Try it. Atma; the Self, breathing out into the absence and breathing into the presence, and nothing happens. Sounds good.

Q: I had these people try to kill me because I did not like Osho...

K: I always poke fun about Osho and I try to make people fight for their guru and the moment they react, they make the guru weak. Whatever you have to fight for becomes weak. If you just stay quiet, it's okay because then your guru is okay. No one fights for Nisargadatta. No one fights for Ramana and for sure no one fights for me. [Laughter] I just trigger and very often people start fighting for the guru. But then they make them small not me. I just have fun. But if you fight for your master you already make him very small because he needs to be fought for. What to do? I have many Osho people who start fighting and get angry and I like it. I even put Ramana down just to see what happens and the moment they fight for him, they make him small.

The truth you have to fight for is not worth fighting for. And the guru that you have to fight for is not worth to be a guru. You can fight for politicians, for your party, for your mother.

Q: Pull all rugs from under my feet...

K: And I say no. Everyone says take my last concept away and I say, who cares? Keep your flying carpet with yourself. Imagine I would have an interest to set you free.

Just be that what you are which is the Absolute guru and that never needed any master or anything. The rest is so much bullshit that you hang on to whatever, enslaved by some ideas. It is not even a question if it's a right guru or a wrong guru. There are only wrong gurus. There can only be false gurus. If there ever was a right guru, that would be hell. Fuck! As if the Self would ever show up as a guru. The Diamond Sutra says Buddha never showed up in this world and if you meet Buddha on the way, kill him by knowing that there is no Buddha walking the Earth – never was, never will be. Everyone now thinks that they have a Buddha inside. If people would really read The Diamond Sutra, they would just be quiet. It says everything.

The Heart Sutra is not much different. It says it all, there is no enlightenment, there's no Buddha. And I would just sit here and tell you that you will not be the first one to make it. There was no one before you who could realize his Buddha nature. Maybe you can realize your butter nature but not your Buddha nature. Everyone has this idea that there were gurus before and there were realized masters and they take it all for real. Then they think I can make it too because before me there was a realized master. Ha, ha, ha. And I can tell you that there was no one before you and you will not be the first one who realizes his so-called true nature. That would be quite something.

The very idea that there are realized ones instantly creates unrealized ones – instantly. Enlightened – unenlightened, awakened – unawakened, all that dreamlike differences. And be happy that you cannot know yourself, come on! You will never realize that what you are. It will just be a real lie again – real*lie*zation.

Q [Another visitor]: Is there anything without a meaning?

K: There's nothing without *me*, so there's nothing without *me*aning. Even nothing is there because there's a *me*. Without the I, there's no definition possible. There's not even nothing without you. Everything and nothing is only in the presence. Where is everything and nothing in the absence? Only in the presence of I there's all that imaginary ideas of nothing, everything, emptiness… all that you can talk about is only in the presence of I. But where is all of that in the absence of it? And who cares if there's an absence of meaning or purpose or any of that? The things that are so precious in the presence and are not there in absence.

Q: Is I the root-thought?

K: Yeah. You have to out-root the root thought I. And how to out-root the I? Does the I have any roots? In what? The I creates a belief system because there's an I, there's a belief system because there's a believer. But what is the root of the believer? How can you out-root that what has no roots? It is so fleeting, it's just a fleeting shadow and it only exists in the present which itself is a fleeting shadow. If it would be real it would be permanent. If the presence is permanent, it should be permanent. And only permanent can be said as that what is real. But that what is Reality is in the presence and in the absence. It doesn't need any presence or absence. It's neither permanent nor not permanent. But everyone has this idea that awareness is permanent. So, what to do with that all?

The famous fuck it all and be what you are! But who can do that? It's all too much. So, you better be quiet again and let the fucker fuck the fucker.

24ᵗʰ July Talk 2
Ladakh

Even acceptance is just trying to control

Q: Is the trinity in presence consciousness?

K: You will never know what is consciousness. Consciousness is realizing itself in Trinity, in three ways. But that doesn't mean consciousness is Trinity.

Q: Then what is consciousness?

K: No one will ever know.

Q: Is consciousness what I am?

K: No. You'll never know what it is. You don't need to know what is consciousness because you're *in spite* of consciousness. Why are you interested in consciousness if you are *in spite* of consciousness? What's the problem? Let consciousness be what consciousness is. Who gives a fuck about consciousness?

Q: The crucifixion is...

K: A fiction!

Q: For who?

K: It's just a fiction – finished. And what is the third question?

Q: I have no third question...

K: That's the true question because what you are has no question. The origin of what-you-are has no question. Otherwise everything comes as a hear-say.

Q: That I know...

K: If you knew that, you would be quiet.

Q: I don't know...

K: Even that is showing off what you don't know. The ones who claim I don't know are especially the worst that you can find; the people who don't know anymore. Hiding behind the not knowing.

The no-question is the most original question because all your questions are hiding behind somebody. They are not yours. What-you-are doesn't own any question – no need for any question. Try to find something what is yours

Q: There is nothing...

K: Even nothing is too much. Now you think that you have some answer but even that is questionable. So, be quiet.

Q [Another visitor]: I went to an enlightenment retreat...

K: With whom?

Q: Adyashanti...

K: Since I saw the video of his awakening, I don't say anything.

Q: You talk about the bitterness...

K: The bitterness is that you take all the bitter pills but they don't work. You did all that you don't like, you did all the enlightenment retreats and the bitter thing is that it never worked. You go to bliss and silence retreat and the bitter thing is that nothing of that worked.

Q: It was all sweet and I thought it is all bullshit and all I have is just ugliness...

K: Compared to all the sweet things, one feels ugly. All the nice and beautiful words and then one thinks, 'What I think, I cannot tell anybody. It's only bad. I want to kill everyone and I cannot show it.' You meditate and you bring light to where demons are. Then the demons appear. It's not like sweet angels come out from that area. It's more like demons popping up; all your so-called bad and nasty ideas and faces and ugliness: what you always try to hide, always putting it somewhere where no one can see it. But when you throw light into it, become aware about it, your awareness brings light to that area, it all pops up. It's not a nice experience. If there's something to do, you have to face your ugliness.

Q: Is the ugliest thing the void?

K: The ugliest is your never-ending greed. That you are the greediest bastard that you cannot imagine. You are always greedy for yourself. So much greed, the businessman inside trying to get all of it, trying to control everything. The greediest bastard you cannot imagine, that's your face. And you cannot get rid of him. You always try to be nice, have a nice day, I love you, blah, blah, blah. Especially in America it's really needed. That's meditation; you go to the darkness, what you always tried not to show. By becoming more fearless you allow it to come up. You don't care about the consequences anymore, your society, your friends. By that you normally lose all your friends and all your enemies too. No friends, no enemies. You become independent. The energy rises and the energy is the ability to face this – Who cares? No consequence for anything. The more you allow it, the stronger it gets until you totally stand alone. No one can give you or take anything away from what you are because you faced your darkness. Then one who goes away is okay and the one who stays is fine.

It seems like it's real. That's John de Ruiter's core splitting honesty. That you have to go to your core splitting honesty and show your real face. And if that's needed, it has to be done. I don't say you shouldn't do it. I don't say that you are already what-you-are and you don't have to do it. If you first have to face your dark side, you have to go there. All your fear is hidden there. All your fear, all what you tried to avoid is hidden there. And you have to meditate on that, that's called *sadhana*. You meditate on your sadness. Your sadness is don't shoot anyone and you have to face that sadness. To face joy is a piece of cake. To face bliss and beauty is a piece of cake. You have to face the other side because where there is joy, there is as much sadness. You realize yourself in Absolute joy and your preference is joy but you have to face what comes with it – as much joy, as much sadness. What you call sadness actually is joy in nature but first you have to...

It's not by understanding. You have to go into it; you have to become the sadness, that what's the nature of sadness. Then you may experience that the nature of sadness is as much joy as joy. There's no difference in nature. But for that you have to, in a way, face it. Milarepa had to face all the demons, all that's bad. He was famous for that. You have to face the devil and you have to recognize yourself in the devil. You have to face hell. It's like Mahabharata; you have to go to hell and in the last you may say – 'May it be as it is.' No tendency left to avoid the hell. Then it's okay. If hell is hell and heaven is heaven then who cares? May it be as it is. Those who always go after nice and beauty, that's called a *sangha*; the oneness, the hugging, blah, blah, blah. But to be alone somewhere in a cave and be alone with your meditation and no one helping you, being totally left alone with all what you are, facing your loneliness and sadness. That's why people go to Himalayas. But you don't have to go to Himalayas, you can do it everywhere. It's not a place. It's something that's normally hidden in your inner direction to a place which is buried somewhere. It seems like you have to go through that. Some don't but some really have to.

Q [Another visitor]: And to do that do we have to avoid external stimulation?

K: No. You can even do it as a doctor in an emergency room. You can even have a family, then that's your hell. Relatives are all hell. By trying to avoid them, you try to avoid hell. Having friends is hell. Being part of a society is hell, being born is hell. Normally you want to go to the unborn, you want to go to the nice side. No, for that you don't have to leave hell, you have to face the hell.

Q: But to go deep into it...

K: It's not going deep into it. It's opening up to it.

Q: That way you lose your enemies?

K: If you don't have friends anymore then you don't have enemies anymore. You have enemies because you have friends. Maybe you lose the discrimination between enemies and friends. Even the closest friend is an enemy. How many times did I have to say, any *me* is an enemy. Who's your friend? Is your mother your friend? Or father? Do you have any friend? Be happy.

Q [Another visitor]: Is there any end to this process?

K: It ends when it ends but there's no promise of ending. It can continue many lifetimes. It's not like one week you go to a darkness retreat and then my monsters are gone. Ha, ha, ha. Keep dreaming! You collected all the demons for thousands of lifetimes and now you want them to go away in one-week retreat?

Q: But does it end?

K: It doesn't matter. You will know when it ends. You are just greedy.

Q: I'm just asking...

K: This answer is the worst answer, 'I was just asking. I have no interest but I was just asking. I'm not interested in your answer anyway.' Why should I sit here and give you any answer anymore if you're just asking? That's offending. 'I'm just asking, actually I don't need it.' Do you want to know it or not? That's quite an arrogant statement, 'I'm just asking.' I'm always surprised that I react to everyone differently.

That is one side but the other side doesn't need anything. Yes, you have to but what-you-are doesn't have to do anything. It may happen by accident and there was never any problem or you have to go the long, long way. There's a short-cut of Ramana; just be what you are or you go all the way around. But who knows what's shorter? Some have to go through all the sadhanas and all the teachers. In the end that goes too and who cares how long it takes? But now you already want to know how it will be so that maybe you don't have to go.

Q [Another visitor]: Do ayahuasca and peyote help in facing the darkness?

K: Don't mix them both. I hate you for that. Don't even put them in one sentence.

Q: What's the difference?

K: Ayahuasca is oneness and being one with everything. It's like being in a church; there's drumming and good feelings. I talk to people who take *ayahuasca* and they go for it again and again for having a good no-time.

Q: And *peyote*?

K: *Peyote* just shifts your perception to the other side, to absence. There's no advantage in it. There's no experience in it. It's just being the Real McCoy with the two sides, the *tonal* and the *nagual* without an interruption. It's working and without working, the presence and the absence. It's not like a drug for me.

Q [Another visitor]: But only because you read the books before?

K: I didn't read anything before. I just read one book *Journey to Ixtlan* and then I took *peyote* every day for five years in champagne, everyday a little sip. But I don't say that you have to do that. We are just talking about what this drug does; otherwise I would just have a *peyote* party here. In Santa Fe there are tribes and chiefs that have a *peyote* party every week like a meditation group. In the beginning you take *San Pedro* to experience your power animal but *peyote* is the end of you having any excuse. It's not about power. It's crossing the eagle even before seeing the eagle, the awareness point, the white eagle.

But I tell you that you don't need one of them.

Q: Or maybe we should go to Mexico?

K: I should be totally frustrated… why am I sitting here? But I just enjoy the failures around me, the leftovers. Even when you tell them there's nothing in it, they still say that I have to go there. Always trying to get an advantage somewhere. Then I go there and I get something, always trying to change to something else. Wonderful! Just go and tell me how it was. I have nothing against it. Always trying to get entertained in a different way, this is working that's not working. You are more interested in what works and what doesn't work and trying to control life all the time. In spite of me telling, the controller cannot be killed. This little caretaker inside who always takes care about his little advantages and trying to avoid bad things. If I didn't see that as the nature of the caretaker, I would maybe mind. You cannot kill him. It will be permanently there. Even by being what-you-are, you cannot get rid of it. There's always this advantage-hunting guy there. I don't want to do anything with him. Just leave him alone and let him be. Then I will not talk to you anymore, I will just be quiet. If you are interested in all of this, then you go for it but don't bother me.

Q: Because...

K: I'm very serious here. I'm not interested in all of that. There is no because.

Q: The experience you had with *peyote*, I never had with *ayahuasca*. It seemed much deeper.

K: But I don't want to hear that. I give a shit about your experiences, you know that. I am not interested in your experiences and your comparison about drugs. I have no interest. And I don't make anything higher or lower; it's just different but it doesn't make any difference. I don't say that is better than this or deeper or higher. Having a body is a drug, there's always a chemical produced in your brain and someday it's good and someday it's bad. The feelings coming from one side and the hormones running from the other side. How do I control my little chemicals here and what do I have to take and what do I have to eat so that I don't feel bad? I always take care about all these little feelings and all these poops and farts of my being. [Laughter] And doctors are the worst, they say. Permanently watching what fart comes out and what stinks and what shall I do with it. What experience was there?

What to do? The moment God wakes up he becomes a dog-tor for himself and caring about his fucking life, about his fucking existence of how it is and what is the memory effect and what was the story and what happened there and how did I feel with that and that guru gave me that *shakti*. Stingy seekers seeking everything for nothing.

Q [Another visitor]: I don't see a point in experience of going for an advantage. You can also just have an experience of joy...

K: You are lying. That was the biggest lie what you just pronounced. Out of joy nothing comes, there's just silence. Whatever comes is just looking for an advantage – every time. And you are just pissed because you don't have that advantage that you are looking for. You are looking for an advantage that you don't need an advantage. But you will never have that advantage. Only that advantage is what-you-are but you will never get it by anything. But you try. And I don't blame you but trying will not bring it. By none of the outside experiences or inside experiences you can be that what-you-are who doesn't need one.

When Ramana says be quiet, be that what you are, it's not an advantage. It's just the absence of one who needs or doesn't need anything. And that's more than an advantage. That's satisfaction by nature but not by any outside event or ecstasy bullshit. So far so bad. I'm not interested in all these bloody experiences and how I manage my world and my life and now I have the answer of how to be better. Then I meet friends and compare what you do for life and how you feel, blah, blah, blah. It's all so exhausting. How high can you fly? How deep can you fall without a parachute? Oh, I fell without a parachute, you still need one?

I hate advanced seekers, I tell you. I hate seekers anyway. The seeking suckers, seeking the next deeper experience. Seeking the next shakti, the next shanti and then comparing it with the next seeker. 'My guru gave me more shanti than your guru can give you. You have to come to my place.' Always comparing, oh God! You just have to sit for a few hours in Tiruvannamalai in a cafe and you know all what goes on.

And it will never end. It's like farmers meeting... whose crop is better and how did they grow that one and my pigs are better than yours. Everyone takes himself so important about his achievements and what he made and his techniques of controlling life. Wonderful! But who wants to listen to that? I watch television and I already see enough. But when I talk about that, I am not here to listen to that.

Every morning before I come here I always think today I will be nice. [Laughter] I will just listen to their stories and achievements and experiences with drugs and gurus and I will just smile. But this fire comes from behind and it doesn't allow anything. Empty promises I give myself every morning. When I talk to myself I don't allow this bullshit; cannot do it. Otherwise I just don't do this anymore. I have no interest. It has to be Absolute and fixed and not this little comparing *my* life. I have heard too many stories and I'm not interested in it.

Q [Another visitor]: It's not much fun being nice actually...

K: Nice is *scheiß; scheiß* means shit in German. In German they say, 'Nice is the brother of *scheiß'* because you are cheating everyone by being nice. But who is not a cheater? They all cheat you. They all want something, all business.

Q: I have noticed that with myself...

K: You cheat yourself I know. One is his own toilet already. Then you wait for enlightenment as a flush so that the shit may go but maybe the flush never happens and you have to live with your bloody shit forever. But the problem is that sometimes you have a flush and you feel there's a clarity and you very quickly fill it up again with shit because you cannot live without shit. That what is a concept needs concepts and stories. As Barren Katie would say, who would you be without your stories?

I am not here to give you more shit for your story. I'm not interested in that. The best thing would be that you may come with all of it and maybe you go back with a little bit less. And less, and less, and less, and less. But not with more stories and putting more on top of that. It's like the hydra; you chop one head and others pop-up. Actually the best chopping is not to chop at all. But sometimes I'm stupid enough to chop it again. What to do?

Today I'd try to be quiet. But then I'd make another story; 'Today it was so nice, Karl was quiet.'

Q: Have you ever done that?

K: Yeah and they still talk about it. One hour in Munich, two hours in Morocco and they still talk about it. It's worse than talking because then they talk permanently about why I didn't talk and it was so nice. But I don't want to be nice. I'm not here to be nice and to make a pleasant experience, come on. I want to torture you with every word I speak. This is a torture chamber here and not a wellness seminar. Since they talk about it and say it was so nice, I don't try to be quiet anymore. You can be quiet alone in your room. You pay for some words here. I'm a

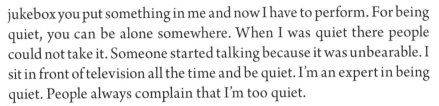

jukebox you put something in me and now I have to perform. For being quiet, you can be alone somewhere. When I was quiet there people could not take it. Someone started talking because it was unbearable. I sit in front of television all the time and be quiet. I'm an expert in being quiet. People always complain that I'm too quiet.

Q: Who are these people? [Laughter]

K: My mother was one of them. I was always too quiet and she complained that my son never says anything. Then when I came back from disco she was still there and asked me to talk to her but I was already exhausted and drunk. Normally people say that he never says anything. I saved everything for this. No one is here with free will. You're raped to sit here. [Laughing] But in spite of the experience of being raped, there is a silence which can never be imprisoned and it doesn't demand anything.

There's absolutely no disadvantage in anything because what-you-are never needs any advantage at all. But that phantom you believe to be, this caretaker always hunts. It's like Shiva goes hunting and it shoots again, the next prey and the next prey and the next prey. Shiva becomes *jiva* and becomes a hunter, hunting all those experiences always trying to bring the biggest prey back to his wife and the wife says you can do better – show me something else; never satisfied. But imagine if Parvati would be satisfied, Shiva would just sit at home watching television and nothing will happen anymore. He would not hunt anymore. All would stop right away. So it needs some Shakti from behind which is the wife, Parvati who pushes Shiva out to do something – bring something home. They say it's Shiva-Shakti but I would say it's Shakti-Shiva. Who controls who? Shiva controls Shakti or Shakti controls Shiva? That's the question. Does the energy control you or you control the energy? So, it's Shakti-Shiva. But everyone wishes for Shiva-Shakti. Ha, ha, ha.

Q [Another visitor]: The beast you refer to, is it the same as the demons?

K: Not really. I prefer to call it the devil, the diabolic *me*. The one who creates separation, the master of time. This little phantom inside, this little or big devil who always creates separation and lives by separation and always tempts you. There's a permanent temptation from that phantom that by this drug, by this understanding, by that you will end separation. The moment you wake up you enter his field, his area. He is the master of all presence.

Q: The moment you talk to someone, then it shows up...

K: The devil has to show up. The *me* cannot hide itself anymore, this nasty one. The one who wants more and more, the one who wants to control God. It's actually the God inside who wants to control God. It's not different from God but the God who knows God is the devil himself because he's in love with himself and then he wants to know his beloved. That is this controlling energy, the God who wants to know God. And he's even jealous about himself because he's jealous of God who doesn't know himself; doesn't need to know himself. He's so angry in itself, in its nature. He's angry with himself that he has to exist. He's not angry about anything else. He's just angry about himself that he has to exist. So, you're angry about yourself that you have to be, that you have to exist. And you want to get out of it, you want to be nice but you only want to be nice because you try to hide this anger inside. You try to hide it, you try to be civilized, you try to tame yourself.

Q: Sometimes it is deep down and it comes from behind...

K: It's just that you cannot hide it anymore. I just talk to it and it cannot hide because there's no corner you cannot know. I know that by heart because I am That. I know how tricky I am and how the devil called intellect works, by heart. And I don't mind it. I have nothing to lose to know myself. I am in no conflict about that. There's no conflict for me. But for you it's still a conflict because you have a preference that not knowing, the absence, would be better. But me being the devil, I have no problem with being the devil. I experience myself as a devil, what's the problem? This is my realm, this is hell and it's only there because I am. The devil and the hell pop up together. And they are not different from what I am. So I'm devil and the hell – *Hell*alujah! What's the problem with the devil? It's not like embracing it or accepting it. You are That! You cannot not be that. You cannot not be that what is God and you cannot not be that what is the devil. But everyone thinks that

I cannot not be That what is God. The devil is no different from me. You are that what is.

You can never accept to be the devil. You can just be that what is the devil and there's no way out of it. Acceptance doesn't work. You try to tame the devil by accepting him but he's totally untameable. You cannot control the devil by acceptance. You can only control the devil by being the devil. And you are the hell, so what's the problem with hell when you are the hell? I ask you.

When you are the presence and the presence means the devil and the hell and me and all what you call this diabolic separation experience. You are that all and there's no way out of that. So what? You only suffer because you want to escape it. You want to escape yourself. You want to avoid yourself and by that you suffer. You should suffer more by that. Even acceptance is trying to control, imagine! That you cannot imagine.

Q [Another visitor]: There are moments in which there is a situation and something triggers what is not adjusted to the moment...

K: Who decides what it is adjusted or not adjusted?

Q: This moment you can just kill somebody...

K: Any moment you can just kill somebody, just needs the right circumstance.

Q: It shows up in some moments...

K: No. It's just that in some moments you cannot hide the anger inside you. Then the killer comes out. But it's always there. You are civilized by lies, by Ten Commandments – you shouldn't, you shouldn't, you shouldn't, you shouldn't. You fear the consequences, that's why you behave. If there would be no consequence, you would kill everyone around you right away. You fear the consequences, that's what stops you. Imagine if there's no consequence; like war. You can shoot everyone without any consequence, you would shoot right away. Everyone would go, phom, phom, phom, phom. Today I shot fifty people. It was all enemies. If I wouldn't have shot them, they would've raped my mother. There's a good reason for you to be bad. You just look for a good reason to be bad.

Q: Sometimes it happens that you say something to someone that would be a totally worst-case scenario for him...

K: Why not? Just create a worst-case scenario. A friend leaves you because you say something or your mother doesn't like you anymore. Then you succeeded. Do your best to get them all away, piss off! The problem is, look at me, I talk to all of them like that and then more and more start coming. It doesn't work.

Q: It's not just that you say something and the other person is disappointed...

K: Why don't you dare to hurt them? Why are you afraid to hurt somebody? Because you don't want to be hurt. You just make a business out of it. You don't hurt me and I don't hurt you. It's just business. That's called friendship.

Q: It always happens with people I know...

K: It doesn't matter what happens. You just make business with existence; I don't hurt people so that I don't get hurt by them. You're just afraid to be hurt so you don't hurt someone else. It's not that because you don't want to hurt them, you're just afraid to be hurt by someone. It's just fear. Civilized people? They just fear the consequences. As the Bible says, don't do to others what you don't want them to do to you. Ha, ha, ha! But you would like to do something to them. What's going on in this circus? You tame yourself by fearing the consequences. That's called being civilized. Otherwise your Stonehenge man is still very active.

Q: Sometimes this thing comes up...

K: It never comes up, it's ever present. It doesn't have to come up. It just hides behind the mask, that's all. It's a masquerade of the devil, this persona. Behind this masquerade of the devil, this persona, is always that what is the devil just having a nice face, a nice hugging guy, hiding behind hugging someone. Having a nice face and smiling. This masquerade of the devil is because you are surrounded by the devil himself.

Q: The quality I mentioned, it doesn't need a reason to say bad to be bad...

K: It is bad.

Q: Sometimes one says something bad to someone and thinks that he has a point but you don't...

K: You are quite arrogant my dear. You think you can do something to someone. Who do you think you are that you have a power to hurt somebody? That someone can get crazy by your doing or not doing. Who do you think you are? What energy do you think you have to have this ability to hurt somebody or you can make someone crazy? Who do you think you are that you have this power? Do you believe that you have an *avatar* inside? Or you think you're stronger than someone else or something?

Q: I don't know...

K: I listen to you and I hear you. You believe that you have some power. You think by your ability, by your words you can hurt somebody. You think you just hold back because if you do something than something will happen to someone. Are you a good guy because you hold back?

Q: I'm not saying...

K: I'm just listening to what you say and I get that.

Q: But these things just come up...

K: Don't excuse yourself. The devil always tries to excuse himself. I just listen and I hear someone who believes that he has some abilities, that he can do something. Otherwise he would not talk about it. You only hold back because you think, 'I only hold back otherwise I'm bad or something or someone can be hurt.' There must be some *shakti* in you and you can use it, like a power. That's a personal thing; friends have this power over each other. One has this ability, if someone says something bad then someone is hurt and he shows it. All these bloody games that the devil plays with himself.

Q: But what I say is something without a reason and mostly with people I don't know...

K: So what? Why always hurt people you know?

Q: I just brought this up to have some clarity about this...

K: And I just made it clear.

Q: For who?

K: For myself. If I hear you, I know where it comes from. There are no nice guys around here and you are not nice. And you don't do it because you don't want to hurt somebody. You want to feel power. You want to be in control, as every devil, every *me*. What's the problem? I just clarify you that there's nothing wrong in being the devil who wants to control. But you will fail. God cannot control God, he can only control his little imaginary shit kingdom and you try to behave in that shit kingdom. But what you really want is to control yourself – that what is God, that what is behind everything. Even by religion, by trying to be good, you want to control goodness, imagine! I'm not bad so I control the bad.

And it works, that's the problem. The illusion that it works comes by the temptation of the devil himself. You're always tempted because something works. For a while it works but then it takes it away again and suddenly it crashes again. I like the song from Johnny Cash, God will cut you down. Sooner or later God cuts you down. All your belief system that you have some power, that you can do something or not, all of that are temporarily gifted by an illusory idea. Then it just takes it away and you crash as you are. By all your so-called – '*My* power of acceptance, *my* power of knowledge, *my* power of whatever.' It was never in anyone's power. It's all given and it will be taken away as nothing. You think now I control my life.

And all these ideas always tempt you. You sit here and think you should, you should. If you just behave like that, if you just understand and then you control life. By the right understanding nothing can happen to you anymore. Even when I was in Bombay with Balsekar, it was all about control. Working mind is better than thinking mind and if by God's will you have a working mind than you control happiness. The little personal happiness you control and then... pang... it will be taken away again I tell you... even in spite of all that psychotherapy.

There are no innocent questions. There is no innocence in this presence – never was, never will be. There's always business. The little businessman inside, the devil wants to rule his hell and tries to find tools to control in whatever you call as separation. But he will never succeed. But he tries. He is bad and he tries to control it by being good. This little doer, it is doershit! Trying to control yourself is a joke. Then everyone who is controlling is complaining that he feels imprisoned by control. What you try to control controls you because now you try to control an imaginary life and that imaginary life controls you. One comes with the other. Then trying not to be bad. It's bad from the beginning. It can only get worse.

This morning again I promised myself to please myself but I cannot. But sometimes I'm tempted to, but it's very quickly gone.

Q [Another visitor]: I'm hoping not to be nice anymore...

K: Don't worry, you never were. [Laughter] I have a bad job because I have to play nasty.

Q: When you spoke about the devil it occurred to me...

K: God knowing himself is a devil.

Q: He could be a saint as well...

K: What is he not? The main thing is that the devil is not different from God. God knowing himself is his own devil, creates his own hell and he cannot give his guilt to anyone else. He's self-guilty from the beginning. He cannot blame anyone else other than blaming himself, to know himself. The moment you know yourself you have to be the devil because it's unbearable. And you already want to find a way out of it, so you fight permanently for everything. You seek a way out of it. But there's no way.

You have to experience yourself as the one who knows himself. It's a *fata morgana* that God falls into that trap, falling in love with its image. The awareness God, the God who knows himself. But how can you not fall being in love with yourself by the presence of yourself? By being in love with yourself you want the best for yourself. The best would be to not be in love with yourself and not to know yourself. You try all the time not to know yourself. But you cannot. This presence is the way you know yourself. Then the absence is not knowing yourself. These are two sides of what-you-are. You are that Real McCoy, God who has two sides – Shiva with his two faces. The moon and the no-moon. The knowing and the not-knowing. What can you do?

But if you fall in love and this presence really becomes your reality, then for sure by nature you want to get out of it. But the more you want to get out of it, you are in it. It's a perfect trap – absolutely perfect!

Q: Who devised this trap?

K: You! Only Self can trap the Self so absolutely, no one else. There is no one else but the Self. The trapper, the trapping and the trapped are not different. You are the perfect trapper and trapping and the trapped. You are that who created the prison but there's no one in it. And you have to play all the roles, the prisoner, the prison, the guard. There's no other actor. So, what to do? Sometimes you play as a nice guard and a nice prisoner because you think maybe I can come out earlier. No! You have an absolute sentence for eternity. You cannot not experience yourself being imprisoned. It's part of what you are. It's not only a life sentence, it's an eternal sentence. Sentenced for eternity to experience yourself in this presence. No way out! As eternal as you are, as eternal is the presence and eternal is the absence and there's no coming and no going. What to do?

And I wish I could open the doors. But in that way I'm unable to lie to myself. If I would say there's a way out, I'd be lying to myself. It doesn't work. Only by being what-you-are, this all ends – instantly. Only because there's an idea of end you suffer. If there's no end of suffering, there's no sufferer anymore. You cannot suffer about what you are. If this suffering is eternal without beginning and without end, your interest is gone. Without the interest, there's no *me* because there's nothing to get out of it. That's why I just sit there and say what to do?

Now your interest is; something becomes better when this is gone, when I'm absence, when I'm prior. But this is eternal as everything. No coming, no going, that's called silence. Silence kills you. Silence kills the sufferer. But there was never any suffering in the first place. There's an idea that you want to get out and then you suffer about trying to avoid yourself. That's the only suffering you can suffer about. But who makes you so stupid? Only love makes you so stupid because love always wants the best for yourself. Love is your biggest enemy; the love for yourself and not hate.

But whenever I say that someone says, 'No... love is everything!' Everyone is so conditioned by love. Everyone is hoping for love. One day love will come and I'll be in an unconditional love and I'll be in an unconditional acceptance and then, and then, and then. The hope becomes bigger and bigger.

Q: And we sit here...

K: And you think you'll get it from me? Ha, ha, ha! I'm in unconditional hate, you know me. It doesn't work either. Neither unconditional love works nor unconditional hate works but it seems like hate comes easy and love needs effort. So, I take it easy, I hate. I'm in unconditional hate, in unconditional unacceptance. I never accept anything.

Q: Why is that?

K: I don't know. It's fine. I'm so lazy that I don't have to know. Unacceptance is natural, I don't accept anything. But trying to accept is so much effort. Everyone gets tired by acceptance. Today I'll accept, tomorrow I'll accept. I have to remember to accept. But that you cannot accept to exist is natural. It's the first experience. The moment you experience that you exist; non-acceptance. You cannot accept that experience.

Q: Then there's this thing about giving...

K: Giving up or giving off? [Laughter] Because it doesn't exist, it's wonderful. I'm giving off. Why not giving down? Why does it always have to be up? Down goes by itself but for up, you have to lift it up. Everyone thinks God is up there, so I'm giving up. I'm giving it to him. He's fed up with your giving up. It's already full up there.

Q: But there's nobody up there...

K: If there would be something, it would be a post office; postponing. God is a post-office. But laziness is what you are! What is laziness? Unknowing, unacceptance.

Q: Isn't laziness stillness?

K: Even stillness is too much. The laziness in nature never needs to be lazy. It doesn't even need laziness. So, I can talk and everything can happen. For not talking, you have to make an effort. Some make an effort to not talk and then they are exhausted after a while. They try to be quiet. Just have a verbal diarrhoea and be happy.

Q: Let the jukebox roll...

K: ...without a record. You have no perception without a record. But you want to feel it; you want to hear it because you try to perceive it. The worst thing you can do to hurt somebody is to call him your friend because the moment you call him your friend, he has to behave. You imprison him with your friendship. Fuck it! What a trick! Friendship is a business. Marriage is the biggest business. It's not freedom if you're afraid to hurt somebody. And who do you think you are to hurt somebody? That's the main question.

Truth never hurts anyone. When I say something here, everyone starts laughing. No one is offended here, that's the main thing. If it really is with trying not to hurt, that hurts. Who do you think you are who can hurt me with what you do or what you say? That hurts. How can you imagine that you have this power over me that you can hurt me with your behaviour? Come on! Who do you think you are? That's what I'm talking about. Why do you make me so small and powerless that you think you can control me by how you behave? Who do you really think you are? It's amazing! But everyone thinks by his behaviour, by his saying or not saying he can control someone's feelings or something. You really hurt someone by trying not to hurt him. It just simply says you are so weak and I am strong and I can hurt you by my behaviour, by what I do or not do. Your life is good or bad. I control your emotions and how you feel. That's quite devilish. I never hurt anyone, ha, ha, ha! Trying not to hurt anyone hurts everyone.

Look at yourself and yourself can never get hurt by anyone's behaviour. That is giving glory to That what your nature is. And not this little personal bullshit, this being hurt or something. His glory can never be hurt by anything, it can never be touched, there's never any spot on the nature of the Self. Behave like that with everyone. And not like he has no power. You always think they are all handicapped sitting somewhere, handicap here, handicap there and you are the doctor giving them a medicine of good behaviour and make them feel good. Dr. Feelgood. Oh God, oh God. Amazing!

Q [Another visitor]: There are parents in San Francisco who treat their children like they are dumb...

K: If you go to Hyde Street, you only meet the vegetables. All the leftovers from the bad trips of LSD. So much about drugs. If you're unlucky then you never come back. If you look at the eyes of people on Hyde Street, there's no one at home. That's why I never say that people should take drugs. Who knows what comes out of it? There's nothing to be afraid of. But what is there to gain by that? For me soberness is the highest ecstasy. What's more ecstatic than being sober? And it's for free! You don't have to pay for it. Sometimes there are people who went for drugs they agree. This silence is uninterrupted. Not trying to escape this presence is not so bad... but maybe you have to try all of that first, escaping by drugs and all those things. Who knows? Love is a drug in that sense.

Q [Another visitor]: I'm so happy to hear these honest words...

K: From the depths of my heart. It's like a devil with a soft voice. And I wish you all the best... as if the other one needs it. [Laughter] It's crazy! Good wishes are the worst; especially birthday wishes. Happy Birthday, ha, ha, ha – Now you're born, asshole! [Laughter] It's like a Happy death day. I'm so sorry that you're born, ha, ha, ha. How can a birthday be happy? Everyone is happy when this shit factory is gone because everyone is doing everything to get rid of it. But it doesn't work. Only enemies around you; especially your family. I know where you came from, says your mother.

Q [Another visitor]: Would you say that future demands the present to happen? That my words are already complete...

K: They are already spoken. The imaginary ownership is the only thing that's imaginary; that there's something that you own. Ownership is a dream, this notion that you own, that there's something that's yours, is false. This *mine*, that's the misery. Then you have guilt with doership and all those things. Otherwise there's no doership or mine or doing or not doing or birth or no birth. You only care because you own it. If you look honestly, it's just life that owns it. Life is the Absolute owner of everything but there's no relative owner in it. And whoever claims it's mine is just a joke. *My* kid, *my* mother, *my* story, *my* whatever. *That's* the dream and not that there are sensational experiences. This relative ownership, that's the dream. My consciousness; imagine if someone says *my* consciousness. Help me!

Try to find what's yours. You cannot find anything. By trying to find your question, you cannot find any question or answer. So, what's there to fear about if there's nothing what's yours?

Q [Another visitor]: It's too much here...

K: Only because of this little notion and you take it as real... it feels too much! This little notion of existence, that becomes real for you. That's all. Such is the notion of awareness it starts with. It always starts innocent, this awareness. Then it becomes really big. This first false I, this awareness I, from that everything follows. That's the root of everything. But what to do? You cannot get rid of it. Try to get rid of awareness. You can only try to get rid of awareness in awareness. There's no need for getting rid of awareness but only in awareness you try to get rid of awareness. So, what to do? You have to be *in spite* of presence or absence of... whatever. And who needs to know if it's good or bad. This story of doing or not doing. It all belongs to this bloody 'I'. I, I, I... Him again!

And he wants to be in control so he wants a confirmation of his existence, permanently. If I can hurt somebody, I exist. If I do something wrong, I exist. If I'm bad, I exist. Or if I try to be good, I exist. Permanently!

Q: When you walk in the morning, for a while it's really nice...

K: It's just a preparation for the next bullshit. Then it really hits you. It's always a preparation. I always know when I'm feeling levitating, I can tell you the same evening or next morning I have a back pain. That's called the pain is back! But for a moment you think now it feels so nice and you're levitating. That's just a preparation... just to hit you. The wish of ease gives you the disease.

The best you can dream about is neither having friends nor relatives nor knowing even yourself anymore. Even the first relationship with yourself is worse. The moment you relate to yourself, it's too late. That's where all the drama starts; when you have a relationship with yourself. It's a hate relationship. The moment you relate to yourself, you're fucked. It's too late.

Q: Because then there's two?

K: Yes. Because then there are two selves. So, any relationship is shit; especially the relationship with yourself. It's never good enough. Then you work on your relationship day and night your whole life but it never satisfies you. Fuck! But you cannot stop it because you cannot stop loving yourself. So, you will try your best but the best is not good enough. You can never be good enough. That's why the Buddhists try to be good. You fail all the time. You try to have compassion but compassion cannot be owned. There's only compassion when you are not, but when 'you' are, there's no compassion. So, what to do? It's like Self is a seaman, seeing all the time and now it became a man then he's fucked. When there's an Absolute seer without a man, no problem. But a seaman? Crossing the seven oceans and always failing.

I'm always amazed. By whatever I say, one gets happy and the other one gets sad. Fantastic! It's unpredictable.

Q [Another visitor]: I have been happy all the days...

K: But just too lazy to show it? When you're happy you don't have to show it. But when you're unhappy, you end up showing it. Happiness is just overrated bullshit.

Q [Another visitor]: Having no idea of not knowing what-you-are and what-you-are-not is an Absolute advantage as compared to...

K: Nothing can be compared to that. That is the nature of nature. There's no comparison in it. No one can compare in that. There is no pair, there are no two. How can you compare that? There's nothing that's not that. It's never an experience. It's just that what-you-are but it's not an experience because there's no experiencer and nothing to experience. There's no one who can compare anything. You're hunting a *fata morgana* because it's not for *you*. You will not be there. By whatever you try, you are not there. You never existed in that. This little fleeting shadow will be gone in that Absolute light which doesn't know any light. And that light which doesn't know what is light and no-light has no shadow anymore. There was never any shadow. How can there be a shadow in that what *is* the light? Only when there's an experience of light, then you create the opposite of darkness. But the experience of light is not light.

Q: So, what about the story of the relative me?

K: What about it? It's already gone. Why worry about something what's already gone? Come on! It never existed. There was never any born body. It's just a shit factory that turns into another shit factory. Nothing will change, nothing will happen. These atoms will turn into another information with another name. This food body that appears now will become food for something else. So, what's this precious thing worth? Nothing! It didn't come by being born, it will not go by dying. Nothing was born in birth and nothing will die in dying. This energy is inexhaustible. This is eternal life here, this body. It doesn't have to know to be eternal life, it *is* eternal life. That what is energy now shows up as this body, that's all. But it's not born by presenting itself as a body. It will be still what it is in whatever.

In coming never anything came and in going never anything goes. How can life come and how can life go? By what? Life shows itself differently by transforming into something else. But that what is transforming into something else is not gone by that. What you are is in never anyway changed. So, what's there to worry about? Comparison is only when there's an ownership of my body, your body. Then there are two different bodies. Then you compare. Your arse is better than mine and then you're in trouble. When two arses meeting, whose arse is better? When men meet it's like whose car is bigger? When women meet it is, whose kid is more intelligent? 'My kid didn't even have to go to school; he was directly admitted to the university.' It's terrible; mothers' meeting is the worst-case scenario. It's like a Tupper party, whose plastic is more? They have these Tupperware parties for selling plastic boxes. Mothers only have kids to meet other mothers. To talk about the little toy you created. 'My toy is better than yours. My toy can already walk in six months. Your toy took one year?' Everything revolves around how the kid is growing and what is happening in school. Because you own something, it's yours. You want the best for it. Then you compare mother love with other love. There's no other love than mother love.

It's a horror! Being alive moment by moment is a terror. It's a horror show. Having a body, whoa! You always have to take care about this. But what to do? You cannot otherwise realize yourself as in this horror show. The hell of separation, the hell of ownership, the hell of mine and yours.

25th July 2018 Talk 1
Ladakh

Blissful experiences are the biggest traps

Q: When I wake up in the morning, it seems very real. I find it difficult to get my head around that this is a dream state...

K: It seems so real. At first you don't want to wake up and then you give up. You're in-between, the twilight. Then you go to the toilet and see yourself in the light. It's all because you're used to these evidences. You need evidence for everything, a proof. Then you find proof everywhere and then you take that evidence as real. There are so many evidences, that you can feel the pain and you can see your face, and it was the same ever since you can remember. It has changed a bit but the eyes still look the same. But you can never be sure if there was a moment before of if there was even a yesterday. You can never know. There's just a memory effect; no one can prove to you that there was a yesterday. That there was anything at all before. Try to prove it.

Q [Another visitor]: Photos?

K: Photos are in this moment. Nothing can prove that there was a yesterday. And you need all the proof. Then you meet people who confirm that you met them yesterday. Wonderful! But no one can really know if there was a yesterday or tomorrow. You cannot even prove that the moment before was real because you cannot go back there. If there was really a Reality of that moment before, you should be able to go back to that Reality. And if there is a real future, you should now already be there. But you are always in this... You need all the help, the surroundings, the photos, the people and all the world who can confirm that yes, there was a yesterday because there was a program in the television yesterday. So, there must be a yesterday. But in Reality you cannot even prove what happens now exists or not. If it would really exist, it should be the same in the next moment as well. How can it change?

This is like your belief system; always changing, never fixed. Yesterday you had a different one and the moment before you believed in something else. All unpredictable. In a way it's all fiction. Whatever needs to be proven, cannot be real. Whatever *needs* to be real, cannot be real. So, what is this? A permanent doubt. It's a permanent existential crisis, you are used to it. That you take this as real because you get confirmations all around. Everyone confirms everyone. It's a conspiracy of ghosts. I confirm you, you confirm me. Good business. I'm relative, you're relative, so let's be relatives.

The scientists could not even prove matter. They have no idea. The quantum physics say they have no idea if it exists or doesn't exist. They're just in a limbo. You go deeper and deeper but still there's nothing to find. The tools get sharper and sharper and more sophisticated and still they cannot prove anything. All guess work. They are just guessing that it's more likely that the carpet exists than it doesn't exist. They can only say it's more likely that there's a carpet. If you go into the carpet, it's gone. So, what's real? If even the biggest intellectual scientists cannot find anything, it's all science fiction. Every theory, every concept is fiction. Every so-called proof is fiction. That the apple falls, is fiction. Everything is fiction. So, what to do with this little phantom who needs permanent confirmation? In fiction, in fiction, in fiction.

Can this fiction give you anything? Can it satisfy you because it's permanently changing? Even the scientists and gurus tell you different things. One guru tells you from one reference point and the other one tells you from another one. If you really look into it, it's all gone. They don't even exist. What is all of that? But still you are! Surprisingly what you are, is in all the changes, in all the doubtful experiences, in doubting, doubting, doubting... you are!

So, where would you rely? Can you rely on the world? Can you rely on anything in this fiction? All permanently changing concepts, every religion changes permanently. Every truth is changing permanently. Today the truth is like this and tomorrow the truth is totally different. So, what is truth? Just another fiction? So, you're with and without truth. Forget truth, forget reality, even forget yourself and still you are. In total forgetfulness and absence of any experience of existence or not, you are. So, what's real? What would you say is the only Reality you can trust? That you are! Everything is fleeting but there's that what-you-are in all those fleeting experiences. And by being that there's neither satisfaction nor non-satisfaction. Both are gone. All the ideas of peace and war – peace off! For all of that, there was never any necessity for what-you-are to have anything. That there is something or not. There was never any need. That is called satisfaction. But you don't even know what satisfaction is. What to do?

In India it's like subtracting – abstracting everything. Whatever you can know becomes fiction. Fiction, fiction, fiction. Even the 'knower' is fiction and then you remain as that what is. And that is always the tradition of all times, the *jñāni* way. First looking at the world, matter – fiction. Then spirit, sometimes there, sometimes not – fiction. Then the awareness sometimes there, sometimes not – fiction. That's *neti-neti*. You do not rely on any of that because your nature is absolutely in spite, with and without. That's being the substratum. That's what you cannot not be; the Absolute substratum. That you can call God or nature or life. It's just that what-you-are. The Self is maybe the most beautiful way to call it but you can even call it underwear. It doesn't mind. That never minds whatever you call it. It never reacts to anything. There's neither action nor reaction in that what-you-are.

The problem for you is that you think that you need something to become That by something. That you need an understanding, that something has to go for you and all of that. No. In going you don't go and in coming you don't come. All of that is, puff, puff, puff... just blow it away. That's Bob Dylan, the answer is blowing in the wind. These are just pointers when I say 'be what you cannot not be', because you are in any... whatever.

But I know about the one who wakes up in the morning. Even to understand it's a dream doesn't work. It's not meant to work. It's just another phrase. At first you say it's a reality and then you say it's a dream. Who calls it a reality and who calls it a dream? Only an illusion or that what is a dream calls it something. Only the unreal needs to know what is real and what is not real. The unreal will never become real, that's all. Because only in unreal is there an idea of existence, the notion of existence. So, how can that what is... not? Because it exists it is not. If you really look into it, it's gone. All existence when you really look into it, it's gone. So, what about all this existence? What is doubtlessness is nature where there is no doubter or no-doubter or whatever can be doubted, because there's neither existence nor non-existence? You neither exist nor do not exist. There's neither knower nor no-knower... that's knowledge that doesn't even know knowledge because it's just another concept. Aware or un-aware... what is that what is aware or unaware? You will never know.

But you cannot *not* know it, because that knowledge that you are is in spite of all your so-called... whatever. No one can give you; no one can take it away. You never lost it, you cannot gain it. You cannot forget that you are and you cannot remember it: there's only forgetting and there's only remembering because you are. But in forgetting you haven't forgotten and in remembering you cannot remember. So what? It's just sport.

Being the Buddha is not knowing any Buddha. Being with and without Buddha is that what is the Buddha. Failing to know yourself, that's the realization of Buddha. Forgetting even Buddha, then even the Buddha drops. But the dropping is not that something has to drop. It is just being *in spite* of whatever you can imagine. Even imagining that everything is an imagination and you are that what is imagining everything, is another imagination. All these beautiful words are... Whatever you can repeat, forget it. Try to repeat silence. Is there any *again* in silence? Or is it just like a flat line that's uninterrupted. Neither being nor not being. Anything else?

Q [Another visitor]: In deep-deep sleep...

K: There's no *in* deep-deep sleep. Deep-deep sleep is the absence of one who sleeps or doesn't sleep. It's the absence of presence or absence. That's why they say the nature of deep sleep doesn't know any deep sleep. An absolute absence of one who is and who is not. In deep sleep, there's still one in deep sleep. In deep sleep, there's still awareness. But in deep-deep sleep, there's not even awareness... and you still are. So you are with and without awareness or not awareness. And then awareness happens again. That's the last thing in the evening and then the first thing... awareness. But there's no one who knows what was in-between those points of awareness. But still you are. There was not even nothing: you cannot even say there's nothing. No one would define himself in deep-deep sleep. There's no definer. And then with the awareness the definer starts, the awareness 'I'. Then the defining starts, the dreaming starts. There *brahman* starts... the creator, and it creates again. But what is it when *brahman* is not?

That's the pointer. Deep-deep sleep is the absence of *brahman*. That's why it's called the *Parabrahman*. The nature of *brahman* is with and without the experience of that what is *brahman*. The nature of *brahman* doesn't need the experience of *brahman* to be *brahman*. That's why it's *Parabrahman* – the nature of *brahman*. That's the only reality. The experience of *Brahman* is already a dream. There are two *brahmans*. How can there otherwise be an experience of *Brahman*? There's an unaware *brahman* and an aware *brahman*. The so-called separation starts very early. When awakeness is there, there's already separation. How to avoid that? That's why Buddha called it a divine accident. You cannot avoid to wake up. So, even *Parabrahman* cannot not become aware. So, what's there to do? The divine accident happens every morning.

To try to be aware of something, you have to be aware already, it's too late. So, even Mr. Tolle's 'now' is too late. It's all too late. Whatever you do now, it just confirms that there's someone who needs to do something. Who needs to do something by being not aware to exist? But now in awareness it's already too late. That's why he called it an accident. No one has any intention in that what he is. No one knows why intention happens. But why not? Then out of that very subtle intention starts the dream. The first that's dreamt is the *Brahman* – the creator, the dreamer. The dreamer is the first part of the dream. Then comes dreaming and that what can be dreamt. But that what is dreaming the dreamer is never part of any dream.

Whatever you try now is fixing a problem which was never there. So many problems and no one has them. There's no ownership of any problem. There's no one here who owns anything. Life cannot be owned and that what is living cannot avoid living itself. Life cannot avoid living itself. God cannot avoid starting to know God. When God knows God it's too late. There are already two Gods. Then he becomes his own devil and creates his own hell of separate events and experiences. Who's there to blame? If nothing ever happened, who's there to blame? It's all by accident. No doership in anything; absolute non-doership. Nothing is ever done by anyone, or not done.

Abiding in that what-you-are which never needs to abide in itself, it's like a paradox. You need to be established in that what never needs to be established in anything. That you cannot get with any intellect. It's crazy! When I say failing is the best what can happen, you fail to know yourself. By failing to know yourself you even fail *not* to know yourself. By failing to know yourself you succeed in being that what is knowledge. In failing you even fail not to be. You cannot unmake you by failing. You even fail to unmake you, confirming your Absolute non-existence. You don't need to understand that. [Laughter] Trying is futile. Stay confused!

Abiding in confusion. Being totally confused, not knowing what-you-are and what-you-are-not. Total chaos... and still you are. Isn't that amazing? And that what needs order, will always fight for order, fight for peace, fight for something. But for what you are, no need. No need of *vipassana*, imagine! But it's all fun.

Q [Another visitor]: You said that awareness creates separation...

K: Awareness is already in separation. It doesn't need to be created. It's not needed to create separation because the experience of separation is already there. Already awareness, this purest notion of existence is an experience... and for an experience it needs two. So, you don't have to look for separation here, it starts very early. The experience of separation starts right away, in the beginning of awareness, when you wake up. When there's awakeness, already you experience yourself, and when you experience yourself there are two. And from there on there's only a dream of separation. But the main thing is, by that experience of awareness or separation, no one gets separated. There's no issue in separation. There's nothing wrong or right about separation. It's just the way you dream yourself or you realize yourself. So what's there to do? If in the beginning you cannot avoid the beginning, what can you do? If the beginning already is separation, whatever follows is separation. It's too late. In the beginning already it's too late. And whatever you do now is futile. Be happy about it that happiness cannot be found in any circumstance, in any sensation.

Q: In that way, *vipassana* and all that training...

K: Is just for failing. They're perfect. Every technique is perfect but in all these techniques you fail and then you go to the next thing and you fail again until you fail of failing. Then you are that who is even in failing what it is. It doesn't need to succeed in anything. In total failing, you succeed in being what you cannot not be. All the techniques of *vipassana* and all the debates and all the Buddhist techniques are just for failing. Compassion is very wonderful because you try to gain compassion. But it cannot be owned by anyone. You fail to own compassion. Whatever you can own is pity. You fail in compassion but the moment compassion swallows you; you will be gone. It's not that you succeed. Compassion *takes* you; you cannot 'have' compassion. So, you fail. And I like Buddhist techniques; they're made for failing. They just kill you. You try very hard, your best but your best is not good enough. You cannot control it, but then life controls you – totally. The relative doership can only be annihilated by failing and not by succeeding. If you succeed in doing your *vipassana* then that would be – 'Look at me, I did it.' But then you again doubt your success. You will fail.

Once a student asked a master what is the difference between us?

The master replied, the student fails sometimes and the master fails all the time. In nature they are not different. Permanent failing is what you are. If you fail sometimes, you have an insight, but it goes again. Normally you fail sometimes to know yourself, like in deep-deep sleep you fail to know yourself; and still you are. Can you be a success in deep-deep sleep? The one who succeeds in his techniques... is there any technique of deep-deep sleep? Tell me. Whatever you succeed in is fleeting and will be gone again. All your achievements, deep understandings, realizations, come and go. You cannot even keep this body. It's already gone, this hard disk that collects everything. All what you can collect is shit, that's all. It's just a shit collector. Call it ignorance or shit, it's the same. Truth cannot be collected, come on! Can there be a collector of truth? Can there be an ownership in truth? Can there be any owner of Reality? Can there be *my* Reality? Tell me. Is there any possibility of owning Reality? Is there anyone who can own Life? What would you say? What is this whatever that you call it *my* life? *My* consciousness, *my* soul, *my* whatever. Just drop the *mine* and you are fine. But can you drop the *mine*? But if it would be possible to drop the *mine*, you would be fine. No ownership, no trouble. If nothing is yours, not even nothing, who cares about anything? But can you do it? No it's not a doing. It drops by itself.

All this ignorance, these events, they come by themselves and they go by themselves and you will still be what you are: you were, you are and you will be. It all came and it will be gone – hello, goodbye. All these precious understandings, precious insights, *shakti* peace experiences; hello, goodbye. All your sitting in front of the wall for a long time will all be just a fading memory of nothing ever happened. It never happened! So, what to do? Trying to memorize more everyday what happened. Does an awakened one have to memorize his awakening permanently? What is this about people sitting there permanently and talking about their awakening; about whatever happened to them? Before I was sitting like this and I had a deep insight and now everything is fine. Then you have to tell it to everyone. I know many of these so-called... whatever. And whenever I meet them, they tell me their story as the first thing. Not love at first sight, the first and the last thing you hear is their story;

'My *guru* told me and *I* woke up! I was in the presence of that one and blah, blah, blah and I woke up totally. *I* woke up to *my* true nature.' I always tell them, bravo! See you next time.

The guru of Rama taught him everything, all the Vedas and he understood everything, I am not the body, I am not the spirit, I am that what is God. Hallelujah! I am God! Then out of gratitude to his teacher, he took his biggest diamond ring and gave it to the teacher. The teacher opens his jar which is already over-flowing with diamond rings and just tells him, 'Okay! See you next time!' Just pointing out that your realization right now will be gone and you will be stupid as before. That story I liked the most. Realized people, realized masters – see you again, hello goodbye. All the Buddhas who walked this earth. And what did Buddha say? There would never be any Buddha walking this earth. Buddha can never be seen by anyone, not even by himself. And now people sit somewhere and claim to be Buddha. They will be punished, for sure. They will be tested in their Buddha-hood... phom... chop-sui. [Laughter]

It's sometimes so much fun that realized people tell their story and they need to be approved by someone who confirms them. Imagine that you are enlightened and you have to tell somebody. Who is there to tell? Everyone gets enlightened for their friends only. You wake up only for your friends and not for yourself. You want to show off with it. [Laughing] 'Look, I made it!' What a show! You show-off this...

Then I like the story of this Zen Buddhist teacher in Japan, always the best. These stories I like most. One disciple from a thousand comes to the master and says that 'I am ready, take whatever you want from me. I am ready for enlightenment, give me enlightenment.' What does the master say? 'Can you give me your little finger?' [Laughter] The master chops off his little finger and the disciple starts to cry, 'Oh my little finger'... The one who was very ready for enlightenment, no one was more ready than him. Then the master asks, 'Are you less now?' The disciple is still crying for his finger and the master chops off his hand. The disciple cries, 'Oh my hand!'...and the question always is, 'Are you less now? Does it make you less having no hand?' Then chopping the whole arm... 'Are you less now?' The disciple cries for his arm, 'Oh my arm!' Then the master chopping the whole head... 'Are you less now?' If I would do that right now, everyone would be enlightened. No one would dare to say 'I am not enlightened' anymore. [Laughter] After that whenever he asked his disciples are you enlightened, no-one had any doubt. In one stroke a thousand people were enlightened. But if you do it these days maybe you have consequences. In that time whatever happened in a monastery stayed in the monastery. There was world that could do anything. I'm always looking for that place again. [Laughter]

So much about people who are ready; advanced seekers being ready. They called off the search, they did everything. They are in total acceptance, 'I accept everything.' When it comes to your little finger, everything is forgotten. 'I am ready to devote everything.' Ha, ha, ha. What is yours to devote anyway? 'I surrendered everything'... but not the surrender-er, that's always too much. All those surrender-ers, they will be dropped like nothing without existence even caring about it. 'I surrendered *my* life' ... as if it was ever yours!

Q [Another visitor]: All the things around come and go and this feeling 'I am' is always permanently there...

K: That's another trick. You land in the uninterrupted but it's still a landing. It's still an 'I' who lands in the I Amness. It's timeless, without time, but then you fall into the trap of being timeless. There's still one too many who's timeless. Even the I Amness is just another trap. 'I am the body' is a trap, then 'I am not the body' is a trap, 'I am something is a trap' and 'I am nothing' is a trap. All traps! But it's very comfortable, getting into the I Am, staying there. It's already without discomfort. It's quite comfortable. In the presence it's quite quiet. Then the next would be the awareness; it's even more comfortable. It's like the KO; the body. And then the OK and then the Okie-dokie. I'm fine in any way.

Q: So what is this I Amness? How is it different from when Ramana said put your attention into I Am?

K: He said *first* focus on the I Amness and you will fail. Because maybe for a while with effort you can stay in I Amness, but you always fall out again into 'I am the body' or 'I am whatever.' So, you fail by the *first*. You fail and then you go to I Amness just for failing. Just put your attention to I Amness but the attention is helpless, it can only stay there by effort and then you fall out again. Once you fall out of I Amness, then you realize that by no effort you can stay there forever. Then who cares?

Q: It seems he says to keep coming back to this I Am...

K: That's the first step. And I tell you that even Ramana was putting you into a circumstance that you fail. It's for failing. It's everywhere, in every tradition. In Buddhism, in Hinduism there's *neti-neti*, it's all about failing. It's not about succeeding. It's not about anything. You put your attention to I Amness but you fail. When attention is free, it just goes by whatever and it comes back. It's like Zazen. You sit in front of the wall for some time and then you have going out of the body experience into the space experience, the pure I Amness. That's a *satori*. So, already you are fine. But the question is *who* is more fine in I Amness then I Am the body? It needs one who has the advantage. And the advantage will go again into a disadvantage. So, even the advantage is a disadvantage because it needs one who has that advantage in some other circumstance. So, try...

Then maybe you see that you have had the *satoris* many times. Going from identified to non-identified. Being the body, being not the body, being space-like. So, discomfort-comfort, like a ping-pong. Then after a while you are not interested anymore in this ping-pong because you know that you cannot control it. Then you stay in the awareness, the blank awareness, the witness state. Then you can stay there for a while because it's very fine. 'I am neither the body nor anything else. All appears and disappears and I am still what I am.' The witness is the best what I can be because Awareness uninterrupted, neither attached nor unattached at all. There's no spot on you, you're just awareness. It's like a screen where everything is dancing. Wonderful! And it can take quite a while. There's not even time involved. It feels like eternity. But by whatever event, by a little trigger, you are unexpectedly back in the market place. In Tao they say that you can stay in the light of awareness for thousands of lifetimes but there will be a trigger and you're back at the same moment that you left because there was not even time involved. You just wanted to have a glass of water and you come back from eternity into this moment and you are as thirsty as before. So what then is the advantage of awareness?

Even awareness is just another landing place that you have to depart again. The eternal tourist cannot stay in any landing place. You are the eternal tourist, Buddha experiencing himself as everything. You have no favourite place, come on. And having a favourite place, a preference is *me*. That's a *me* preference and by that you suffer already. That's the only way of suffering because there's one who has a preference. But what-you-are never has any preference and it will just go to another place. Then you go to the prior. Then you're in Samadhi of being prior.

Q: So, the I Amness is okay and the trouble is that we make a preference out of it?

K: How can this *me* not make it a preference?

Q: It's very hard...

K: It's impossible! You want to stay there. Your intention in this life is having no intention. Then there's pure spirit, no intention. This no intention becomes your Absolute intention.

Q: But that's a trap...

K: Of course! Everything is a trap, come on! You are the trapper, the trapping and the trapped, permanently. How can you not be trapped by yourself? Try not to be trapped by yourself. But who cares about being trapped by oneself? It's just for sport, come on! It's just for fun. Who takes it seriously? 'Me!' [Laughter] The permanent question is who has it? And who needs it? That's 'who am I?' Who needs it? Who has an advantage? The answer is always *me*. And once you put a light on the 'me', it's gone. The phantom always needs something. But how to get rid of that phantom? How to get rid of something what doesn't exist? It's sometimes there, sometimes not.

Q: Sometimes you really see that there's a phantom...

K: You are the phantom of being in love with yourself. You know that. The love for yourself is a phantom experience. Love for yourself is your issue, not the phantom. When there's love, there are two; you are the lover and the beloved: that's two. This big love is the biggest trap you can be in. Your heart has to be broken. The love for yourself needs to be broken. But who can break it? By trying to break it, you make it real. By trying not to break it, you make it real again. So what's the way out? Being *in spite* of that; that's all. Not *because* of a lover loving in that love affair, you are. The more you believe that this has to go, it's there. Consciousness will always have a love affair with itself. There'll always be a lover loving the beloved and trying to know itself. Consciousness inquiring into consciousness will never stop. It never started, it will never stop. It will always be different, sometimes a love affair, sometimes a hate affair. What an affair!

Just to be what you cannot not be which is in spite of presence or absence of any... whatever. Consciousness starts with awareness and ends with awareness but you do not. You do not start with it and not end with it, so just be that. But no one can claim to be That. Who claims to be that? Then we land again somewhere. That's why I say you have to absolutely fail to know or not to know yourself: it's neither knowing nor not knowing yourself. Not knowing what you are and not knowing what you are not. This is the middle way; neither knowing nor not knowing. This is Buddha's middle path. That's Nisargadatta's: on one side there's love that tells me I'm everything, on the other side there's wisdom that tells me I'm nothing. But they have nothing to offer. Life flows between them. What I am just flows between them. They always want to tempt everyone but they have nothing to offer. They are just advisors that cannot make you wiser than you are. You are wisdom itself, how can they make you wiser?

Then there are positions of gurus, someone is a love guru – the open-heart guru and then there are wisdom gurus. And both are empty as nothing. What can they give you? Just promising something that you don't need. You are nothing – bullshit wisdom! You are everything, bullshit love. But your life is absolutely independent of all of that. But you have to experience it yourself. No one can give you that. You have to look into wisdom and you have to see it's empty. And you have to look into love and see it's empty. Love doesn't give you the satisfaction of your nature and wisdom doesn't give you anything. Your satisfaction is absolutely independent of all of that. May it be as it is!

But the first step is failing in I Amness, as always. Then you fail everywhere. Then you land somewhere, you depart again. But everything is permanently there: there's always love and there's always wisdom. But where there's love, there's hate and where there's wisdom, there's ignorance. Both come together, but you are neither. You can just be astonished... Wisdom, wow! Love, wow! Okay! What to do with you? Do you want something?

Any questions from the ones fighting for yourself; peace fighters everywhere. All the wars in this world are made by peace fighters. So, peace off! And be what you cannot *not* be.

[Pointing to a visitor] Welcome back! Where did you come from right now? Where were you when you were gone?

Q [Another visitor]: Some kind of absence...

K: So, there's an absence and a presence. Isn't it fantastic? You can shift between the presence-absence and nothing happens. You are in the absence and you are in the presence. And none of them can make you more or less. Fantastic! There's nothing more to it. You can never be more or less as you are, by anything. Absence is just another experience of death. So you experienced death and this presence is what you call life. You are in life and you are in death. Neither life can make you alive nor death can make you dead. What is there to fear? Is there anyone who's born in absence? No. And now in presence there's someone who's born. So you're with and without someone who's born and not born.

It's more than simple. It's here-now, here-now: there's absence and presence, form and formless, life and death. They are only there because you are. They cannot make you alive or dead. Nothing more! Fear not. What is there to fear if you are absolute independent of presence or absence or any idea of imagination? None of that can either make you nor unmake you. But the main problem is that you want to own that experience, you want to own yourself because you're so in fucking love with yourself. Love wants you to know yourself. What a fuck! All this misery comes from love. No one ever imagined that. How can love make me miserable? This relative love for yourself is the worst-case scenario. Nothing is worse than that. What else can make you so stupid to look for yourself? Only the love for yourself makes you ignorant. Love, love, love...

And when I hit it all the time, they say Karl has no love, he has no heart. They are right, I have no heart. I don't even know what is heart and what is not heart. But everyone wants to open his heart; heart surgery. For what? For what do you want to open your heart? What bullshit has to come in there? Maybe you have to open it to get the bullshit out! But does heart contain anything? Heart is not a container, come on! How can heart contain something? What has to leave heart? How many ideas can one destroy in one moment?

Q [Another visitor]: So what slips from what into what?

K: That one who has a slip. [Laughter] Whatever has a slip is slippery... slipping in and out. Mr. Slipper and Mrs. Slipper. When you're horny for yourself, you are slippery. Out of love for yourself you become horny, and by being horny you are the devil who wants to know himself. That is being horny and being slippery and slipping in and out. That's what they call as sex – slip in, slip out. It's a horny devil.

Q: Can I ever be satisfied?

K: You can never be satisfied and no one needs you to be satisfied. So, don't worry; not even you. It's a horny devil – me – always slips in and slips out. It's very slippery. The moment you want to catch him, it's gone. It's so slippery that guy.

Q: When you sit here, the little Karl steps aside?

K: No. I cannot step aside. The little just becomes very big. But it's always very big. [Laughing]

Q: So, there's no difference between sitting there and sitting here?

K: There's no difference between karl and Karl, he's always total radi*karl*. Just be total. Be as you are, be Absolute, be total. That's all. But no one can *be* that. And just by being neither Karl nor no-Karl, you are just what is total. Who plays that ping-pong? Who's in and who's out? Too much?

Q [Another visitor]: How can it be too much?

K: It still takes the breath away. *Atma* cannot breathe anymore, the air is gone. In English they say you are my heir... ha, ha. Even gurus say, 'You are my heir, my successor. You will fulfil my legacy, my lineage.' In Tiruvannamalai there were two or three persons who were confirmed by Mooji. Life is so funny, I love it. If it would not exist, I would even invent it. But who doesn't want to be a successor from a very famous guru? And confirmed by so many other *gurus*? And so many other people come. They cannot all be wrong! I like the Upanishads – What's the biggest master? Shit! Because so many flies cannot be wrong. I do everything so that masses do not come but maybe I will fail. Who knows? Attracting masses is like a massage for your ego.

[Pointing to a visitor] It's your birthday today. How does it feel to be dead? Happy Dead day! Because whatever has a daddy is dead. Why not celebrate a dead day? The moment I died – when I was born. It's better to have a dead day than a mother's day.

Where did Jesus go when he went up? Into the blue. Blue is a symbol of not knowing what-you-are and what-you-are-not, going into the blue. Out of the blue you came and into the blue you will go. And in between there are blues: you are in a sad music of a sad existence which is called blues.

Q [Another visitor]: You say that this moment repeats itself...

K: It's not a repetition. This moment didn't come and it will not go. It doesn't repeat itself. It didn't come in coming and will not go in going. It's eternal. It's never created.

Q: Is it like a block of cement?

K: Block of... whatever. [Laughter] It's not meant to be cement. That's too mental. It's as concrete as concrete. But even concrete becomes dust again.

Q: So, what gives us the idea of movement and choice?

K: The dream of coming and the dream of going. It's like a dream of being born, the dream that this moment comes. It's an experience but it's not real. In the coming it doesn't come and in going it doesn't go.

Q: So we don't live in a block of concrete?

K: It's like a video recorder; the movie is already there. By coming it's already there and by going it's not gone. It's just an infinite loop. It will come back again because it's not gone when it's gone. That's why there's this symbol of eight – the eternity. It's like a loop. Nothing comes and goes in it and maybe you are just the perception which is in one point. And you experience this moment but this moment didn't come, it was already there and by going it doesn't go. It's like an infinite loop. That's why the holy number of Shiva is one-zero-eight. The one in absence experiencing the infinite eight. You are That what is in the absence of form; information appears in front of you but it's already there.

Q: But who would create such a stupid thing? [Laughter]

K: Who calls it stupid? It's perfect and Absolute. It's Absolute perfection – no way out. That's why the holy number of Shiva is one-zero-eight. That's the realization of that what-you-are. You realize yourself in one-zero-eight. As awareness – one, zero is formless spirit and the eight is the infinite loop of information. And no way out of it. So what to do? I don't have to invent anything because it's already written in so many Vedas and Upanishads and Avadhuta Gita and all the Gitas. I just repeat myself all the time. I cannot invent anything. I never created any word. It was never my knowing or not-knowing or knowledge or anything. I don't have to worry what comes out next because it's already there. That's called peace. There's an absolute non-doership in every word. The words are already spoken, you just experience them. They are never yours or not yours. Who wakes up in the morning? And no *ayahuasca* will end things, I tell you.

Q: I have a practical problem. I get emotionally attached to objects and start collecting everything. Now I have thousands of goods, magazines...

K: You're just a big collector. You are so much in love with your things. You extend, extend, extend. The next time you need a warehouse for all of that. Wonderful! As long as you can pay for it, no problem. There are collectors who keep collecting, then after awhile they really don't know anything anymore. They cannot let go of anything and after a while it becomes very messy.

Everyone has it more or less. Everyone has some precious things he will never let go, just in case. This tendency you cannot destroy. Last year I was trying to sell a house and for days and days I had to pack. Then I always thought, 'Will I need this sometime, should I put it in a storage?' It's hard work. If it's just your body, it's okay. You can just put it over another place. But your body doesn't end here. [Laughter] You are a Messiah, without a mess you cannot exist. You need your mess. What would you do without a mess? You would not be a Mess-iah. You need a messy world to be a Messiah – come on! To clean it up again, to make a new earth. When I say Eckhart is a new Messiah I mean it, and he needs that this should be a mess, that something is wrong here. What would you do if nothing is wrong? What would a Messiah do if there's no mess? He creates his Church with many masses.

Q: How can I be sleeping and listening to you at the same time? [Laughter]

K: You don't have to know that, you do it anyway. It happens all the time. How does it happen?

Q [Another visitor]: You practised karate?

K: I still do. Earlier it was the empty-hand karate, now it's the empty-tongue karate. In karate emptiness fights you and emptiness always wins. A dead samurai always wins. You cannot kill a dead samurai; he always wins. It's like an empty tongue, the one who doesn't have to defend what he says. It's not different. I exercised in Kumite. In that the one who attacks first always loses because that what is emptiness always knows it before the attack. The defence is always faster than the attack.

Q: Is it same as *aikido*?

K: *Aikido* takes the energy of the other one and winning against him by his own energy. That's a bit different. In aikido you step out of the way and he loses against himself. Just use his energy against him.

Q: So the weakness is always in the attack?

K: The weakness is always that there's one who wants to win. You have to be that what doesn't lose in losing and doesn't win in winning. It has no advantage of winning and no disadvantage in losing. It's a nice technique.

Q: In *aikido* every posture has to be divine movement...

K: Beautiful. Beauty always wins because beauty is harmonic. It has no resistance. It's just a beautiful movement. Karate is more like a hammer, everything has to be straight. Karate is hitting with totality not with your body. Then body is just a tool. Tai Chi is the basic and then comes Kung Fu. Kung Fu is the material art, but before that you have to master your spiritual part. If *it* hits, it breaks but when *you* hit, nothing happens. I can start a school of empty tongue karate.

Q: Are reasons bullshit?

K: Reason in German is *grund*. You try to become a gigantic intellect by reasoning. Like your mother wants to reason with you, always dominating. It's like an S-M show. Be reasonable, be able to reason. Don't be Abel, don't be Cain. God loves Abel but not Cain. Cain tried to please God but God was never pleased with him trying to please Him... and Abel just enjoyed himself lying under the tree and God was pleased like hell. When you enjoy yourself, God enjoys himself. But if you try to please God then he's really angry because you try to control him. God hates nothing more than someone trying to control him with his behaviour. You really get your ass kicked I tell you. If you just enjoy yourself it would be fine. God enjoys himself because you don't want anything from him. But if you try to please him – watch out! By all your good behaviour, by all your bhajans. Then he really comes, 'What do you want?' [Laughing]

Q: We try to have a fixed idea, God is like this...

K: If you want to entrap him into a fixed concept he would show you how fixed he is... the moment you want to control him. Even by praying you want to control him. He hates that actually, if you ask him. I would hate that someone prays when he wants something. It's just business.

Q [Another visitor]: That's begging and not praying...

K: It's all begging. Every prayer is begging. Just be quiet, then you please him.

Q: Or say thank you...

K: Thank you is the biggest bullshit you can tell him, as if he has given you something. As if he would care to give you something. Who do you think you are who can thank God? Arrogance needs to be beaten up.

Q [Another visitor]: Isn't that gratitude?

K: Gratitude is the biggest bullshit ever. Gratitude for what? Then you say that someone is blessed by God because he got more things from God – gratitude! Always arrogance and always being apart and being special to someone else. It always sounds good but it's all bullshit.

It's amazing what this little phantom always come up with. 'I have so much gratitude, God loves me.' Watch out when God loves you, you will be loved to death. If God has sex with you, watch out!

Q: Does that happen? [Laughter]

K: Some people claim, 'God *came* to me, since then I'm full of gratitude. I opened myself up to God and then he went into me.' When one thinks he's blessed by something, it's really a trap.

Q: But when there's gratitude...

K: There's no gratitude. You already confirm that you are a slave of someone else when you have to thank God or someone; that's slavery. It's a sensation of slavery that you have to thank somebody for something. That you are a slave of a master or something, or a slave of a guru. Maybe the gratitude comes naturally but still you confirm someone there. It's a trap to confirm one who's getting something from somebody. It's crazy! Then you feel special and blessed and then you are more apart from life.

Q: It's a good feeling...

K: Good feeling are always lies. Good feelings are always traps. Special blessings and blissful experiences are the biggest traps on earth.

Q: Happiness...

K: It's a fake happiness. You think happiness is not a trap? Shit happens. Your story of being a seeker and all that is part of it. What to do? Like being in a warm water and feeling nice. Then the water gets freezing again. But who do I tell that to? All the traps are made by yourself. And all are slaves for yourself. You are the master and the slave. You're enslaved by yourself. Who cares being enslaved by oneself? But you have to be all of that, the master and the slave. It will always be like slavery and rape. You feel raped to do something what you never wanted to do. But who cares being raped by what one is? Being the raper the raping the raped. The master, the slave and the slavery. But what to do? Gratitude... famous words... and I'm always so sorry to demolish them. Terminator – killing whatever is in time. It's a false happiness you're looking for all the time because happiness is your very nature and can never be gained by anyone. Never be given by any fucking master I tell you.

And be happy about it that no master, no guru or any special guru purnima cannot help you. What-you-are never needed any of this guru, guru, guru. What else can I tell to myself? Shall I tell him that you should go to this master and that master and get yourself enslaved and then maybe you become what you are? Then I would really kill myself! Talking to a depending self and making him more depending. There are a handful of people, not even a handful. Nisargadatta said I'm not here to make bloody disciples; I'm here to make gurus. I'm talking to the guru and by talking to I am, maybe you are that what-you-are. But not by having disciples around me sucking whatever can be sucked. No one has to have any gratitude by being around. I would rather take everything away from you than give you anything.

Q: Do we suck from you?

K: You are a sucker for sure. Stupid questions get stupid answers. You were a baby and now you are a bigger baby, still looking for a bigger tit, you know that. Then you look for *Brahman*, the biggest tit.

Q: Is gratefulness just a result of...

K: An illusion. It's all an illusion. There's a belief that you got something from someone. You are grateful for something what was given or not given. Even if you think I take something away from you then you're grateful that I took something away from you. But it's still one too many who is grateful for some advantage. It's always about advantage and disadvantage and God getting something for an advantage. Then having some advantage... then the ownership is confirmed. And ownership is owner-shit – *my* gratefulness. It always starts with an *I* or *my*. What to do? I can just point to it. I cannot take it away. I have no interest.

Q: Assuming that this moment was not God's perfect choice...

K: Even perfection is just a fucking idea. Forget perfection and be what-you-are. Perfect creates imperfect. Love creates hate. You will be angry again because what you want is not there anymore and you get angry again. It's always unstable and fragile.

Be grateful that you don't have to be grateful to anyone or anything to be what-you-are. But it's not felt. That is what-you-are. It's not a feeling, it's never a feeling. Enjoy that you never need to enjoy anything to be what-you-are. That's the nature of joy; it never needs to enjoy anything. And everything else is dependency.

Q: Can gratitude be another name for complete absorption?

K: No. Keep hoping!

Q: Maybe one is grateful for not believing in anything...

K: That's still one too many. It's always maybe, maybe, maybe and whatever is a maybe is a fiction. Come on! Fishing for something. You want to fish for a bigger fish. Then maybe you are grateful that you got a bigger fish or no fish. I could not catch the fish. I'm so grateful that there's no fish to catch. Just another illusion. What else can it be? Whatever has a difference is a delusion. The *me* always creates a delusion, always drunk by hope. Maybe, maybe, maybe: always fiction waits for you. Next life or this life and then and then...

Q [Another visitor]: What about no-hope?

K: Then you hope for no hope. It's the same bullshit. Gratitude and no gratitude is the same. All belongs to that presence and presence already is a dream. Life is just a piece of cake and if you wait for eating, you will just starve. So, just eat it.

27ᵗʰ July 2018
Ladakh

∾